Knowledge, Communication and Creativity

SAGE STUDIES IN
INTERNATIONAL SOCIOLOGY

Editor
Julia Evetts, University of Nottingham, UK

Knowledge, Communication and Creativity

Edited by
Arnaud Sales and Marcel Fournier

SAGE Studies in International Sociology 56
Sponsored by the International Sociological Association/ISA

SAGE Publications Ltd
1 Oliver's Yard
55 City Road
London EC1Y 1SP

SAGE Publications Inc.
2455 Teller Road
Thousand Oaks, California 91320

SAGE Publications India Pvt Ltd
B 1/I 1 Mohan Cooperative Industrial Area
Mathura Road
New Delhi 110 044

SAGE Publications Asia-Pacific Pte Ltd
33 Pekin Street #02-01
Far East Square
Singapore 048763

Library of Congress Control Number: 2006928579

British Library Cataloguing in Publication data

A catalogue record for this book is available from
the British Library

ISBN 978-0-7619-4306-8
ISBN 978-0-7619-4307-5

Contents

Biographical Notes

The Editors

Arnaud Sales holds a Doctorat d'État ès Lettres et Sciences Humaines, from Université de Paris 7-Denis Diderot. He is Full Professor and Head of the Department of Sociology, Université de Montréal. He is author, co-author or editor of several books and issues of academic journals, among them *La Bourgeoisie industrielle au Québec* (PUM, 1979); *Développement national et économie mondialisée* (Editor, *Sociologie et Sociétés*, 1979); *Décideurs et gestionnaires* (Éditeur officiel du Québec, 1985); *La recomposition du politique* (Co-editor, PUM/L'Harmattan, 1991); *Québec, fin de siècle* (Co-editor, *Sociologie et Sociétés*, 1994); *The International Handbook of Sociology* (Co-editor, Sage, 2000); *New Directions in the Study of Knowledge, Economy and Society* (Co-editor, Sage, 2001). He is a specialist in economic sociology focusing on administrative and economic elites, knowledge workers and the relation between the public and private spheres. He was Vice-Dean of the Université de Montréal's Faculty of Graduate Studies (1987–1992); and Vice-President, International, of the Society for the Advancement of Socio-Economics (1995–1998) where he founded the Knowledge, Economy and Society Network. He was elected Vice-President for Research (1998–2002) of the International Sociological Association and chaired ISA Research Council.

Marcel Fournier received his doctorate in sociology from the Ecole Pratique des Hautes Études-Sorbonne in Paris, France, in 1974 (with Pierre Bourdieu). He is a Full Professor in the Department of Sociology at the Université de Montréal, Canada, and in 2006–2007, professor at the Univerité de Metz, France. He received various distinctions: Member of the Canadian Royal Society; in 2001–2003, Killam Fellowship and Visiting Professor (Sociology Department) and Pathy Chair, Princeton University, NJ; 2004, Prize Pouliot (ACFAS). He is editor of the international French journal *Sociologie et Sociétés*. His fields of interest are the History of Sociology, Sociological Theory, Sociology of Culture, and Sociology of Science. His books include *Marcel Mauss* (Paris, Fayard, 1994); (with Michèle Lamont) *Cultivating Differences* (Chicago, University of Chicago Press, 1992); (with D. White) *Quebec Society* (Scarborough, Prentice Hall, 1996); *Marcel Mauss: Écrits politiques* (Paris, Fayard, 1996); (with Philippe Besnard) *Émile Durkheim: Lettres à Marcel Mauss* (Paris, PUF, 1998); *L'Entrée dans la Modernité: Science, culture et société au Québec* (Montréal, Saint-Martin, 1986); (with Yves Gingras) *Sciences et médecine au Québec* (Montréal, IQRC, 1986); and *Durkheim, Mauss & Cie* (Paris, Fayard, forthcoming). He is a member of various scientific associations, as the Executive Committee and Program Commitee of the International Sociological Association (ISA), the American Sociological Association (ASA), the Association canadienne des sociologues et anthropologues de langue française (ACSALF) and the Association internationale des sociologues de langue française (AISLF).

The Contributors

Roxane Bernier is a Researcher in the Department of Sociology at Université de Montréal. She was affiliated with the Centre d'étude et de recherche sur les expositions et les musées at the Université Jean-Monnet (France) for three years in the mid-1990s, and since 2003 has been a fellow member at the Centre interuniversitaire de recherche sur les sciences et la technologie (Québec). Bernier investigates the users' perception relating to interactive content presentations within a museum setting. In general, her research involves the sociology of knowledge on information technologies, multimedia professions, visitor studies, online museums, and cultural institutions. Her expertise led to the coordination of a special issue on IT for the European museology journal *Publics et Musées* in 1998. She has published articles, among others, in the *Journal of Educational Computing Research* and *Behavior and Information Technology Journal*; more recently a book chapter in *E-Learning and Virtual Science Centers* and several entries for the *Encyclopaedia of Portal Technology and Applications*. She also served as a peer reviewer for the *International Formal Methods Europe Symposium*, the *Journal of Educational Computing Research* as well as for the *Cultural Attitudes towards Technology and Communication Conference*.

Philippe Breton is Docteur d'État en sciences de l'information et de la communication, researcher at the CNRS (Laboratoire cultures et sociétés et Europe, Université Marc Bloch, Strasbourg) and chargé de cours at Université Paris 1, Sorbonne. His publications include *L'incompétence démocratique* (La Découverte, 2006); *Éloge de la parole* (La Découverte, 2003); *L'argumentation dans la communication* (La Découverte, 2003); *La parole manipulée* (La Découverte/Boréal, 1997; 2nd edn, 2004; this book won the 'Le dissez de Penanrun' Award of the Académie française des sciences morales et politiques in 1998); *Histoire des théories de l'argumentation* (with G. Gauthier, La Découverte, 1999). Translation in Spanish, Portuguese, Russian, Arabic, Vietnamese, Hungarian, Greek, Italian, Serbian, Korean, Rumanian and Brazilian.

Craig Calhoun is President of the Social Science Research Council and University Professor of Social Sciences at New York University, where he was previously Chair of the Sociology Department. He received his doctorate from Oxford University and taught at the University of North Carolina, Chapel Hill from 1977 to 1996, where he was also Dean of the Graduate School and founding Director of the University Center for International Studies. His publications include *Nationalism* (Minnesota, 1997); *Critical Social Theory: Culture, History and the Challenge of Difference* (Blackwell, 1995); *The Roots of Radicalism* (Chicago, forthcoming); and the co-edited anthologies *Understanding September 11th* (New Press, 2002) and *Lessons of Empire?* (New Press, 2004). He was the editor of *Sociological Theory* from 1994 to 1999 and is currently editing a history of sociology in America for the American Sociological Association's Centennial.

Randall Collins is Professor of Sociology at University of Pennsylvania, where he also holds positions in the departments of Comparative Literature, Religious Studies, and History and Sociology of Science. He has formerly taught at University of California Riverside, UCLA, Virginia, Harvard, and Chicago. His 15 books include *The Credential Society* (1979); *The Sociology of Philosophies* (1998); *Macro-History* (1999); and *Interaction Ritual Chains* (2004).

Steve Fuller is Professor of Sociology at the University of Warwick, England. He was awarded a Ph.D. in History & Philosophy of Science, University of Pittsburgh (1985). Fuller has been a Visiting Professor at UCLA, Gothenburg University, Lund University, Copenhagen Business School, Tel Aviv University, and Tokyo International Christian University. He is the founding editor of the quarterly journal, *Social Epistemology*, and the founding president of the Knowledge Management Consortium International. Fuller is the author of about 200 articles, which have appeared in fifteen languages, and the author of over a dozen books: *Social Epistemology* (Indiana, 1988; 2nd edn, 2002); *Philosophy of Science and Its Discontents* (Westview, 1989; 2nd edn, Guilford, 1993); *Philosophy, Rhetoric and the End of Knowledge* (Wisconsin, 1993; 2nd edn, Lawrence Erlbaum, 2004); *Science* (Open University and Minnesota, 1997); *The Governance of Science* (Open University, 2000); *Thomas Kuhn: A Philosophical History for Our Times* (Chicago, 2000); *Knowledge Management Foundations* (Butterworth-Heinemann, 2002); *Kuhn vs Popper: The Struggle for the Soul of Science* (Icon and Columbia, 2003); *The Intellectual* (Icon, 2005); *The Philosophy of Science and Technology Studies* (Routledge, 2006); *The New Sociological Imagination* (Sage, 2006); *New Frontiers in Science and Technology Studies* (Polity, 2007); *Science vs Religion?* (Polity, 2007); *The Knowledge Book: Key Concepts in Philosophy, Science, and Culture* (Acumen, 2007).

Joshua Guetzkow is Assistant professor of Sociology at the University of Arizona. After completing his dissertation examining the connections between welfare and criminal justice policy in the US over the last 40 years, he was a Robert Wood Johnson Post-Doctoral Scholar in Health Policy at Harvard University, where he studied the interpenetration of the criminal justice and mental health systems. His collaborative research on categories of worth in the social sciences and humanities has appeared in the *American Sociological Review*, Poetics and Research Evaluation. His research interests include the sociology of culture and knowledge, the governance of social marginality, the law and psychiatry, and the role of ideas in policymaking.

Jerald Hage received his Ph.D. in sociology from Columbia University. He is presently director of the Center for Innovation at the University of Maryland— College Park. His present research objective is to write an evolutionary theory of societal change that combines three levels of analysis—micro (role theory), meso (organizations and networks), and macro (institutions and society)—around the role of knowledge and technology as a causal force. The theory is comparative with concerns about alternative pathways and distinct historical periods. The primary focus is on the interface between organizations and institutions. To develop the expertise to write such a theory, Hage has worked in the following specialties: economic sociology, institutional theory, organizational and network theory, and theory construction. His most recent book is *Innovation, Science, and Institutional Change* (co-edited, Oxford, 2006) and before this two other books with the same theme were: *Post-Industrial Lives* (co-authored, Sage, 1992) and *Organizations Working Together* (co-authored, Sage, 1993). He has published 16 books and over 100 articles or chapters in books. Hage's co-authored book *State Intervention in Medical Care* won the prize for the best book in Comparative Public Policy from the International Political Science Association in 1991. He was elected President of the Society for the Advancement of Socio-Economics (1998–1999). He has been a visiting professor at various European Universities (Bocconi, 1995; Ecole des Mines, 1975–1976; Eindhoven Technological, 2001; Tilburg, 2004) including holding the BP Centennial Research Chair, London School of Economics 1994 as well as having several fellowships including the Netherlands Institute for Advanced Studies (1998–1999); the Japan Society for the Advancement of Science (1997); Rockefeller for Bellagio, Italy, 1996.

J. Rogers Hollingsworth is Professor of Sociology and History and former chairperson of the Program in Comparative History at the University of Wisconsin. Awarded honorary degrees by the University of Uppsala (Sweden) and by Emory University, he is the author or editor of numerous books and articles on comparative political economy. One of his major research interests is the study of how organizational and institutional factors influence different types of innovations. His recent publications include *Contemporary Capitalism: The Embeddedness of Institutions* (with Robert Boyer, 1997); *Governing Capitalist Economies* (with Philippe Schmitter and Wolfgang Streeck, 1994); *Advancing Socio-Economics: An Institutionalist Perspective* (with Karl H. Müller and Ellen Jane Hollingsworth, 2002); and *Fostering Scientific Excellence: Organizations, Institutions, and Major Discoveries in Biomedical Science* (with Ellen Jane Hollingsworth and Jerald Hage, 2008). He is past president and also honorary fellow of the Society for the Advancement of Socio-Economics.

Michèle Lamont is Robert I. Goldman Professor of European Studies and Professor of Sociology and African and African American Studies at Harvard University. She taught at Princeton University for fifteen years before joining the Harvard faculty in 2003. During the 2006–2007 academic year, she is holding the Matina Horner Distinguished Professorship at the Radcliffe Institute for Advanced Study, where she is completing her book *Cream Rising: Finding*

Excellence in the Social Sciences and the Humanities (to be published by Harvard University Press). This book concerns institutionalization of excellence in American higher education, studied through the prism of peer review process. She has also written on the role of culture in generating social inequality; the cultural strategies of stigmatized groups for coping with racism; culture and poverty; how culture mediate the impact of discrimination on health, and many other topics. Her most recent book *The Dignity of Working Men: Morality and the Boundaries of Race, Class, and Immigration* (Harvard University Press, 2000) won one of the top awards in sociology, the C. Wright Mills Award from the Society for the Study of Social problems. Her articles have appeared in the *American Sociological Review, the American Journal of Sociology, Sociological Theory, Annual Review of Sociology, Ethnic and Racial Studies*, and numerous other journals. Professor Lamont has been a fellow of the John Simon Guggenheim Memorial Foundation, the Center for Advanced Study in the Behavioral Sciences, and the German Marshall Funds as well as a visiting scholar at the Russell Sage Foundation, the Institute for Advanced Study, and the Schomburg Center for Research in Black Culture. She is serving as Chair (2006–2009) of the Council for European Studies, the learned society of social scientists and humanists studying Europe. She is also co-director of the Successful Societies Program of the Canadian Institute for Advanced Studies and the director of the European Network on Inequality of the Multidisciplinary Program on Inequality and Social Policy at the Kennedy School of Government (Harvard University).

Grégoire Mallard is a Ph.D. candidate in sociology at Princeton University and Ecole Nationale des Ponts et Chaussées (LATTS). His dissertation explores how American experts in foreign policy have addressed questions of sovereignty when designing nuclear non-proliferation policies in Europe and the Middle East. He is editor of *Sciences et Souverainetés* (Co-editor, *Sociologie du Travail*, 2006); and *Global Science and National Sovereignty* (Co-editor, Routledge, forthcoming). He has published articles in the *American Sociological Review, Sociologie du Travail* and *Critique Internationale*. He has served on the editorial board of *Contexts Magazine* since June 2004.

Yan Sénéchal is a Ph.D. candidate in the Department of Sociology at the Université de Montréal. At the intersection of social problems theory and political theory, his thesis explores the sociological analysis of public problematizations in democratic societies. His research interests evolves around the relationship between questioning, knowledge and society. Among his various editorial activities are *Le savoir à l'usage du changement social?* (with Charles Gaucher, CELAT, 2003) and *Impertinence et questionnement* (with Jonathan Roberge, Botakap, 2001). He also contributed to the 'Débat' section in the international French journal *Sociologie et Sociétés* (with Jonathan Roberge). He is co-founder of the Groupe de Recherches et d'Etudes sur la Gouvernance Urbaine et Métropolitaine (GREGUM, with Pierre Hamel) and of the Groupe de Recherches et d'Études sur la Philosophie en Sciences Sociales (GREPSS, with Jonathan Roberge and Stéphane Vibert). Since 2006, he is fellow at the Chaire Approches Communautaires et Inégalités de Santé (CACIS, Faculté de médecine, Université de Montréal).

Nico Stehr is Karl Mannheim Professor of Cultural Studies at the Zeppelin University, Friedrichshafen, Germany. During the academic year 2002/2003 he was Paul-F.-Lazarsfeld Professor at the University of Vienna, Austria. Among his recent book publications are *Governing Modern Societies* (with Richard Ericson, University of Toronto Press, 2000); *Werner Sombart: Economic Life in the Modern Age* (with Reiner Grundmann, Transaction Books, 2001); *The Fragility of Modern Societies: Knowledge and Risk in the Information Age* (Sage, 2001); *Knowledge and Economic Conduct: The Social Foundations of the Modern Economy* (University of Toronto Press, 2002); *Wissenspolitik* (Suhrkamp Verlag, 2003); *The Governance of Knowledge* (Transaction Books, 2004); *Biotechnology: Between Commerce and Civil Society and Knowledge Politics: Governing the Consequences of Science and Technology* (Paradigm Publishers, 2005, edited with Christoph Henning and Bernd Weiler), *The Moralization of the Markets* (New Brunswick, New Jersey: Transaction Books, 2006); (ed. with Bernd Weiler), *Who owns Knowledge?* (Transaction Books, 2007) and *Moral Markets. How Knowledge and Affluence Change Consumers and Producers.* (Paradigm Publishers, 2007).

John Urry is Professor of Sociology and Director of the Centre for Mobilities Research, Lancaster University. Recent books published include *Sociology Beyond Societies* (Routledge, 2000); *Bodies of Nature* (Sage, 2001); *The Tourist Gaze* (2nd edn, Sage, 2002); *Global Complexity* (Polity, 2003); *Performing Tourist Places* (Ashgate, 2004) with J-O Baerenholdt, M. Haldrup, J. Larsen); Tourism Mobilities (Routledge, 2004, with M. Sheller); *Mobilities, Networks, Geographies* (Ashgate 2006, with J. Larsen, K. Axhausen); *Mobilities* (Polity, 2007).

Section One

Introduction

1

Knowledge, Communication, Reflexive Creativity and Social Change

By Arnaud Sales, Marcel Fournier and Yan Sénéchal[1]

Knowledge, communication and creativity in their many forms are among the great obsessions of contemporary societies. Indeed, life in human societies has always called upon knowledge, communication and invention. No group, no community has ever been formed without representations, information and knowledge, without ties being forged and without the exchange of words, emotions, feelings, symbolic goods and materials, while innovations, including even minor ones, often serve to ensure the continuity of social life. Even if contemporary societies, in this regard, are not totally different from past societies, social change and historical processes transform social configurations. Whatever names are used to characterize our societies – *Knowledge Society, Information Society, Network Society* – they are based to an unparalleled degree on knowledge, high technology and research, along with ongoing, fast-paced creativity in every field, creativity that is at once innovative, destructive and adaptive. As Hans Joas stated, creativity, with considerable ambivalence, contradictions and exclusion processes, plays an ever-increasing role in the understanding of contemporary societies. This is true for more and more individuals in the new generation who seem to have adopted creativity as a central value or aspiration, beyond the instrumentality of their professional lives (Joas, 1992/1996: 255–56). This is true too for many institutions that cannot survive without innovation. Does this mean that we are living today in a 'Creative Society' as suggested by Richard Florida (2002)?

The extraordinary pace of social change requires, if only for adaptive purposes, placing creativity, or the power to produce new realities (Joas, 1992/1996: 74), at the core of social practices, developing organizational units centred on resolving complex new problems, and massively engaging all those whom Robert Reich (1992: 167) called symbolic analysts, those who have the ability to maintain the pace of innovation, devising solutions for unresolved problems, or transforming institutions either incrementally or rapidly. In this regard, artists and cultural workers emerge, on a par with research scientists and workers in technoscientific fields, as the ideal type of workers in a knowledge economy. Artistic work, which had until then been considered a negligible economic entity, could in many respects increasingly be seen by some 'as the most advanced expression of new production methods and new employment relationships resulting from recent changes to capitalism' (Menger, 2002: 8). The cardinal values of creation – imagination, play, improvisation, atypical behaviour, or creative anarchy – have invaded other worlds of work.

These processes, relationships and fields of knowledge are intimately tied to the powerful role of communication, which acts as the main catalyst for reflexive creativity, through training and diffusion, exchange, recombination, integration of knowledge and innovation. Creative processes, specifically those tied to knowledge production, which is one of the themes of this collection of essays, entail different types of communicational exchanges at various levels and stages: the capacity of individuals to work within and communicate across several fields of activity simultaneously; their ability to become part of intellectual, scientific, professional and artistic networks. It also implies the support they receive from research institutions characterized by scientific diversity, strong social integration and ongoing exchanges among members.

In light of these observations, the focus of this collection of essays is to connect these issues and realities from a sociological point of view. The objective is not to present a unified perspective with regard to these themes, but rather to analyse from various angles the transformations seen in today's societies by shedding light on the conjunction of these highly interdependent elements, which are at once the source and result of social change: knowledge, communication, networks and creativity. This introductory chapter will therefore put these essays into perspective, in addition to presenting their most significant contributions.

The first section of this book focuses on the role of knowledge that is defined as a capacity for action, creation and transformation in the production of societal change. The authors look at how the impact of the general increase in knowledge affects individuals, lifestyles, institutions,[2] and of course technological development. The second section shows the impact that the new communication and information technologies have had on the transformation of social relations and contemporary communities, as well as the development potential of an international public sphere. These analyses lead to a critique of advanced societies as knowledge societies and a questioning of the concepts of innovation and creation. The third and final section focuses on creativity and communication in the production of knowledge. One of the essays revisits the great debate relative to the role of communication in the production of knowledge types. The issue of diversity and the intensity of communicational, intellectual and scientific exchanges, along with the role of the 'high cognitive complexity' of research scientists in the making of major discoveries are addressed. Another essay in the section then considers the creativity of networks, over and above the great scientific thinkers and eminent intellectuals. Finally, this volume concludes with an examination of the role of the processes involved in evaluating creativity in the production of knowledge. Let us now take a more in-depth view of these three major sections.

Knowledge and Social Change in Contemporary Societies

Legacy of the Industrial Society and the Knowledge Variable

One of the major legacies of industrial society was to give knowledge a central role and to constitute, to an unprecedented level, a reflexive capacity with regard to creativity. Through the implementation of sophisticated and secular education systems and the institutionalization of scientific research, which permit both the dissemination and the development of formal knowledge, industrial societies have put in place a mechanism of social auto-transformation, assuring that society, its agents and institutions could deliberately 'create creativity' (Touraine, 1969: 10).

The first movement entailed the introduction of 'exo-education as a mandatory standard' (Gellner, 1983), as opposed to local and religious-oriented education. In other words, the passage from an oral society to a schooled society led to considerable growth in human capital through the dissemination and extension of universalistic, often sophisticated knowledge to a large part of the population. Aspirations, professional interests and production, values, social demands and consumption of goods by the population have been largely transformed by this movement. The second movement occurred with the 'institutionalization of science as a professional career accompanied by the transformation of the university, and specifically the creation of research laboratories' (Freundhental, 1991/1997: 99), combined with decentralization, which promoted competition (Ben-David, 1991/1997: 132). The irruption of science in production processes also emerged from this movement (Chandler, 1962; Moscovici, 1968) along with the institutionalization of industrial research and development. The emergence of applied sciences in the nineteenth century was the turning point in the use and development of production-oriented science. Starting with scientific knowledge, it was feasible to quickly develop, from a unique technological basis, a vast array of new products using the same set of scientific and technical skills and existing methods of production (chemistry and pharmaceutical, electrical, communication and information equipment, aerospace, military and civilian nuclear research, biotechnologies, etc.). Companies in these industries progressively institutionalized R&D, whereas universities placed basic research at the heart of their mission, and the state intervened in various ways to expand research activities. The dialogue among these three institutional actors has since led to talk of a 'Triple Helix System' (Etzkowitz and Levdesdorff, 2000) involving universities, corporations and governments.

Knorr-Cetina and Preda (2001) stressed that the most developed theories on the role of knowledge were those that addressed its socio-economic impact. The crisis surrounding the Fordist model, the need to restructure capitalism, and the rise of new industrialized countries led economists, management researchers and of course company leaders 'to question the sources of development and prosperity' (Amable *et al.*, 1997: 10–11). Research on the role of technical change and especially innovation developed, giving birth to a micro-economy of innovation, as well as research into the role of knowledge, whether scientific, applied, formal, tacit, relational, instrumental, technical, or organizational, etc.

In their search to understand growth,[3] economists identified a 'knowledge' variable related to the quality of a country's labour force and its technological capacity. The most global explanation involves the theory of the disappearance of the classical comparative advantage, which for some time had been used to explain the geographical location of an industry. According to this theory, the location of production depended upon two main factors: the wealth of natural resources and

portion of factors of production, that is, the relative abundance of capital
our. Today, in developed countries, the existence of natural resources and a
labour force are no longer deciding factors in the determination of location.
... . mainly counts is the capacity and competence to develop and use ideas pro-
ductively (Centre for Educational Research and Innovation/OECD, 2000). What
counts is qualifications and knowledge, the main sources of competitive advantage
today (Thurow, 1996). The technology parks and techno-suburbs, the transnational
services, specifically financial services have developed because the intellectual
resources were close at hand. What counts is creativity and innovation.

Knowledge has always been a crucial dimension for the transformation of human
society (Popper, 1956: 11). What is new, however, is the notion that within
contemporary societies, knowledge acts on knowledge. 'Knowledge is now being
applied systematically and purposefully to define what new knowledge is needed,
whether it is feasible and what has to be done to make knowledge effective. It is in
other words being applied to systematic innovation' (Drucker, 1993: 42). Knowledge
strengthens creativity, whereas knowledge production demands creativity. And since
the 1980s, we have observed the accelerating, deliberate diversification and spread
of selective kinds of knowledge creation, deployment and use (specifically, scientific
and technical knowledge) and their implications in and for many spheres of life
worldwide. Overall, this group of observations strongly indicates that knowledge has
acquired a specific place and status within contemporary societies, to the extent
where they can be qualified as Knowledge Societies. Nico Stehr develops this theme
in Chapter 2, *Modern Societies as Knowledge Societies*.

Knowledge as a Generalized Capacity for Action, Creation
and Transformation

In knowledge societies, the material basis of social action has been displaced by
a symbolic basis. As we have just seen from an economic perspective, knowledge
has diminished the significance of capital as a central strategic resource. What
counts today, is the availability of knowledge, along with a highly skilled
workforce. For Stehr, the advantages are not just economic: knowledge is also one
of the most significant sources for building an open society, a theme that is
explored later from other perspectives by Philippe Breton and Craig Calhoun. The
increase in the level of knowledge constitutes an immense factor in the openness
of societies, which can be related to what Tomlinson calls 'the general experience
of cultural disembedding' (1999: 105).[4]

Knowledge, in Stehr's view, is neither an academic or encyclopaedic accumulation
of information, nor a simple productive force in the Marxist sense, but rather a
generalized capacity for action: 'the potential to initiate new things' – or one could
add the potential for creativity – 'and a model for reality'. Knowledge is the
capacity for action that transforms or creates reality. Biotechnical knowledge
transforms natural realities and creates new ones. The result, which is not necessarily
positive, is that the application of scientific knowledge in a society requires that
social conditions and the existing conditions for action adjust to this knowledge or
be transformed in accordance with standards established by science.

In return, scientific knowledge is practically always being challenged. And despite the centrality of knowledge-based occupations, one should not, says Nico Stehr, conclude that we are in the process of becoming a technocratic society. On the contrary, in a knowledge society, individuals and small groups benefit from an extraordinary increase in their capacity for action. And there is certainly a connection with the fact that the hegemonic power and the capacity of institutions as powerful as the state, the army and the church to control social life have been weakened by the appropriation of knowledge by individuals. This questioning of hegemonic power obviously goes hand in hand with the rapid development of information and communication technologies, which have allowed the infringement of national boundaries, while the proliferation of power centres, called 'the differentiation of organizational populations' by Jerry Hage, which have an increasing capacity for action and have given rise to a multi-centred world (Badie and Smouts, 1992; Rosenau, 1988), has had an impact on the power of traditional hegemonic institutions. This theme is explored in greater depth in the following chapter.

Knowledge and Social Change: The Multiplication of Power Centres

In the late 1970s, there were already some 10,000 multinational corporations (Stopford and Dunning, 1983). In 2004, the *World Investment Report* issued by the United Nations Conference on Trade and Development (2004: 39) specified there were 61,000 transnational companies and more than 900,000 foreign affiliates, a six-fold increase in parent companies, thereby bearing witness to the power of globalization. If the expansion of international or global activities into numerous fields has played a part in the increase in this type of power centre, particularly economic centres, one should in no way limit their role to this factor. The role of knowledge is at least as crucial, if not more important, given the increasing number of organizations whether local, national, or transnational. Jerald Hage in Chapter 3, *Knowledge and Societal Change: Institutional Coordination and the Evolution of Organizational Populations* examines the role of knowledge in the production of societal change by way of the evolution of organizational populations. These organizational populations are defined as industrial sectors that share a similar technology and marketplace. The general pattern of evolution for these populations is a historical shift from consolidation to differentiation.

Consolidation leads to a decrease in the total number of organizations. Consolidation occurs, for example, either as a result of integration or absorption strategies that create a higher concentration in the sector, or as the result of a major innovation such as Ford's invention of the assembly-line process, which imposed new requirements for entering or staying in the market and hence decreased the number of competitors. *Differentiation*, which would be the predominant trend for decades, leads to an increase in the total number of organizations in the organizational population, despite the ongoing power of the concentration movement. Differentiation occurs when, for example, a new technology, such as molecular biology, precipitates the founding of new firms; when development reaches a level that promotes the tertiarization of the economy; or when significant deregulation is effected to counter monopolies, as seen in recent decades.

The impact of consolidation and differentiation differs in terms of the intensity of capital investment, level of R&D, degree of bureaucratization, the role of innovation in facing competitive forces, establishment of market niches and the level of workforce qualifications. In a knowledge society, where the capacity to adapt is vital to the growth and survival of firms, competitive advantage necessitates complex forms of innovation, along with rapid and multiple responses not only to new scientific and technological knowledge, but also to consumer demands. This is the level where knowledge, communication and network issues start to become intertwined. The demands of this new environment increase the intensity of inter-organizational relationships, particularly the sharing of knowledge for the purposes of innovation. Although globalization has triggered an expansion of inter-firm trade and competition, we are also witnessing an expansion of business networks, technological alliances, complex supply chains, in short inter-organizational cooperation, which is becoming a major economic resource. Some huge consortiums, such as COVISINT in the automobile industry, with its 22,000 partners, have been formed to share resources through an Electronic Data Interchange used for the acquisition of raw materials, parts and data, and logistics and administrative processes.[5] Furthermore, knowledge is shared among technological alliances or within the University–Corporation–Government Triple Helix.

These relationships are controlled by a new, expanding form of non-market governance. To advance a knowledge-based theory of social change, according to Hage, one needs to account for organizational populations as well as institutional modes of governance.

Increased levels of knowledge within society have affected individuals and institutions, as well as the dynamics within society. As underlined by Karin Knorr-Cetina: 'A knowledge society is not simply a society of more experts, of technological infra- and information structures, and of specialists rather than participant interpretations. It means that knowledge cultures have spilled and woven their tissue into society, the whole set of processes, experiences and relationships that wait on knowledge and unfold with its articulation (Knorr-Cetina, 1997: 8; see also 1999). The result has been a differentiation in social categories and consumer tastes that interact with offerings from producers, who through their investment in R&D, have shortened the useful life of products and hence tastes of consumers who have become hooked on technological developments.[6] Pressure for differentiation rather than consolidation is related to the variety of tastes, how taste changes over time and the variety of materials and production technologies.

What role then does knowledge play in the area of organizational consolidation and differentiation? According to Hage, it has not been frequently associated with changes specific to the new economy or knowledge society. The emphasis has essentially been placed on organizational learning within the firm or inter-organizational networks. This is clearly based on the fact that when knowledge increases within a society, technology and markets are transformed, placing greater emphasis on organizational learning. Hage therefore maintains three hypotheses as regards (a) an increase in levels of education and income; (b) a rise in R&D investment; and (c) the interaction between these main factors.

These hypotheses play a central role in the historical reversal from consolidation to differentiation. There are, however, variations in the way this transpires in different societies. And that is where non-market modes of governance come into play. Initiated either by the state, by different types of associations, or by different organizational networks, these modes of governance partially explain intersocietal differences for the same technological–market nexus with regard to the consolidation/differentiation processes of organizational populations. Hage maintains also that it is the conjunction of innovation and organizational differentiation that has specifically led to the development of information technologies. Section 2 of this collection addresses the effects of the development of information technologies on the transformation of communicational modes and social relationships in general.

New Information Technologies and Communication, Communities and the Public Sphere

Communicational Infrastructure and the Transformation of Social Relations

Knowledge not only transforms institutions and cultures, but it also has a considerable effect on sociality through communicational innovations that accentuate the role of machines. The integration of micro-electronics, information systems and telecommunications, in conjunction with the development of transportation systems, had made it possible to build an integrated communicational infrastructure that literally or figuratively cuts across societal boundaries (Castells, 1996; Urry, 2000: 33) that are becoming more and more decompartmentalized (Laïdi, 2004; Sassen, 1999). In association with privatization, deregulation and trade-liberalization processes (Sales and Beschorner, 2005), the communicational infrastructure facilitated and sustained globalization by linking and integrating global space. This infrastructure comprises a network of players, organizations, technologies and machines that include the interconnected nodes through which a large number of flows pass and are relayed. It compresses time and space, and permits the movement of people, information, images, sounds, music, knowledge and money. It connects individuals at unprecedented levels, in addition to organizations, without borders.

To take stock of this impact, one has to delve first into the micro-sociological level of integration, as discussed in Chapter 4, *Mobilities, Networks and Communities* by John Urry. The author examines the transformation of relationships and modes of communication to understand how complex connections in a networked society are implemented and maintained, where new mobile technologies lead us to revisit the concept of community not only in terms of the notions of co-presence and absence, but also the combination of humans and machines.

If the frequency and scale of indirect machine-mediated relationships have experienced considerable growth in recent decades, there remains a certain nostalgia for the times when social relationships entailed essentially face-to-face encounters within local social groups. Social science researchers have focused on such situations, noting a profound alteration in social ties, a sense of community and, more broadly, the lifeworld (see Adikhari and Sales, 2001; Calhoun, 1992). These alterations were generally interpreted in reference to the monetarization and bureaucratization of the lifeworld by political and economic systems (Habermas, 1981/1984), but also relative to contemporary experience of life marked by the universal principles of cognitive rationality and technology.

Many including Calhoun (1992) and Urry are opposed to the overly pessimistic representation of the new forms of social relationships and integration, because in most societies relationships have involved various types of remote connections that are more or less mobile, and more or less mediated through messengers, material means and machines. John Urry specifically notes that social relationships are not necessarily specific to a location, but are constituted through various 'circulating entities' (Latour, 1999). Connections occur in many forms of social space. With new technologies, individuals are, moreover, involved in a much broader environment and organizations are striving for large-scale integration. New technologies are involved in the organization of a large part of contemporary life through indirect relationships. But as Urry says, one should not believe that such relationships are sufficient. Mobility is central to the way in which people live in a networked society. The nature of networked connections must be considered, particularly those formed through various forms of circulating entities, including travel patterns whether corporeal, imaginary, virtual, or communicative via letters, faxes, email, or mobile phones.

Co-presence and types of communities: People networks cannot completely ignore face-to-face relationships. As has already been mentioned, even the representation of a community is often very limitative. There is, as Urry maintains, a propensity for proximity, because nothing helps forge strong relationships better than co-presence, which allows for the display of multiple signs of understanding or misunderstanding. Co-presence is in fact not negated by indirect relationships regardless of the weight such relationships carry today.

This does not prevent the formation of virtual communities, virtual in the sense that these communities do not *a priori* involve frequent co-presence, as in the case of friendships or even long-distance love relationships. Although not all discussion groups are virtual communities, it should be acknowledged that the Internet has led to the creation of small worlds involving individuals who are geographically far apart, for example, groups of people who have been cut off from their homeland through immigration. Through computers, long-distance ties are maintained with the expectation or hope of meeting again some time in the future. From this perspective, the Internet, says John Urry, should be considered in continuity with other social spaces. The compulsion for proximity also plays a role in these communities where people do meet face to face if they can. The relationships that the Internet generally helps to forge are not limited to cyberspace.

A more thorough examination is needed to account for some major phenomena that are all too often sidelined, even blacklisted, in sociological conceptualization: these phenomena entail the way in which means of technical communication and mobile machines are combined with humans to form mobiles or machinic hybrids, hence new material worlds, while 'knowledge cultures centrally turn around object worlds to which experts and scientists are oriented' (Knorr-Cetina, 1997: 8), are intertwined with culture and practices.

In this respect, the twenty-first century will, regardless of what we want, probably be an era of manned machines, miniaturized, privatized and digitalized mobile machines, adapted to the body with prosthetic features constituting various types of digital nomads. These machines, which will have an effect on social relations, creation, innovation and transactions, will serve to reorganize space–time and generate 'a liquid modernity of interdependent flows'. People will therefore, inhabit information, image and mobility networks, through these knowledge machines. But as Fuller questions, is this mobility and innovation not leading to a 'downgrading of institution and upgrading of community as supporting concepts'? That, according to Fuller, would entail an anti-institutional perspective. But would such a perspective not reflect the great pace of change today, leaving more room for movements and flows than for structures, which was the prime focus of sociology in the 1970s?

Globalization, New Technologies and the International Public Sphere

Information and communication technologies, as we have just seen, have contributed to the profound transformation of communities and the types of private inter-individual exchanges. Could these technologies also contribute to the formation of an international public sphere, as a forum for reasoned critical debate where opinions are formulated on issues and policies involving the public good in the emerging transnational social space? How can national public opinions regarding the power of corporations, the state and international organizations be expressed at this scale given such human diversity? Major decisions are made by super- and supra-national organizations, without necessarily any representation by citizens. International economic regimes that ignore local living conditions are being put in place. The state's traditional regulatory safeguards are falling apart, and there is still uncertainty as to how to replace them. States may end up having less control over many phenomena, but citizens even more so. In many cultures, the ability to form and express opinions, a fundamental condition of democratic life, has been altered by religious practices, and authoritarian regimes. Today, with the premises of a globalized human society gradually becoming established, how are the terms of global solidarity to be defined and how can the hard-won democratic gains endure in the new societal order currently under construction? The issue of the development of a global public sphere arises, which is central to post-societal creativity: owing to (a) the capacity of the public space to sustain the formation of opinions, identities, a common culture as well as lifestyles; (b) its diversity if not divisions; and (c) its potential role in maintaining democratic life in this new globalized world.

In Chapter 5, *Information Technology and the International Public Sphere*, Craig Calhoun proposes to clarify the nature of the ties that bind these two terms in the context of globalization and the shifting foundations of production and dissemination of knowledge. If globalization results from the considerable transnational expansion of the private sector (Sales and Beschorner, 2005), it has also been driven by the intensive development of information, communication and transportation technologies in a movement that dates back to sixteenth century. Radical change has occurred in the past twenty years as a result of computer-mediated communications and has led to the emergence of an economy operating in real time and based on networked firms (Castells, 1996). Economic agents, far more than citizens, are the ones who benefit most from Information Technology (IT) and electronic media. Moreover, as Calhoun states, the 'dark sides of globalization' are using these technologies, thereby creating new risks and hazards. Global interconnections, for example, have transformed war. The forces of terrorism are using technology to their own ends, forcing societies to employ far more radical security and surveillance measures. Calhoun analyses a number of these dangers, and then finally identifies reasons for hope, including the formation of a public space, namely an international civil society supported by the Internet and other means of communication, particularly television.

Although corporations are the ones that benefit the most intensively from information technologies, these technologies have helped create a vigorous international public sphere. From this perspective, it is true that discussion groups and web sites supported by powerful search engines have facilitated the exchange of information in terms of interests and opinions regarding social issues and debates both locally and globally. On the other hand, the ability to reach very large groups of people is facilitated by email. The Internet, a system that does not lend itself to state control, seemingly plays the role of eighteenth-century cafés alluded to by Habermas (1962/1991; 1981/1984) in his thesis on the public sphere. It is also true that democratic states can relay public aspirations with regard to human rights, social policies and the environment in the transnational space. But says Calhoun, this does not account for the 'partnership of corporate powers and national governments backed by international agencies serving that partnership and a global culture heavily shaped by neoliberalism'. Limitations on the expression of opinions and the debate in the transnational space should not therefore lead us to exaggerate the power of such a civil society. It would be difficult for the channels of such expression to find in the transnational space an interlocutor comparable to the national state. Civil society retains a definite national character and national governments are the ones that echo opinion movements with considerable ambiguity from their respective societies. Nevertheless, information technologies provide opportunities and specificities to at least develop this forum, namely the global public sphere. They facilitate, both locally and globally, openness, self-organization, cultural creativity and even forms of solidarity.

Calhoun's analysis is qualified but essentially optimistic: while noting the inequalities introduced by information technologies, Calhoun indicates that they also provide means of creativity, for engineers and designers, as well as for other users, including artists who use the Internet as a new way of creating and disseminating their work. Dotcoms, he says, offer greater freedom than governments or even universities. The potential associated with information technologies is not just political, but also cultural: they offer means for re-imagining the nature of social relations and cultural creativity.

A Critical Look at Knowledge Society and Innovation

Developed societies' obsession with discovery and innovation and consequently the development of systems to foster creativity and knowledge, has led to a reflection on the conditions and means for stimulating knowledge-based research and innovation. For example, researchers have proposed the model of the national systems of innovations (Freeman, 1995; Lundvall, 1988; 1992; Nelson, 1993); the system of relations and networks associated with the university-industry-government Triple Helix (Etzkowitz and Levdesdorff, 2000), which is key to the mastery of the innovation flow; and the differentiation between two modes of knowledge production (Gibbons *et al.*, 1994). Mode 1, essentially the former academic system, is characterized by researchers working in isolation, the compartmentalization of disciplines and the fragmentation of knowledge; whereas Mode 2 is associated with application and utilization, the ability to handle uncertainty and is carried out within many synergistic institutions, in a transdisciplinary context, by self-organized, mobile, temporary teams connected via flexible networks.[7]

In Chapter 6, *Creativity in an Orwellian Key: A Sceptic's Guide to the Post-Sociological Imaginary*, Steve Fuller takes pleasure, and not without reason, in criticizing this somewhat caricature-like distinction used time and again as a basis for national scientific policies.[8] He is specifically concerned with the ever-increasing importance placed on transforming universities into 'engines of economic growth'. Fuller maintains that an Orwelian regime of Newspeak demeans our understanding of life in society. The emergence of concepts such as 'information society' and 'knowledge society' used to describe contemporary societies on the basis of a single assumption constitutes the most revealing symptom of such 'Newspeak'.

Sociology has not remained untouched by this movement, under the effects of not only a post-sociological discussion centred on key notions of 'mobility' and 'innovation' – two phenomena that retain their own intrinsic value, independent of their consequences – but also through the resurgence of interest in the concept of community, as noted above, to the detriment of the concept of institution, a reversal that is particularly deceptive in the eyes of the author. However, for Fuller, the construction of institutions has shaped societies more than individual or communitarian mobilities, a perspective that could lead to some lengthy discussions.[9]

Innovation, presented as the key to competitiveness, is, in the eyes of Fuller, merely 'the first global policy craze of the twenty-first century'. The contemporary cult of innovation is simply the celebration of business over industry, a 'normative economic strategy' and the 'prerogative of losers'.

On the basis of Schumpeter's idea that 'innovation is creative destruction', Steve Fuller has formulated the thesis that 'innovation is correlated with a devaluation of what things have been in favour of what they might become.' He believes that there is a 'mystique' surrounding innovation that promotes the presumed genius of the Schumpeterian entrepreneur, who assumes the risks of innovation and leaves precursors in oblivion. In many cases, it is an absence of collective memory that makes people capable of 'recognizing achievements as innovative', and many innovations are simply a form of repackaging. One may well ask whether there are indeed that many truly innovative companies. The proposals Fuller advances to conclude his thesis seem paradoxical and recall the introduction to Francis Bacon's essay on vicissitude:[10] (a) innovations are 'reactivated lost futures' or as Plato's Meno said, they are 'forms of reminiscence'; (b) 'a highly innovative society wastes its potential by making poor use of its past.'

Fearing that sociology would be reduced to a 'genetically programmed version of rational choice economics', he reasserts his conviction that, as the founders of sociology intended, the discipline must distance itself from biology. Innovations emerge less from some social biologism, than from planned collective effort aimed at the well-being of humanity. This would broaden human potential. The state would then have the obligation to 'seed innovation – in the form of publicly financed education – as an extension of its transgenerational stewardship over part of that potential'. In the end, and paradoxically, everything happens as if the issue was to edify true knowledge societies, a theme taken up by Nico Stehr in Chapter 2.

Creativity and Communication in the Production of Knowledge

Sociology has rarely broached the idea of creativity, which has for some time been the private preserve of philosophy and psychology. The role it plays in classical sociology is marginal. Gabriel Tarde at the end of the nineteenth century defends interpsychology against Durkheim and his school, and considers inventions as a factor of change. For Durkheim, society is the breeding ground for 'creative effervescence' (1912/1990: 611) and holds a creative power that no observable being can equal (1912/1990: 637).[11] Although economists have frequently worked on technological or organizational innovations, sociologists have been far more active in investigating the production of knowledge and artistic production. More recently, Hans Joas expanded the concept of creative capacity to include the entire realm of human action. He believes that 'a third model of action should be added to the two dominant models of action, namely rational action and normatively oriented action. What I have in mind is a model that emphasizes the creative character of human action. Beyond that, I hope to show that this third model overarches both the others' (Joas, 1992/1996: 4).

Joas shows that the idea of creativity, specifically the ability to imagine new, risky paths through uncharted territory has all too often been viewed as attributing creative properties to a concrete form of action to the exclusion of all others. That applies to the three main metaphors for creativity, namely *expression* (the idea of authenticity), *production* (objects) and *revolution* (radical restructuring of societal institutions).[12] On the contrary, one must think of creativity as the 'analytical dimension of human action'. Every human action is potentially creative.

This theme is broached in this collection of essays only from the perspective of the *production of knowledge*. The first two sections of this book focus on the role of formal knowledge, reflexive creativity and communicational innovations in social transformations at various levels ranging from organizations, communities and the public sphere. The third and the last section delves into the relationship between creativity and communication in the production of knowledge.

Should discovery be perceived as unsocialized, as a product of solitude and illumination, or rather as an eminently socialized activity tied to networks and/or institutions? What status should be attributed to creative individuals and what are their attributes? What role do intellectual discussions and debates play from a communicational perspective in the development of scientific discoveries and intellectual developments? What role do the gatekeepers and the audience play? Is creative capacity tied simply to the strength of an intellectual or scientific network? What are the features of the most creative institutions? In this final section, the reader will come to understand the relationship between creativity, communication and knowledge production from various angles.

Creativity, Communication and Knowledge Status

The relationship as regards the status of knowledge has been the object of debate and controversy since ancient Greece. Philippe Breton in Chapter 7, *Between Science and Rhetoric: A Recurrent Debate on the Role of Communication and Creativity in the Definition of Knowledge*, goes back to the sources of this relationship to integrate it into contemporary debate on the status of knowledge. From this perspective, the starting point must be the Aristotelian distinction among (a) science based on demonstrative syllogism with definite premises; (b) reasoning from probable premises based on dialectics and rhetoric; and finally (c) poetics, the production of fiction. This distinction leads to three types of knowledge in terms of their relative importance in relation to the division of reality. It opens a space for scientific thought, a space for plausible knowledge and a space for fiction.

If we exclude fiction, a central distinction emerges between what is a scientific statement and what is opinion. Aristotle associated opinion on the one hand to dialectics and on the other to rhetoric. Bear in mind that in the classical sense, dialectics, which is different from, yet still oriented towards, the scientific method (Chrétien-Goni, 2002: 291) is a method of argumentation reserved for open debate with a view to producing new knowledge, supplemental to a given opinion.[13] Opinion is also tied to rhetoric, the persuasive use of language to influence an audience.[14]

What status therefore do dialectics and rhetoric occupy in relation to intellectual creation and discovery? Stated simply, for any idea or statement whether certain or probable there are two phases – *inventio* and *dispositio*: 'it is one thing to invent ideas, and arguments, another to structure them appropriately so as to communicate them' (Chrétien-Goni, 2002: 291). *Inventio* defines content for a subject, whereas *dispositio* is the phase where the subject is given form. Opposition between these two moments (which entail intense toing and froing) often leads to associating solitude with the process of discovery,[15] which for many would be unsocialized and incommunicable. This explains why heuristics in the nineteenth century has been reduced to a psychology of discovery, and suggests that communicational processes do not come into play until after the solitary *inventio* phase. Soundly argued discourse to describe the discovery would therefore be developed in a second phase (*dispositio*). Following the sequences of the art of rhetoric, the discourse is then drafted (*elocutio* or Style) and finally presented to an audience or in a public debate in a structured form (*actio* or Delivery).

With respect to the role of communication in the production of knowledge, Philippe Breton sees the relationship with the audience as a determining dimension of knowledge production. Continuing with the Aristotelian perspective, Breton shows that the solitary scientific approach differs from that of the dialectician or rhetor,[16] who from the outset takes his relationship with the audience into consideration: 'reception is an essential mechanism to production itself.' And even more so for the humanists in the Renaissance era: 'communication and production of opinion become inseparable' because knowledge is conceived as being co-produced as part of a debate. 'Knowledge, for Breton, becomes a matter of network, at least as far as opinion is concerned. It is from there that some started to think that all knowledge, including scientific knowledge, is produced within networks', a thesis also advanced by Randall Collins later in this collection.

This position goes a long way in understanding heuristic procedures and leads to a contemporary re-examination of the moments and conditions of creativity. As regards the moment of invention, without denying the role of the turning point or moment of 'illumination' and the presence of creative individuals, today we cannot ignore the institutional framework, which consists of departments, laboratories and research groups and the role of its intra- and inter-communicational quality. Reflexive creativity cannot be implemented in organizational isolation. This helps explain the contemporary institutional configurations of the innovation processes where interactions, networking, coordination and intensive communication between scientists, intellectuals and organizations are so central. Such configurations include multidisciplinarity and hybridization of scientific fields (Dogan, 2000; Dogan and Pahre, 1990; Hollingsworth and Hollingsworth, 2000; Latour, 1987), inter-organizational cooperation, strategic technological alliances and techno-economic networking around scientific, technical and market nodes (Callon, 1991; 1992).

The status of knowledge: For Philippe Breton, it is essential to strive to understand the contemporary status of two major constituents of knowledge, namely scientific statement and opinion. The advantage of scientific statements is that they can be verified through argumentation and evidence, and can be taken into consideration by the scientific community because the author of such statements is in a position to 'reject any opposite and contradictory statement on the same referent' (Lyotard, 1979: 43). Opinion[17] does not have the same conditions for legitimization.[18] It does not benefit from the laboratory arsenal.[19]

Philippe Breton questions whether there is a place for opinion as knowledge appropriate for public affairs between scientific research for truth itself, and the pure field of fiction, since the opposition between scientific and literary cultures endures, without any place given to opinion and rhetoric. This opposition is not just discipline related; what differentiates the perspectives resides even more in the distinctions among three positions on the status of knowledge.

The first position, an objectivistic point of view, ranks scientific statement and opinion (at a much lower level) as forms of knowledge. This perspective tends to see the humanities and social sciences or the political world as generators of 'degraded' knowledge because it is not feasible to construct scientific statements. Knowledge in these areas is still too strongly tied to opinion.

The second position, which is relativistic, maintains that the production of scientific statements is equal to the production of opinions, because the relevant rules of operation are identical. According to this position, the focus should be on the rhetorical dimension of scientific discourse. There would be no difference between an objective fact and an opinion, both of which are derived from knowledge, which is always built on rhetoric. The production of knowledge is an eminently social activity linked to the role of the community of peers. Legitimization is obtained by way of rhetorical processes and power games. Breton, however, wonders whether this position in the end degrades all knowledge.

The third position defends the idea that there is symmetry between science and opinion because the fields being investigated are different. The scientific statement would be reserved for physical and natural sciences, whereas opinion would pertain to the social world, particularly the humanities and social sciences.

Sociologists cannot help but think that the variable legitimacy of opinion as well as that of science has something to do with the societal context, which leads Breton to hypothesize that there is a close link between the status of knowledge and the social context for a macro-historical perspective. The status of opinion and the status of the scientific proposition can only be asserted within a favourable social context. Breton maintains that opinion-related heuristics only have meaning in democratic societies that are open to political and legal debates, as well as to debates on the values of the society. Civil society – an area where opinions are shaped and even more so where social creativity emerges – can only thrive in open, democratic social contexts. The affirmation of opinion in the debate is in direct opposition with social closure, orthodoxies and the most regressive forms of authoritarianism and fundamentalism. Opinion blossoms, on the contrary, in multiple forms where there is freedom. From this angle, which is one of the themes taken up by Nico Stehr, knowledge contributes to opening up societies, hence the association between knowledge societies and democratic life.[20]

The production of knowledge is independent from neither the community of peers nor the broader audience targeted by the researcher. Knowledge is only readily produced within macrosocietal contexts that are open to debate, particularly in the case of the social sciences. How Chapters 8 and 9 broach the role of research institutions, personal characteristics of the great scientific thinkers and the role of networks, will be discussed in the following paragraphs.

Scientific Discoveries and High Cognitive Complexity:
Diversity, Multidisciplinarity and Communication

Rogers Hollingsworth focuses on major biomedical discoveries in Chapter 8 *High Cognitive Complexity and the Making of Major Scientific Discoveries*, leading us to the heart of scientific creativity and raising more concretely the issue of society's capacity to create creativity.

Hollingsworth looks at social factors underlying innovation, and like Randall Collins he places the emphasis on intermediate or mesosociological levels of analysis. Hollingsworth first considers the social and institutional contexts that foster major discoveries, a theme he developed in his previous works. Then he examines the properties of laboratories. The primary focus of this chapter, however, from both psychosociological and neurophysiological perspectives is on people; those research scientists who have made major scientific discoveries. His research covers more than 290 scientific discoveries, in the basic biomedical sciences in France, England, Germany and the United States, and takes into consideration the institutional and organizational properties of the laboratories and the personal characteristics of the researchers, for example, their socio-cultural origin and the diversity of their fields of interest and avocations. The main thrust of his study is the concept of 'high cognitive complexity', namely a person's capacity to understand a complex world, establish 'connectivity among phenomena in multiple fields of science', and transpose ideas from one field of knowledge to another.

Hollingsworth distinguishes two types of laboratories in terms of their organizational features: Type A laboratories, which are characterized by greater 'cognitively scientific diversity'; Type B laboratories, which have more restricted areas of research and remain essentially oriented towards a single discipline. His conclusion is clear: the probability of a discovery being made in a Type A laboratory is far greater than in Type B laboratories. It is remarkable to observe that integrating significant scientific diversity is essential for addressing issues relative to different scientific fields. Hollingsworth demonstrates the importance of multidisciplinarity, and the central role of communication and scientific dialogue within research institutions for strengthening the integration of knowledge and expanding intellectual horizons. Diversity and integrating diversity are inextricably linked to communication and intense interaction not only between researchers within the same laboratory, but also among laboratories within the same institution. And if the internalization of a 'high level of cognitive complexity' is a necessary condition for major discoveries, it is essential to understand the variation in 'high levels of cognitive complexity' among research scientists themselves.

Hollingsworth devotes much of his essay to resolving this enigma. His analysis is derived from various sources: interviews with various research scientists in various countries, a study of archives and various documents (autobiographies, etc.). The hypothesis he is attempting to verify is that 'cognitive complexity tends to have its roots in various social psychological processes.' The two processes he is investigating are: the internalization of multiple cultures and the practice of non-scientific avocations.

According to Hollingsworth, the 'multiple cultural identity' builds one's capacity to 'live intuitively in multiple worlds simultaneously' and to 'observe the world in more complex terms'. This leads to a greater potential for innovation. The example he provides is that of German–Jewish scientists, whose exceptional achievements cannot be explained only by the importance given to reading and formal learning within Jewish families. Their double interior/exterior identity and status as strangers have played a major role, as seen with certain Nobel Prize winners such as Gertrude Elion and Rosalyn Yalow. Marginality definitely played a role, so also determination fuelled by sacrifice, discipline and a huge curiosity for new things: these are the socio-psychological conditions for innovation in science. Diversity is not just about religious or ethnic diversity; it can also be linked to social origin.

The second dimension pertaining to the concept of 'high cognitive complexity' involves 'non-scientific avocations'. Hollingsworth's hypothesis is that whenever research scientists have other fields of interests and practices – art, crafts, music, literature and even politics – these have a positive effect on the research they undertake because such avocations serve to expand their cognitive complexity and foster intuitions from non-scientific fields. Major discoveries could therefore be partly tied to an ability to establish unexpected connections among different fields.

If internalizing high cognitive complexity is a necessary condition for making major discoveries and if research scientists who have this characteristic do not achieve such major discoveries, we need to explore why the results among researchers vary. Hollingsworth therefore connects, on the one hand, the results of his study of the process of discovery and high cognitive complexity, and on the other, recent results in the fields of neuroscience and cognitive psychology. To explain cognitive variation observed among research scientists with high cognitive complexity, Hollingsworth hypothesizes that besides chance and contingency 'the starting point of this literature is that every brain is unique and distinctive', specifically because of the very complexity of the brain, which provides multiple combinations of interconnections between its different parts and leads to extensive, ongoing differentiation. The institutional dimension serves to combine these personal characteristics, providing research scientists with high levels of cognitive complexity an opportunity to work together in centres and laboratories that foster diversity, communication and interaction in the quest to understand particularly complex phenomena. With their capacity for dialectics and rhetoric, they will then be in a position to translate their knowledge for the scientific community, which will, where applicable, recognize it as a major discovery.

Hollingsworth's study remains as he himself acknowledges 'essentially at the stage of hypothesis and/or theory generation'. Efforts can be made to promote specific types of laboratories, or specific types of organization, but given that major discoveries are rare, it is clear that, as Fuller also underlined, planning a discovery is difficult to accomplish: discoveries seem to emerge from chaotic processes, associated with risk and contingency. Reflexive creativity cannot be viewed in a deterministic manner, independent of ongoing interaction between individuals and institutions. Major discoveries are made by individuals with remarkable characteristics, but as Hollingsworth's research shows it is not possible to disregard the role of 'structural and cultural environments where the scientist's potential can be realized'.

Beyond the Great Research Scientists: Network Creativity

For Rogers Hollingsworth, the chances of making a major scientific discovery are associated with individuals who have internalized multiple cultures, have the capacity to integrate knowledge from many scientific fields, and are sustained by research institutions that foster multidisciplinarity and intense scientific dialogue. However, for Randall Collins, the creativity of intellectual networks is paramount. In Chapter 9, *The Creativity of Intellectual Networks and the Struggle over Attention Space*, Collins focuses on intellectuals, particularly philosophers. The author sees creativity as synonymous not with discoveries or problem-solving, but rather with the definition of new topics, or the development of new tools of argument, and the opening of new avenues of research for new generations of intellectuals. The primary condition of creativity is not, he challenges, the presence of brilliant individuals or geniuses; the main actor and creator is the network, that is, the fairly dense system of relationships and interactions that operates like a fraternity or a clan.

Thinkers should not be thought of as being in splendid isolation, but rather as participants in a network, which is itself defined as the actor on the intellectual stage. Networks should be defined as intergenerational groupings incorporating the eminent master surrounded by his or her disciples and their equally eminent students; as well as in terms of the ideas, intellectual movements and emotional energy that circulate through these networks, are placed by contemporaries at the centre of attention and transformed from generation to generation. Within this attention space, 'creativity occurs by conflict among rival positions' with regard to the same problem set. The eminent thinker, canonized by history, is merely 'a concentration, a distillation of what the network has done.' Collins therefore questions the role of the genius *per se* in the history of ideas.

His general hypothesis is: 'eminence attracts eminence.' Eminent intellectuals are defined as those who are connected with other eminent intellectuals, whether vertically through the generations or horizontally with other intellectuals on their way to making their mark historically. Collins defines eminence as the influence intellectuals exert on future generations, as seen through the dissemination of their written works and the place their name acquires in the history of their discipline.

Intellectual networks are characterized by the circulation and rearrangement of ideas, intense arguments, as well as emotional energy and powerful ambitions and rivalry. The great thinkers are those who are rewarded for what occurs within the network. These relationships, which are at once cognitive and emotional, are often so intense that they could be qualified using Durkheim's expression 'collective effervescence' around the great thinkers who exercise charismatic power as a result of their level of concentration, the energy they place in intellectual production, and their total commitment to their work. Through these networks, students for their part acquire intellectual sophistication, as well as emotional energy from their masters. This brings us back to the importance of solitude alternating with social contacts in intellectual production. What leads actors to reach the top of the attention space above the mass of intellectuals is their immense emotional energy and the long, intense reflection that results in a major rearrangement of ideas. Collins therefore like Hollingsworth stresses that thinkers are involved in the 'internalized conversations of the network' and that 'creativity is a process of making coalitions in one's mind, fitting together arguments that feel successful.' For Collins, however, all processes of intellectual creativity exhibit a collective character: it is the network that carries the action, even if the ideas, at any particular instant, are in someone's brain, or are being formulated by an individual.[21] This is where dialectics and rhetoric come into play in the networks that communicate, distribute, combat and transform ideas. Collins stresses the conflictual character of intellectual life: without conflict, there is no creativity, only tradition! What distinguishes those who reach the top is their high level of concentration, their emotional energy and their 'fanatical focus'. The network itself generates opposition and rivalry, which draws attention to issues raised by the network. Creativity, Collins says, occurs when energy is growing, in conjunction with a positive reception in the attention space.

Processes for Evaluating Creativity

As noted earlier, the community of peers contributes to legitimizing the intellectual or scientific process. It accomplishes this in a mass system by way of an evaluation system. Originality in research and publications is one of the main criteria used to evaluate creative and research work, in art, literature, the humanities and science. Is this not the primary goal of research and an institutional standard of science? There is clearly, primarily in the sciences, a race to be the first to present new findings or new interpretations. The process is all the more competitive because success translates into multiple recognition, not to mention the resources needed to pursue one's research. Latour and Woolgar (1979) dubbed this the 'credibility cycle'. Included among the major social and cultural factors leading to inventions and innovation identified by sociologists are the mechanisms used to evaluate research. These evaluations place the work before an 'effective' audience, which Michel Meyer differentiates from the 'projective' audience (2004a: 38–42; 2004b: 134–36);[22] the effective audience is represented by those who evaluate journal articles, research projects, or are responsible for awarding the prizes or awards. The effective audience, in the form of the Peer Review System, or Gatekeeping, has the singular function in the sciences to evaluate, select and legitimize research projects and findings from the perspective of creativity, innovation, relevance and originality, a function that reflects the dialectics stage discussed earlier. But what do we really know about how this particular audience operates?

Michèle Lamont *et al.*, in Chapter 10 *Evaluating Creative Minds: The Assessment of Originality in Peer Review* suggests a way of analysing the peer-review process from the standpoint of originality, as it applies to the award of grants by the peer review panels formed by the major social sciences and humanities funding organizations in the United States and Canada. It is generally recognized that the determining factor in awarding grants and prizes is the quantity – not only for the reasons outlined by Collins, but also for bureaucratic reasons – as well as the quality of a researcher's work and publications, which is more complex to evaluate. One of the main criteria consists in acknowledging the innovative and original character of the research. But what exactly is meant by originality? In the sciences, originality is often associated with the making of new discoveries, but how is originality defined in the humanities and social sciences? And what kind of expertise is needed for recognizing originality and innovativeness? Originality is not obvious, and that is precisely what made Lynn Dirk say, 'there is double jeopardy: the difficulty in being original is made all the more difficult by the problem of evaluating originality' (Dirk, 1999: 766). It is well known that within scientific environments that are not free from dogmatism, there is considerable resistance to change, which corresponds to an 'essential tension' between tradition and change in the sciences (Kuhn, 1977). Whenever a new paradigm is needed, the definition of originality is the subject of conflict and endless negotiations. In an attempt to understand how originality is evaluated, Lamont *et al.* conducted interviews with members of evaluation panels from various disciplines (including interdisciplinary fields).

The authors demonstrated the impact of three elements. First, the evaluation process is conducted in a bureaucratic context and consists of well-established procedures as well as explicit rules; second, the evaluation not only addresses the specific characteristics (subject, theory, method, hypotheses, etc.) of the proposals themselves, but also addresses the candidates' characteristics (their personal and moral qualities, such as integrity, courage, independence, sense of responsibility, audaciousness and other qualities such as brilliance). The interesting issue here is that this shift from project characteristics to the candidate's qualities indicates that the peer-review panel contravenes its own desire to maintain its objectivity by not complying with the Mertonian diktat according to which a strict distinction must be observed between the proposals and the proposers. Finally, the panelists' decision entails elements of trust towards the candidate and along with an emotional response (enthusiasm, excitement, etc.) towards the proposals. Originality elicits strong feelings ranging from admiration to objection.[23] The emotional load associated with evaluating research work is all the stronger because it entails the evaluation of work by researchers who are often competitors. In conclusion, the authors postulate the existence of the same 'rhetoric of excellence' among the various disciplines, thereby putting into perspective the differences previously raised in the literature, at least as far as the discourse of originality in concerned. They point to other avenues of research for the sociology of knowledge and science, including the study of decisionmaking within the dynamic context of the evaluation process.

Conclusion

Modern societies are generating and absorbing change at an accelerated pace. This seemingly disorganized race towards advanced modernity is driven essentially by knowledge, communication and creativity. A significant part of this collection of essays is devoted to understanding and analysing knowledge and communication as the sources and effects of social transformations. Although the focus today is often on globalization, the essays presented in this collection support the idea that as much importance should be placed on knowledge, innovation and the immense development in communications if we are to understand the transformations affecting communities, organizations and economic institutions, the opening up of societies and the transformation of the public sphere, all of which are discussed at length in this collection. As Nico Stehr states in Chapter 2, we live in fragile societies and they are fragile, not because they are liberal democracies but because they are knowledge based. If this has freed up capacities for action, it also contains enormous risks and uncertainty, and consequently social and political problems along with central moral issues.

Beyond these analyses, this book devotes special attention to understanding ties between creativity and communication in the production of knowledge. The sociological perspectives presented in these essays are clearly separate from a heuristic approach that is reduced to the psychology of discovery and creativity. The authors weigh in on the role of individuals, intellectual and scientific networks and the community of peers and institutions. It would be unrealistic to view intellectual and scientific creativity as purely solitary pursuits driven by the individual genius of actors. At the same time, in attempting to understand creativity, one cannot overlook the fact that 'the actor is never just a social being: he is not in society but facing it and mostly facing the power hidden within its institutions, standards and interests' (Touraine, 1999: VI). Solitude and illumination, terms that frequently crop up in reports describing highly creative moments, cannot be seen in any other light. But although cognitive complexity, which Hollingsworth associates with great discoveries, is built as a habitus within individuals and becomes one of their defining characteristics and strengths, it is still forged through strong social and intellectual experiences. The concept of reflexive creativity specific to advanced knowledge societies cannot be defined in a deterministic manner independent of ongoing interaction among individuals within networks and institutions. The large infrastructures put in place within the framework of research policies are clearly indispensable, but they cannot lead to discoveries, innovations, or the definition of new problems without this high quality of communication which is neglected in many academic settings. Networks are not however a simple grouping of relationships and exchanges. The circulation of ideas, conversations, debates and conflicts that occurs within research institutions and networks mobilize individuals, some of whom, perhaps thanks to their high cognitive complexity, will succeed in producing creative rearrangements which will change thought, culture and social practices.

Endnotes

1 We would like to thank André J. Bélanger for his incisive and insightful comments on the first version of this chapter. We would also like to thank Lottie White for her work on the translation.

2 Organizations and institutions can be described as sets of embedded knowledge which include technology, administrative procedures, organizational structures and hierarchical relations (Lam, 2004).

3 In general, the new growth theories have recognized the importance of knowledge, but it must be said that they have not, however, delved very far into an understanding of what makes it productive. In practice, knowledge has diverse forms and its relationship with economic production is highly complex.

4 One of the significant consequences of a more sophisticated education is that in the long term it has the capacity to make individuals less dependent on the national system in which they were raised.

5 See Sales (2005) and Amsellem (2007). COVISINT which seemed to be in the automotive industry a model of integration for electronic trade and Business-to-Business (B2B) eMarket place, failed because of 'a lack of trust and acceptance among automotive suppliers'.

6 Steve Fuller in Chapter 6 takes a highly critical view of this theme.

7 'In Mode 1 problems are set and solved in a context governed by the, largely academic, interests of a specific community. In contrast, Mode 2 knowledge is carried out in a context of application. Mode 1 is disciplinary while Mode 2 is transdisciplinary. Mode 1 is characterized by homogeneity, Mode 2 by heterogeneity. Organisationally, Mode 1 is hierarchical and tends to preserve its form, while mode 2 is more heterarchical and transient. Each employs a different type of quality control. In comparison with Mode 1, Mode 2 is more socially accountable and reflexive. It includes a wider, more temporary, and heterogeneous set of practitioners, collaborating on a problem defined in specific and localized context' (Gibbons *et al.*, 1994: 3).

8 For a particularly stimulating critique of the Mode 1 and 2 models as well as the 'Triple Helix' model, see Shinn (2002); see also Godin and Trépanier (2000).

9 See for example Urry (2000) or the literature on world systems and transnational flows.

10 'Salomon saith, There is no new thing upon the earth. So that as Plato had an imagination, That all knowledge was but remembrance; so Salomon giveth his sentence, That all novelty is but oblivion' (Bacon, 1625/1985).

11 This concept of social creativity is moreover not a question of caprice for Durkheim, given the importance he places on the concept of the ideal, of which creation is what allows society to make and remake itself, incessantly: 'A society can neither create nor recreate itself without creating an ideal' (1912/1990: 603).

12 One could perhaps expand on Joas' idea by showing that artistic, literary and other forms of creation are the articulation of expression and production, whereas innovations are the articulation of production and revolution. All major technological innovation – to wit printers, steam engines and computers – lead to (cause and effect) not only an increase in productivity but also and especially to a transformation in production relationships and in organizational and institutional changes.

13 'Dialectics is therefore the "art of discussion and examination", and although the goal is not to seek the truth, in focussing on opinion it provides a set of instruments that make it possible to argue any topic and as such dialectics ends up being a general methodology for researching and understanding principles' (Chrétien-Goni, 2002: 291).

14 'Rhetorics is the art of expressing something to someone, the art of acting through words on opinions, emotions, decisions at least within the limitations and standards governing the mutual influence of the interlocutors in a given society. Rhetorics is also the discipline underlying the methodical exercise of this art, by learning to prepare an appropriate discourse. The underlying principle of rhetorics is philosophical reflection on the eloquence and power of language in human societies and the capacity to adjust our representations to those prepared by other' (Douhay-Soublin, 2002: 927).

15 And moreover one's own search for truth regardless of the audience's opinion.

16 But are research scientists not also called upon to be dialecticians and rhetor, beyond the 'illumination' phase?

17 Opinion should not be confused with dogmatic statements, because unlike the latter opinion can be debated.

18 Perelman said that unlike 'demonstration, which can be presented in the form of calculations, argumentation is designed to persuade or convince others, and is only conceivable in a psychosociological context' (1968: 367).

19 Let any human being have enough information and exert enough thought upon any question, and the result will be that he will arrive at a certain definite conclusion, which is the same that any other mind will reach under sufficiently favorable circumstances. ... There is, then, to every question

a true answer, a final conclusion, to which the opinion of everyman is constantly gravitating (Peirce quoted by Habermas, 1968/1971: 126).

20 This central link, however, may be deeply affected by the breakdown in the traditional public and private dialectics tied to the transnational expansion of the private sector. This breakdown deconstructs the role of national civil societies, hence the demands to build an international public society, as discussed by Craig Calhoun.

21 It is interesting to note that certain research pschyologists have adopted this position. The work of Mihaly Csikszentmihalyi in this area is significant: 'My goal in this chapter will be to argue that while the mind has quite a lot to do with genius and creativity it is not the place where these phenomena can be found. The location of genius is not in any particular individual's mind, but in a virtual space, or system, where an individual interacts with a cultural domain and with a social field. It is only in the relation of these three separate entities that creativity, or the work of genius, manifests itself' (1998: 39; see also 1996).

22 The projective audience is the audience targeted by the research and its impacts (a discipline, a society, a community, etc.).

23 This could well be explained by what Nietzsche said of originality: 'What is originality? To *see* something that does not yet bear a name, that cannot yet be named, although it is before everybody's eyes. As people are usually constituted, it is the name that first makes a thing generally visible to them. – Original persons have also for the most part been the namers of things' (Nietzsche, 1882/1910: 207–08).

References

Adhikari, K. and Sales, A. (eds) (2001) 'New Directions in the Study of Knowledge, Economy and Society', Sage Studies in International Sociology, Monograph 2. *Current Sociology*, 49(4): 1–218.

Amable, B., Barré, R. and Boyer, R. (1997) *Les systèmes d'innovation à l'ère de la globalisation.* Paris: Economica.

Amsellem, D. (2007) La construction de la confiance dans l'e-business B2B: Les Mécanismes d'autorégulation, Department of sociology, M.Sc. thesis, Université de Montréal.

Bacon, F. (1625/1985), 'Essay LVIII: of Vicissitude of Things', *The Essays.* London: Penguin Books.

Badie, B. and Smouts, M.-C. (1992) *Le retournement du monde. Sociologie de la scène internationale.* Paris: Presses de Sciences Po/Dalloz.

Ben-David, J. (1991/1997) *Éléments d'une sociologie historique des sciences.* Edited with an Introduction by G. Freudenthal. Paris: Presses Universitaires de France.

Calhoun, C. (1992) 'Introduction', in C. Calhoun (ed.), *Habermas and the Public Sphere.* Cambridge, MA: MIT Press, pp. 1–48.

Callon, M. (1991) 'Réseaux technico-économiques et irréversibilités', in R. Boyer, B. Chavance and O. Godard (eds), *Figures de l'irréversibilité en économie.* Paris: Éditions de l'Ecole des Hautes Etudes en Sciences Sociales, pp. 195–230.

Callon, M. (1992) 'Variété et irréversibilité dans les réseaux de conception et d'adoption des techniques', in D. Foray and C. Freeman (eds), *Technologie et richesse des nations.* Paris: Economica, pp. 275–324.

Castells, M. (1996) *The Information Age: Economy, Society and Culture.* Vol. 1, *The Rise of the Network Society.* Cambridge, MA/Oxford, UK: Blackwell Publishers.

Centre for Educational Research and Innovation/OECD (2000) *Knowledge Management in the Learning Society.* Paris: OECD.

Chandler, A. D. (1962) *Strategy and Structure: Chapters in the History of the American Industrial Enterprise.* Cambridge, MA: The Belknap Press of Harvard University Press.

Chrétien-Goni, J. P. (2002) 'Heuristique', *Encyclopaedia Universalis.* Vol. 11. Paris: Édition Encyclopaedia Universalis, pp. 291–96.

Csikszentmihalyi, M. (1996) *Creativity: Flow and the Psychology of Discovery and Invention.* New York: Harper Collins.

Csikszentmihalyi, M. (1998) 'Creativity and Genius: A Systems Perspective', in A. Steptoe (ed.), *Genius and the Mind: Studies of Creativity and Temperament.* Oxford: Oxford University Press, pp. 39–64.

Dirk, L. (1999) 'A Measure of Originality: The Elements of Science', *Social Studies of Science*, 29(5): 765–76.

Dogan, M. (2000) 'The Moving Frontiers of the Social Sciences', in S. R. Quah and A. Sales (eds), *The International Handbook of Sociology*. London: Sage Publications, pp. 35–49.

Dogan, M. and Pahre, R. (1990) *Creative Marginality: Innovation at the Intersections of Social Sciences*. Boulder, CO: Westview Press.

Douhay-Soublin, F. (2002) 'Rhétorique', *Encyclopaedia Universalis*. Vol. 19. Paris: Édition Encyclopaedia Universalis, pp. 927–31.

Drucker, P. (1993) *The Post-Capitalist Society*. New York: Harper Business.

Durkheim, E. (1912/1990) *Les formes élémentaires de la vie religieuse*. Paris: Presses Universitaires de France.

Etzkowitz, H. and Leydesdorff, L. (2000) 'The Dynamics of Innovation: From National Systems and "Mode 2" to a Triple Helix of University–Industry–Government Relations', *Research Policy*, 29(2): 109–23.

Florida, R. (2002) *The Rise of the Creative Class: And How It's Transforming Work, Leisure, Community and Everyday Life*. New York: Basic Books.

Freeman, C. (1995) 'The "National System of Innovation" in Historical Perspective', *Cambridge Journal of Economics*, 19(1): 5–24.

Freudenthal, G. (1991/1997) 'Introduction', in J. Ben-David, *Éléments d'une sociologie historique des sciences*. Edited with an Introduction by G. Freudenthal. Paris: Presses Universitaires de France, pp. 99–101.

Gellner, E. (1983) *Nations and Nationalism*. Ithaca, NY: Cornell University Press.

Gibbons, M., Limoges, C., Nowotny, H., Schwartzman, S., Scott, P. and Trow, M. (1994) *The New Production of Knowledge: The Dynamics of Science and Research in Contemporary Societies*. London: Sage.

Godin B. and Trépanier, M. (eds) (2000) *La science: nouvel environnement, nouvelles pratiques?*, thematic issue of *Sociologie et Sociétés*, 32(1): 1–170.

Habermas, J. (1962/1991) *The Structural Transformation of the Public Sphere: An Inquiry into a Category of Bourgeois Society*. Cambridge, MA: MIT Press.

Habermas, J. (1968/1971) *Knowledge and Human Interest*. Boston, MA: Beacon Press.

Habermas, J. (1981/1984) *The Theory of Communicative Action*. 2 vols. Boston: Beacon Press.

Hollingsworth, R. and Hollingsworth, E. J. (2000) 'Major Discoveries and Biomedical Research Organizations: Perspectives on Interdisciplinarity, Nurturing Leadership, and Integrated Structure and Cultures', in P. Weingart and N. Stehr (eds), *Practising Interdisciplinarity*. Toronto: University of Toronto Press, pp. 215–44.

Joas, H. (1992/1996) *The Creativity of Action*. Chicago, IL: The University of Chicago Press, p. 40.

Knorr-Cetina, K. D. (1997) 'Sociality with Objects: Social Relations in Postsocial Knowledge Societies', *Theory, Culture and Society*, 14(4): 1–30.

Knorr-Cetina, K. D. (1999) *Epistemic Cultures: How the Sciences Make Knowledge*. Cambridge, MA: Harvard University Press.

Knorr-Cetina, K. D. and Preda, A. (2001) 'The Epistemization of Economic Transactions', *Current Sociology*, 49(4): 29–44.

Kuhn, T. (1977) *The Essential Tension: Selected Studies in Scientific Tradition and Change*. Chicago, IL: University of Chicago Press.

Laïdi, Z. (2004) *La grande perturbation*. Paris: Flammarion.

Lam, A. (2004) 'Conocimiento tácito, aprendizaje organizacional e innovación. Una perspectiva social', in M. Á. Briceño Gil (ed.), *Universidad, Sector Productivo y Sustentabilidad*. Caracas: Universidad Central de Venezuela/Consejo de Desarollo Cientifico y Humanistico, pp. 189–222.

Latour, B. (1987) *Science in Action: How to Follow Scientists and Engineers through Society*. Cambridge, MA: Harvard University Press.

Latour, B. (1999) 'On recalling ANT', in J. Law and J. Hassard (eds), *Actor Network Theory and After*. Oxford: Blackwell/Sociological Review.

Latour, B. and Woolgar, S. (1979) *Laboratory Life: The Social Construction of Scientific Facts*. Los Angeles, CA/London, UK: Sage.

Lundvall, B.-Å. (1988) 'Innovation as an Interactive Process: From User–Producer Interaction to the National System of Innovation', in C. F. G. Dosi, C. Freeman, R. Nelson, G. Silverberg and L. Soete (eds), *Technical Change and Economic Theory*. London: Printer, pp. 349–69.

Lundvall, B.-Å. (ed.) (1992) *National Systems of Innovation: Towards a Theory of Innovation and Interactive Learning*. London: Pinter.

Lyotard, J.-F. (1979) *La condition postmoderne: Rapport sur le savoir*. Paris: Minuit.

Menger, P.-M. (2002) *Portrait de l'artiste en travailleur: Métamorphoses du capitalisme*. Paris: Seuil.

Meyer, M. (2004a) *La rhétorique*. Paris: Presses Universitaires de France.

Meyer, M. (2004b) 'Argumentation, rhétorique et problématologie', in M. Meyer (ed.), *Perelman et le renouveau de la rhétorique*. Paris: Presses Universitaires de France, pp. 123–38.

Moscovici, S. (1968) *Essai sur l'histoire humaine de la nature*. Paris: Flammarion.

Nelson, R. R. (1993) *National Innovation Systems: A Comparative Analysis*. Oxford: Oxford University Press.

Nietzsche, F. (1882/1910) *The Joyful Wisdom*. Edinburgh/London: T. N. Foulis.

Perelman, C. (1968) 'Argumentation', *Encyclopaedia Universalis*, Vol. 2: 367–68.

Popper, K. R. (1956) *The Open Universe: An Argument for Indeterminism*. Totowa, NJ: Rowman and Littlefield.

Reich, R. B. (1992) *The Work of Nations: Preparing Ourselves for 21st Century Capitalism*. New York: Vintage Books.

Rosenau, J. N. (1988) 'Patterned Chaos in Global Life: Structure and Process in the Two Worlds of World Politics', *International Political Science Review*, 9(4): 357–94.

Sales, A. (2005) 'L'impact de la globalisation et de l'économie du savoir sur la question linguistique au Québec', in A. Stefanescu and P. Georgeault (eds), *Le français au Québec: Les nouveaux défis*. Montréal: Conseil supérieur de la langue française/Fides, pp. 147–89.

Sales, A. and Beschorner, T. (2005) 'Societal Transformation and Business Ethics: The Expansion of the Private Sector and its Consequences', in N. Stehr, C. Henning and B. Weiler (eds), *The Moralization of the Markets*. New York: Transaction Books, pp. 227–54.

Sassen, S. (1999) *Globalization and its Discontents: Essays on the New Mobility of People and Money*. New York: New Press.

Shinn, T. (2002) 'The Triple Helix and New Production of Knowledge: Prepackaged Thinking on Science and Technology', *Social Studies of Science*, 32(4): 599–614.

Stopford, J. M. and Dunning, J. H. (1983) *Multinationals: Company Performance and Global Trends*. London: Macmillan.

Thurow, L. (1996) *The Future of Capitalism*. New York: William Morrow and Company.

Tomlinson, J. (1999) *Globalization and Cultures*. Chicago, IL: University of Chicago Press.

Touraine, A. (1969) *La société post-industrielle*. Paris: Denoël.

Touraine, A. (1999) 'Préface', in H. Joas, *La créativité de l'agir*. Paris: Cerf, pp. I–VII.

United Nations Conference on Trade and Development (2004) *World Investment Report 2004: The Shift towards Services*. New York/Geneva, Switzerland: United Nations.

Urry, J. (2000) *Sociology Beyond Societies*. London: Routledge.

Section Two

Knowledge and Social Change in Contemporary Societies

2

Modern Societies as Knowledge Societies[1]

By Nico Stehr

In advanced societies, in the last couple of decades, the capacity of the individual to say no has increased considerably. At the same time, the ability of the large social institutions to get things done has diminished. These developments are related. Appropriating Adolph Lowe's astute observation, we are witnessing a change from social realities in which 'things' at last from the point of view of most individuals simply 'happened' to a social world in which more and more things are 'made' to happen. In this brief contribution, these new realities are described as representing the emergence of advanced societies as knowledge societies. I will describe these transformations not only as real and unprecedented gains from the perspective of the individual and small groups but also what may be described as a rise in the fragility of society.

First, I will refer to the concept of knowledge societies and examine the notion of knowledge, defined as a capacity to act and examine some of the objections that might be raised against my perspective. Second, I will describe the reasons for the importance of scientific knowledge as one among various forms of knowledge in advanced societies and refer to the limits of the power of scientific knowledge. Finally, I describe some of the features of the changing economy before turning to the consequences of the advancing 'knowledgeability' of actors in modern society.

Introduction

> *In some way or other, any knowledge, and especially all common knowledge of identical objects, determines in many ways the specification (Sosein) of society. But all knowledge is ultimately also conversely determined by the society and its structure.*
>
> Max Scheler, 1924/1990: 17

John Stuart Mill, in *The Spirit of the Age* (1831), published after his return to England from France, where he had encountered the political thinking of the Saint-Simonians and of the early Comte,[2] affirms his conviction that the intellectual accomplishments of his own age make social progress somehow inevitable (Cowen and Shenton, 1996: 35–41). But progress in the improvement of social conditions is not, Mill argues, the outcome of an 'increase in wisdom' or of the collective accomplishments of science. It is rather linked to a general diffusion of knowledge:

> Men may not reason better, concerning the great questions in which human nature is interested, but they reason more. Large subjects are discussed more, and longer, and by more minds. Discussion has penetrated deeper into society; and if greater numbers than before have attained the higher degree of intelligence, fewer grovel in the state of stupidity, which can only co-exist with utter apathy and sluggishness.
>
> (Mill, 1831/1942: 13)

Mill's observations in the mid-nineteenth century, a period he regarded as an age of moral and political transition, and in particular his expectation that increased individual choice (and hence emancipation from 'custom') will result from a broad diffusion of knowledge and education, strongly resonates with the notion of present-day society – the social structure that is emerging as industrial society gives way – as a 'knowledge society'.

The foundation for the transformation of modern societies into knowledge societies is to a significant extent based on changes in the structure of their economies. The source of value-adding activities increasingly relies on knowledge. The transformation of the structures of the modern economy by knowledge as a productive force constitutes the 'material' basis and one of the justification for designating advanced modern society as a 'knowledge society'.

Objections

The term 'knowledge society' is a broad historical concept. Aside from the claim that there are much more appropriate conceptual labels to describe modern society or that we manage to cope in much of our ordinary lives without much of an understanding, for example, why technical things work (see Hardin, 2003), there are at least two related and apparently powerful objections to the term 'knowledge society'.

The most frequently heard reproach is that of historical repetition. The sceptics quickly offer the observation that we have always lived in knowledge societies. The term and the theoretical platform 'knowledge society' is not new; nor does it afford, as a result, any fresh insights into the architecture of present-day social systems and its forms of life. Even the rise of distant civilizations, for example, those of the Aztecs, the Romans and the Chinese, was always also a matter of their superior knowledge and information technology. Power and authority were never merely processes based on physical superiority alone. Moreover, knowledge is an essential characteristic of all forms of human activity.

The second objection refers to the concept of knowledge. It is seen as ill defined, perhaps as too ambivalent and contradictory to allow the construction of a theory of society. Knowledge is an essentially contested term. It is therefore doubtful whether it can become a foundation stone for the analysis of social conduct.

The first objection is fair but hardly decisive. Knowledge has indeed always played an important role in human relations. This, therefore, is not at issue. What needs to be asked is why the role of knowledge has recently, that is in advanced modern societies, emerged as constitutive and increasingly displaced and modified those factors that have until now been basic to social existence. The material foundation of social action is being displaced by a symbolic foundation. Capital largely deposed land during the industrial revolution; today knowledge diminishes the significance of both factors. Constitutive for social integration and not only for the creation of new economic value is knowledge. But it is surprising that knowledge and technological change continue to constitute the Achilles' heel of contemporary economic theory. More about the category knowledge in a moment.

So despite the fact that there have also been societies in the past based on knowledge-intensive action, the idea that modern society is increasingly a knowledge society is meaningful and has practical relevance. It is as meaningful to refer to modern society as a knowledge society as it was to refer to 'industrial societies', even though there had been past social systems that were based on the work of 'machines'. If knowledge is not just a constitutive feature of our modern economy but a basic organizational principle of the way we run our lives, then it is justifiable to talk about our living in a knowledge society. This means nothing more and nothing less than that we organize our social reality on the basis of our knowledge.

Loss of Political Power through Knowledge

In the 1950s the sociologist Helmut Schelsky (1954: 24) sketched out his version of a nightmare: the use of electronic calculating machines raises the spectre of the totalitarian state, he claimed. 'Such a government machine can demand absolute obedience, since it will be able to predict and plan the future with perfect reliability,' he prophesied, and 'in the face of technically guaranteed truth, all opposition is irrational.' Half a century later the American entrepreneur and futurologist Bill Joy (2000) is warning us of a development that possesses similarly nightmarish characteristics: his greatest fear is that nanotechnology might start to evolve independently of its human creators. This and other technologies of the future could put the human race on the endangered species list, he claims. Schelsky's prediction was right in line with the Zeitgeist prevailing in the middle of the twentieth century – and as Joy's admonitions show, this Zeitgeist is showing no signs of ageing. This phenomenon is the result of a symptomatic overestimation of the power of modern knowledge and technology. Yet paradoxically knowledge and technology are perhaps the most significant sources of the open, indeterminate society that is growing up around us today. Despite all pessimistic predictions we now find ourselves compared to past historical epochs witnessing the end of the hegemony of such monolithic institutions as the state, the church and the military. The conduct of the latter's representatives betrays a growing scepticism as to their continuing capacity to regulate social conditions: controlling, planning and predicting social conditions are becoming increasingly more difficult. Society has become more 'fragile'. Yet it is neither globalization nor the economization of social relations that is responsible for this state of affairs but the loss of political power through knowledge (see Stehr, 2001: 59–64; Weber, 1922/1964: 339).

Knowledge

In order to fully demonstrate and appreciate the significance of knowledge for societies and social action, particularly in advanced societies, and therefore for the assertion that knowledge is not merely the master key for unravelling the secrets of nature and society but the becoming of a world, it is necessary to first formulate a *sociological* concept of knowledge that differentiates between what is known, the content of knowledge and knowing itself.

One can define knowledge as 'the capacity to act', as the potential to 'start something going', and as a model *for* reality. Thus scientific or technical knowledge is primarily nothing other than the ability to act.[3] The privileged status of scientific and technical knowledge in modern society is derived not from the fact that scientific discoveries are generally considered to be credible, objective, in conformity with reality, or even indisputable, but from the fact that this form of knowledge, more than any other, incessantly creates new opportunities for action.

Science is not merely, as once widely thought, the key and the solution to the mysteries and miseries of the world, but is the becoming of a world. The idea that knowledge is a capacity for action that transforms or even creates reality is perhaps almost self-evident in the case of social science knowledge but less persuasive in the case of the natural sciences. But in the case of contemporary biology one is more and more prepared to acknowledge that biological knowledge extends to the fabrication of new living systems. Biology does not simply study nature. It transforms and produces novel natural realities. Biology and biotechnology are closely linked.

Knowledge, as a generalized capacity for action, acquires an 'active' role in the course of social action only under circumstances where such action does not follow purely stereotypical patterns (Max Weber), or is strictly regulated in some other fashion. Knowledge assumes significance under conditions where social action is, for whatever reasons, based on a certain degree of freedom in the courses of action that can be chosen.[4] Karl Mannheim (1929/1936) defines, in much the same sense, the range of social conduct generally, and therefore contexts in which knowledge plays a role, as restricted to spheres of social life which have not been routinized and regulated completely.[5]

It would be misleading to conclude that the conception of knowledge as a capacity for action and not as something, using the most traditional contrasting image, that we know to be true, thereby supports a reversal of the metaphor 'knowledge is power' into 'power equals knowledge'. Indeed, the implementation of knowledge requires more than knowing how to put something into motion. The realization of capacities of action and power, better, control over some of the circumstances of action, are allies. The relation is not symmetric. Knowledge does not always lead to power. Power does not lead to knowledge and power does not always rely on knowledge.

If one images 'society as a laboratory' (Krohn and Weyer, 1989: 349) in order to capture the idea that research processes and the risks associated with them, for example, in the case of nuclear technology, the planting of genetically modified seeds or the use of chemicals with certain undesirable side effects, are moved outside the established boundaries of science into society, such an image alerts us to the observation that the replication of laboratory effects outside the laboratory requires as a basic pre-condition the ability to control of the very conditions under which the effect was produced or observable, in the first instance. This implies that one needs to reproduce – outside the laboratory, for example, on a field – the experimental conditions that made the initial observation possible, in the first instance. It is only then that the initial observation of an effect can be duplicated. This also means that every 'realization' of knowledge, not only of major experiments, requires the ability to control the circumstances of action. Put differently, the 'application' of scientific knowledge in society demands an adjustment to the existing conditions of action or social conditions that have to be transformed according to the standards set by science. Given the social prestige of natural science knowledge, it is much more likely that conditions of societal action conform to and are adjusted in ways to conform to requirements of such knowledge rather than social science knowledge.

In the sense of my definition of knowledge, *scientific and technical* knowledge clearly represent 'capacities for action'. But this does not mean that scientific knowledge should be seen as a resource that lacks contestability, is not subject to interpretation, travels without serious impediments (e.g. as in the sense that knowledge travels even more effortlessly than money and spreads instantly), can be reproduced at will and is accessible to all nor that scientific and technical knowledge primarily convey unique and generally effective capacities for action.

What counts in modern societies, especially in the sense of gaining advantages in societies that operate according to the logic of economic growth and are dependent on the growing wealth of significant segments of the population, is access to and command of the *marginal additions to knowledge* rather than the generally available stock of knowledge.[6] Knowledge need not be perishable. In principle, a consumer or purchaser of knowledge may use it repeatedly at diminishing or even zero cost.

The Age of Knowledge Work

Scientific discoveries do not usually live up to the reputation of infallibility they possess: they are very often disputed, and despite its social standing, scientific knowledge is almost always questionable. For this very reason it is continually losing, at least temporarily, its practical relevance. Scientific interpretations must come to a 'conclusion' – only then do they have any practical value. In our modern society, this task of bringing trains of thought to a conclusion and rendering scientific insights 'useful' is carried out by 'knowledge workers'.

Knowledge-based occupations should not be seen as passive media obtaining, collating, systematizing, or in some other way neutrally 'operating' on knowledge, and then transmitting that knowledge to various receivers. Of course, they engage in all those activities. But the outcome is that their work on knowledge changes it. Knowledge is never an unproblematic 'currency' which can be easily exchanged. The exchange controls and restrictions are often formidable and enforced. Experts selectively invoke their interpretation of knowledge. Therefore, the definition of the priorities of action and the definition of the situation by clients are often mandated by experts consulted for advice. The knowledge that is passed on, in some way, undergoes changes as it is transmitted. Experts transmit and apply knowledge, but they do so in an active fashion. It is this activity that needs to be examined quite closely, as the transformative activity is one of the keys to any comprehensive and systematic understanding of the function of experts, and of the conditions for the demand for experts and their knowledge in advanced societies.

The centrality of knowledge-based occupations or, to use a narrower term, experts in knowledge societies does not mean that we are on the way, as social theorists have feared in the past, to a technocratic society. A technocratic model of society and its major social institutions, which 'sees technicians dominating officials and management, and which sees the modern technologically developed bureaucracies as governed by an exclusive reliance on a standard of efficiency' (Gouldner, 1976: 257) is but a nightmare, an ideal type or a utopia. Quite a number of arguments can be deployed to demystify the threat of technocracy and a new ruling class made up of faceless experts. The most persuasive argument is social reality itself, which has failed to support the transformation of society in this direction. The long-predicted emergence of technocratic regimes has not materialized. What then are some of the consequences of a more widespread dissemination of knowledge in modern societies?

Living in Knowledge Societies

The conviction that a widespread dissemination of knowledge and skills constitutes enormous emancipatory potential was one of the basic motives of the Age of Enlightenment. A curious yet persistent feature of various contemporary discussions of the social role of knowledge, of information and of skills in modern society is its one-sidedness as well as the lethal proximity to conspiratorial theories of history. Knowledge is frequently not seen as a capacity to act, it is rather perceived as incapacitating and not as enabling but as restraining or as subservient to capital.

There typically is a preoccupation with the repressive potential or the dangers associated with an increase of human knowledge and technical artefacts, especially when its control almost naturally flows to and is employed by powerful aggregate social agents such as the ruling social class, the state, multinational corporations, the class of intellectuals, the military–industrial complex, the professions, the estate of science, the Mafia, political parties, the managerial class and so on. Knowledge becomes a prominent force of generalized repression and manipulation.

Similarly, at the opposite end of the social spectrum, discussions about the social distribution of knowledge tend to emphasize and in fact reflected the dispossession of individual actors in everyday life from access to expertise and technical competence, thereby reducing them to the role of helpless victims, exploited consumers, alienated tourists, bored students, deskilled workers, manipulated voters and therefore to the role of individuals that are constantly overwhelmed by the magnitude and pervasiveness of the power of large organizations whose power now also rests on their command of scientific knowledge and expertise.

This trend towards the development of fragile social systems is the result of an (uneven) extension of individuals' capacity for action in modern societies. The power of large institutions is being increasingly undermined and replaced by small groups with a growing capacity for action. The extension of the capacity to act in the case of individuals and small groups is clearly considerable, especially since the enlargement of options to act can be small and yet have a major impact, for example, in situations of conflict with major corporate actors.

As Dorothy Nelkin (1975: 53–54) has shown in her study of the competitive use of technical expertise in two major controversial political decisions to extend a large airport and to develop a power plant in the United States, 'those opposing a decision need not muster equal evidence.' That is to say, 'it is sufficient to raise questions that will undermine the expertise of a developer whose power and legitimacy rests on his monopoly of knowledge claims or claims of special expertise.' In both public controversies studied by Nelkin about the political decision at hand involving the extension of a major airport and the development of a power-generating station, the ambivalences, uncertainties and disputes among different experts that became manifest in hearings were both a major stimulus and justification for the political challenges brought to bear in the conflict situation by affected citizens as well as for the ultimate decisions arrived at in the hearings. The disputes in the court were of greater importance than the original plans that generated the conflict, in the first instance. In the end, the additional runway requested for the airport was not constructed and the nuclear power plant was not built although a coal plant was completed on the site instead.

Using the term 'fragility' to designate this state of affairs is intended to underline the fact that not only has the capacity of supposedly powerful institutions to 'control' society declined as has their capacity to predict social developments. But what has caused society's centre of gravity to shift in this way? What forms is this development taking, and what consequences will it have?

I submit that these social changes are coming about because knowledge is no longer simply a means of accessing, of unlocking, the world's secrets but itself represents a world in the process of coming into being – a world in which in all spheres of endeavour knowledge is increasingly becoming both the basis and the guiding principle of human activity. Of course all interpersonal relationships are based on the principle that people possess knowledge about each other. And political power has never been based purely on physical force; it has always relied in part on superior knowledge. Social reproduction is not just a physical process but is also a cultural process. It implies the reproduction of knowledge. In this sense one can also consider past social structures as early forms of 'knowledge societies'.

Knowledge societies arise not as the result of simple, one-dimensional processes of social change. Though modern developments in communication and transportation technology have brought people closer together, regions, cities and villages are still by and large isolated from each other. The world may be opening up, and the circulation of fashions, goods and people becoming more intense, but differing convictions as to what is 'sacred' still create insurmountable barriers to communication. The meanings of such concepts as 'time' and 'place' are undergoing transformation, but borders separating people continue to be objects of intense respect and even celebration. Though fascinated by globalization, we also live in an age obsessed by identity and ethnicity. The trend towards the global 'simultaneity' of events is accompanied by a territorialization of sensibilities and a regionalization of conflicts.

The Social Role of Knowledge

As I have indicated in the previous section, attempts to comprehend the social functions of modern science and technology have always come up against a dead end. Both conservative and liberal analyses of modern society conclude with sombre prophecies of a world dominated by science and technology. This vision predicts not simply the destruction of humanity's natural facilities, its emotional life, but also of its intellectual facilities and its capacity for exercising free will. Modern theories of history posit a reduction rather than a broadening of opportunities for development in today's society. However, if one is to understand contemporary political, social and economic processes, then one must cast aside such clichés. For it is not the reduction of our capacity for action that is currently radically transforming the institutions of modern society but a tremendous expansion of this capacity. Collective unease, obstacles to action and individual unease and restlessness are the flip side of the transformation to knowledge societies.

Extending individual opportunities for action does not necessarily open the door to contentment – as shown by tourism, the burgeoning information media and consumerism in general. But in discourses generated by many politicians, theologians, philosophers and social scientists, the individual is posited as a defenceless 'victim' of powerful institutions. It is argued that people lose the capacity for action in proportion as science and technology triumph, fostering isolation, invading people's privacy and generating a sense of helplessness.

The Fragility of Society

I would want to argue that the processes triggered by the growth of science and technology have the opposite effect. They increase rather than reduce our capacity for social action. What is equally striking is the growing 'fragility' of social structures. Modern societies are characterized above all by 'self-generated' structures and the capacity to determine their futures themselves. But modern societies are not politically fragile and socially volatile because they are 'liberal democracies', they are fragile because they are 'knowledge-based' societies. Only knowledge is capable of increasing the democratic potential of liberal societies.

One peculiarity of the many and varied debates on the roles of knowledge, information and technological know-how in our modern society is their one-sidedness. They emphasize the problems caused by the individual's being cut off from specialist knowledge and technical competence – resulting in the individual's allegedly being forced into the role of 'victim': exploited consumer, alienated tourist, incapacitated patient, bored school kid, or manipulated voter. The proponents of such a viewpoint also delight in exposing the 'repressive' potential of the growth of scientific knowledge and the proliferation of technological artefacts – especially when the latter are exploited by such supposedly powerful entities as state and industry to exercise total social control. Yet dire prophecies that these entities would establish themselves in unassailable positions of power have not been fulfilled. For too long, debate among social scientists on the social role of knowledge was centred on social class, the state, the professions and the sciences. Yet a realistic evaluation of the social role of knowledge must come to the conclusion that the spread of knowledge has not only brought with it 'enormous' risks and uncertainty but also a 'liberating capacities for action'.

Uncertainty through Knowledge

But all these do not mean that from now on every consumer, patient and school kid will immediately be able to recognize, understand and control opportunities for action that come their way. An increase in opportunities for social action should not be misconstrued as bringing with it the elimination of all risk, accident and arbitrariness – in general of circumstances over which the individual has little control.

The flip side of emancipation through knowledge is the risks posed by the emancipatory potential of knowledge. The increasing spread of knowledge in society and the concomitant growth in opportunities for action also generate social uncertainty. For science cannot provide us with indisputable 'truths', and can provide only more or less well-founded hypotheses and probabilities. Thus, far from being a source of secure knowledge of certainty, science is a source of uncertainty and thus of social and political problems.

Knowledge societies will be characterized by a wide range of imponderabilities, unexpected reversals and other unpleasant surprises. The increasing fragility of knowledge societies will generate new kinds of moral questions, as well as a question as to who or what is responsible for our society's oft-cited political stagnation. The promise, challenge and the dilemma knowledge societies pose for every individual derives from the need to cope with, and even welcome, greater transience and volatility, the recognition that uncertainty is a necessary by-product of the search for any elimination of disagreements, and the need to accept the transitoriness of virtually all social constructs. Efforts to arrest or reverse these processes are likely to result in conditions that are worse than the alleged disease.

If knowledge is the main constitutive characteristic of modern society, then the production, reproduction, distribution and realization of knowledge cannot avoid becoming politicized. Thus one of the most important questions facing us will be how to monitor and control new or additional knowledge. This will entail the development of a new branch of policy science: knowledge policy. Knowledge policy will regulate the rapidly growing volume of new knowledge in our society and influence its development (see Stehr, 2004). The massive difference in and additions to human capacities to act within just a century may well be represented by two 'bookmarks': In 1945 humans had produced the capacity to destroy life on earth on a grand scale, while by 2045 or earlier it might be possible to create life on a grand as well as a minute scale (see Baldi, 2001: 163). Thus, it seems, the speed with which new capacities to act are generated forces us to alter our conceptions of who we are and, even more consequentially, may in fact change who we are. The promises and anxieties raised by these prospects are the motor of knowledge politics in modern societies. The boundaries of what was once clearly beyond the control of all of us are rapidly shifting.

Conclusions: A Look Ahead

History has by no means ended, but it has certainly changed. The old rules, certainties and trajectories no longer apply. Of course, there are few opportunities for fresh starts in history. Nonetheless, the future of modern society no longer mimics the past to the extent to which this has been the case. That is to say, the future is made from fewer fragments of the past. As a result, sentiments with respect to history that are becoming more pervasive are those of fragility and dislocation. History will increasingly be full of unanticipated incertitudes, peculiar reversals and proliferating surprises; and we will have to cope with the ever greater speed of significantly compressed events. The changing agendas of social, political and economic life as the result of our growing capacity to make history will also place inordinate demands on our mental capacities. The fit or lack of fit between our knowledgeability and what society, the economy and culture mentally demand is one of the major challenges of knowledge societies.

   I have described the extent to which these transformations of modern societies into knowledge societies, in particular the rise in the fragility of society, constitute a real and unprecedented gain from the perspective of the individual and small groups. The stress on rights, and the growing ability to assert and claim such rights, is one of the salient manifestations of the transformations I have examined. The same developments are responsible for a crisis in mastering, planning and managing common problems and for a decline in the sense of individual responsibilities. However, there is a trade-off; the decline in the steering capacity of large social institutions and growing difficulty with which they impose their will on society leads to a rise of the importance and efficacy of civil society. The civil society sector is able to gain in strength at the expense of the once-dominant large social institutions.

Endnotes

   1 This essay was written for oral presentation. A much more extensive analysis of some of the points made in this essay may be found in Stehr (2001; 2002).
   2 Mill (1873/1924: 115) discusses the importance for his own thinking of Saint-Simonian systemic theory of history in his *Autobiography*.
   3 Based on the basic idea that knowledge constitutes a capacity for action, one can, of course, develop distinctive categories or forms of knowledge depending on the enabling *function* knowledge

may be seen to fulfil. I believe Lyotard's (1979/1984: 6) attempt to differentiate, in analogy to the distinction between expenditures for consumption and investment, 'payment knowledge' and 'investment knowledge' constitutes an example of such a functional differentiation of more or less distinctive forms of knowledge.

4 Luhmann's (1992/1998: 67) observations about the conditions for the possibility of decisionmaking perhaps allow for an even broader use of knowledge. Decisionmaking 'is possible only if and insofar as what will happen is uncertain'. Assuming or depending on whether one assumes that the future is most uncertain, the deployment of knowledge in decisions to be made may extend to many more social contexts, even those that are otherwise characterized by nothing but routine attributes and habitual conduct.

5 From an 'interactionist' perspective, organization or any other social structures constitute 'negotiated orders' (Strauss *et al.*, 1964). However, this cannot mean that any and every aspect of the social reality of an organization is continuously available or accessible to every member for negotiation. Only particular, limited aspects of the organizational structure are available for disposition, and only with respect to these contingent features of social action can members mobilize knowledge in order to design and plan social conduct with a view to realize collective practical tasks; compare also Mead's concept of 'reflexive action' (1964: 555).

6 It is worth noting that Peter Drucker (1969: 269) sees the economic benefits of knowledge in 'knowledge economy' extend to all forms of knowledge and to an equal degree. What counts, he adds, is the applicability of knowledge, not whether is it 'old or new'. What is relevant in the social system of the economy is 'the imagination and skill of whoever applies it, rather than the sophistication or newness of the information'. My assertion, in contrast, is that it is meaningful to distinguish between the stock of knowledge at hand and marginal additions to knowledge. The process of the fabrication, implementation and return of each is not identical.

References

Baldi, P. (2001) *The Shattered Self: The End of Natural Evolution*. Cambridge, MA: MIT Press.

Cowen, M. P. and Shenton, R. W. (1996) *Doctrines of Development*. London: Routledge.

Drucker, P. F. (1969) *The Age of Discontinuity: Guidelines to Our Changing Society*. New York: Harper and Row.

Gouldner, A. W. (1976) *The Dialectic of Ideology and Technology: The Origins, Grammar and Future of Ideology*. New York: Seabury Press.

Hardin, R. (2003) 'If it Rained Knowledge', *Philosophy of the Social Sciences*, 33(1): 3–24.

Joy, B. (2000) 'Why the Future Doesn't Need Us', *Wired*, 8(04): 1–11.

Krohn, W. and Weyer, J. (1989) 'Gesellschaft als Labor: Die Erzeugung sozialer Risiken durch experimentelle Forschung', *Soziale Welt*, 40(3): 349–73.

Lyotard, J. F. (1979/1984) *The Postmodern Condition: A Report on Knowledge*. Minnesota: University of Minnesota Press.

Mannheim, K. (1929/1936) *Ideology and Utopia: An Introduction to the Sociology of Knowledge*. London: Routledge and Kegan Paul.

Mead, G. H. (1964) 'Two Unpublished Manuscripts', *The Review of Metaphysics*, 17(4): 536–56.

Mill, J. S. (1831/1942) *The Spirit of the Age*. Chicago. IL: University of Chicago Press.

Mill, J. S. (1873/1924) *Autobiography*. New York: Columbia University Press.

Nelkin, D. (1975) 'The Political Impact of Technical Expertise', *Social Studies of Science*, 5(1): 35–54.

Scheler, M. (1924/1990) 'The Sociology of Knowledge: Formal and Material Problems', in V. Meja and N. Stehr (eds), *Knowledge and Politics: The Sociology of Knowledge Dispute*. London: Routledge, pp. 17–36.

Schelsky, H. (1954) 'Zukunftsaspekte der industriellen Gesellschaft', *Merkur*, 8(1): 13–28.

Stehr, N. (2001) *The Fragility of Modern Societies: Knowledge and Risk in the Information Age*. London: Sage.

Stehr, N. (2002) *Knowledge and Economic Conduct: The Social Foundations of the Modern Economy*. Toronto: University of Toronto Press.

Stehr, N. (2004) *Knowledge Politics: Governing the Consequences of Science and Technology.* Boulder, CO: Paradigm Press.

Strauss, A. L., Schatzman, L., Bucher, R., Ehrlich, D. and Sabshin, M. (1964) *Psychiatric Ideologies and Institutions.* New York: Free Press.

Weber, M. (ed.) (1922/1964) *The Theory of Social and Economic Organization.* With an introduction by Talcott Parsons. New York: Free Press.

3

Knowledge and Societal Change: Institutional Coordination and the Evolution of Organizational Populations

By Jerald Hage

For the past 15 years, working both alone as well with others, I have slowly brick by brick been constructing a theory of societal change that would be sensitive to historical periods and cultural variations as well as connect across three analytical levels: micro, meso and macro. The central theme has been the differential growth in knowledge relative to power and wealth as basic societal resources (see Alter and Hage, 1993; Hage and Alter, 1997; Hage and Hollingsworth, 2000; Hage and Powers, 1992; Hage *et al.*, 1989). But in these various books, papers and doctoral dissertations, there has been a missing link that would connect the quite different theories about societal change found in macro-institutional analysis and meso-organizational analysis, a link that is necessary for synthesizing the large literature on the industrial revolution and its consequences with a theory about the new economy. Institutional analysis assumes that organizations are largely constrained and societal change is incremental and path dependent. On the other hand, organizational and management theory especially in the past (Chandler, 1962; Child, 1972; Hage, 1980; Lawrence and Lorsch, 1967; Perrow, 1967) allowed for independent organizational actors or some agency but ignored the implications of this for macro-institutional patterns and, beyond this, societal change. Clearly there is some truth in both these assertions.[1]

In this essay I want to supply this last brick or missing link that reconciles these two different theories of societal change, placing them in both a historical and a cultural context. Specifically, I want to focus on the role of knowledge in producing social change via its impact on the evolution of organizational populations across time in the context of non-market institutional governance modes. Organizational populations are defined as all organizations that share a similar technology and marketplace or technological regime (Archibugi and Pianto, 1992; Breschi and Malerba, 1997; Guerreri and Tylecote, 1998; Kitschelt, 1991; Malerba and Orsenigo, 1993; 1997). This theoretical problem is not only a strategic site for uniting the various social sciences including economics and political science but also the more mundane task of synthesizing the meso organizational and macro institutional literatures within sociology, a long-term objective in the social sciences.

Why is the evolution of organizational populations within the context of various modes of non-market governance a useful vantage point for uniting such a diversity of social science disciplines and their macro and meso literatures?

To most people this seems like an arcane interest and far removed from the recent major issues such as globalization, the new economy and the problems of development in the Third World. One thesis of this essay is that one pattern of evolution, consolidation, is more appropriate for an institutional theory of incremental societal change, and another pattern, differentiation is more appropriate for an organization theory of societal change built around the ability of organizations to shape their institutional environment. Furthermore, it is not only knowledge that defines the new economy but also that there has been an historical shift from consolidation as a general pattern of evolution to a pattern of differentiation.

This angle of vision provides a number of new insights on the major themes of this book, specifically knowledge, communication and creativity. Essentially what is suggested is that the growth in knowledge is making scientific communication more and more difficult and because of this creativity as reflected in product innovation more problematic. The best demonstration of this is the growing gap in some countries between various measures of scientific output and industrial innovation with the US trade deficit a prime example (but also see the European Commission, 2004). What helps explain this gap is the growing differentiation of organizational populations across time and across the idea innovation network (Hage and Hollingsworth, 2000; Kline and Rosenberg, 1986; van Waarden and Oosterwijk, 2006), that is the knowledge specialization and hence differentiation of organizations involved in basic research, applied research and product development.

A second thesis is that the non-market modes of governance are themselves associated with various kinds of societal change. In particular, a major impact of knowledge is the creation of inter-organizational relationships as a new and increasingly dominant non-market governance mode, inter-organizational relationship (Alter and Hage, 1993; Doz and Hammel, 1998; Dussauge and Garrette, 1999; Gomez-Casseres, 1996; Hagedoorn, 1993; Harbison and Pekar, 1998; Mockler, 1999; Perry, 1999; Powell, 1998; Powell and Brantley, 1992) which is facilitating the globalization processes while exacerbating the problems of developing countries because of commodity chains (Gereffi and Korzeniewicz, 1994; Korzeniewicz, 1994; Korzeniewicz and Martin, 1994).[2] A parallel impact is the creation of knowledge communities (Mohrman and Monge, 2005; Mohrman, Gailbraith and Monge, 2006), which transform at different stages in the development of a new scientific speciality or arena of research such as parallel processing or molecular biology. A satisfactory theory of societal change should explain these dynamic changes as witnessed by the growth in inter-organizational networks (Alter and Hage, 1993; Harbison and Pekar, 1998; Powell and Brantley, 1992) and in knowledge communities since they are now the context in which effective communication can lead to creativity.

Consistent with this intellectual agenda, this essay is divided into four sections Korzeniewicz and Martin (1994), the first two focusing on the organizational population level and the second two on the governance mode level. The first section provides a definition of the two dominant patterns of organizational evolution, consolidation and differentiation and addresses the issue of why there has been surprisingly little intellectual work on patterns of evolution in organizational populations despite the use of this phrase in various recent titles.[3] The second section contains a set of hypotheses that explains which evolutionary pattern, that is consolidation or differentiation, is more likely to be dominant in a particular technology–market nexus and more specifically the role of knowledge in predicting the pattern of differentiation. The third section provides a definition of the arenas in which non-market governance mode can intervene and reviews briefly the increasingly large amount of work on non-market governance modes (Campbell *et al.*, 1991; Hage, 2006; Hall and Soskice, 2001; Hollingsworth, 1991; Hollingsworth and Boyer, 1997; Whitley, 1992a; 1992b). The fourth section contains a set of hypotheses about how the state, associations and interorganizational relationships can impact on the evolution of organizational populations, accounting for variations across societies within the same industrial sector or technology–market nexus (also see Hage, 2006). As one can easily observe, the analysis of nonmarket modes of governance quickly allows us to move into economics and political science, as well as synthesize the meso- and macro-sociological literatures.

The essay ends with a somewhat long sketch of the relevance of this four-component model for integrating organizational and institutional theory into a multi-level theory of societal change. Here the emphasis is also on how the consolidation versus differentiation processes synthesize a large number of different theories in the social sciences.

Evolutionary Pathways and their Consequences for Population Characteristics

Definitions of Evolutionary Pathways

The distinction between consolidation and differentiation is easy to draw and therefore the definitions are quite simple:

Consolidation$_{df}$ = the decrease in the total number of organizations in the organizational population across time.

Differentiation$_{df}$ = the increase in the total number of organizations in the organizational population across time.

The process of consolidation can sometimes occur quite rapidly, typically when a standard technology or design is invented and accepted in the market place. For example, the pasteurization of beer brewing occurred in the 1860s quickly followed by a rapid decline in the number of breweries in the United States (Hannan and Freeman, 1989).[4] A better known example is Ford's invention of the assembly-line process of automobile construction, which led to a rapid fall-out in this industry (Chandler, 1977).

Differentiation can also occur in a relatively short time-span when a new product or service is developed that precipitates the founding of many new firms. Many of the bio-tech companies founded in the 1980s (Powell, 1998; Powell and Brantley, 1992) came after the break-through in biological research associated with molecular biology while the dotcoms flourished for a while in the 1990s because of the commercial possibilities offered by the Internet (van Waarden and Oosterwijk, 2006; Van Waarden, F. *et al.*, 2001).

However easy it is to define these two generic pathways of evolution in organizational populations across time, little research or theory about them has been developed. In the last few decades, the people who were most responsible for placing at least the terms 'organizational evolution' on the intellectual map were Nelson and Winter (1982). However, their model is one of *organizational* evolution and not the evolution of *organizational populations*. In contrast, while the organizational ecologists (see review, Baum, 1996) use the term organizational evolution (Aldrich, 1999; Hannan and Freeman, 1989) and actually report research findings about organizational populations across time, to date all of their analyses have been historically discrete rather than attempting to develop a general theory about the evolutionary patterns of organizational *populations* as distinct from the survival analysis of specific populations.[5] Fortunately, the range of studies of organizational populations has included automobiles (Hannan *et al.*, 1998a; 1998b), newspapers (Carroll, 1987), breweries, labour unions, restaurants (Hannan and Freeman, 1989), credit unions (Barron *et al.*, 1994), small businesses (Brüderl and Schüssler, 1990), hotels (Ingram and Baum, 1997), wineries (Delacroix and Swaminathan, 1991), insurance companies (Lehrman, 1994), telephone companies (Barnett, 1990; 1997), etc. (Baum, 1996), which allows me to summarize much of their work. One exception to this general lack of attention to generic evolutionary processes has been a recent study of the demise of the non-rubber footwear industry in the United States because of globalization (Hage and Hadden, 2001). In summary, to date a general theory about the evolutionary pathways of consolidation versus differentiation that allows for societal differences has yet to be developed.

Probably the major reason why not much attention has been paid to alternative evolutionary pathways for organizational populations is that so much of the thinking in industrial economics, management, economic history (Chandler, 1977) and organizational theory has concentrated on the large organization. Since it is the consolidation process that produces large powerful organizations, by implication the process of differentiation has been missed. Another reason for the relatively greater emphasis on studies of consolidation in organizational ecology (see Baum, 1996) is that in the past this was the more typical process. Since the industrial revolution, consolidation has occurred in beer making, steel, grain processing, cigarette manufacturing, banking, telephone services, railroads, insurance companies, automobiles, hotel chains, glass making and in many other technology–market nexi or industrial sectors, as Chandler (1977) has so well described, naturally the organizational ecologists would be describing this process and not the other. The differentiation pathway, although it has always existed as, for example, in chemical products and electrical products, has been somewhat rare and has only recently become a typical process in the new economy.[6]

Consequences for the Population Characteristics

Even though the topic of evolutionary patterns in organizational populations has been ignored, knowing which evolutionary pathway unfolds in an organizational population – consolidation versus differentiation – allows us to predict *a priori* to a number of organization and population characteristics that have been important in the various literatures cited above. Among other properties, these are the following:

- the total number of organizations in the population;
- the average size (assets) of organizations;
- the rank order of each organization in terms of share of market;
- the relative importance of organizational age and size in predicting mortality rates;
- the founding rate of new organizations;
- the concentration ratio in the organizational population;
- the average investment in physical equipment per worker in the organizational population;
- the average importance of bureaucracy as a mechanism of internal control in the organizational population;
- the average distribution of skills in the organizational population;
- the historical pattern of strike behaviour in the organizational population;
- the number of generalists and specialists or market niches;
- the amount of product and process innovation in the organizational population.

I would submit that this is hardly a non-trivial list of organization and population characteristics. Furthermore, as indicated in the last section, knowing these characteristics allows us to begin to address a number of important macro-institutional literatures about historical societal changes that have increasingly occurred over the past century and a half.

A description of the generic evolutionary processes indicates how these various characteristics emerge more or less automatically. Clearly, if the evolutionary pattern is one of consolidation, which means a high failure rate or merger rate, the total number of organizations decreases creating a large concentration ratio with a greater average investment in equipment reflecting a standard technology combined with a relatively unskilled labour force and a bureaucracy of managers as Chandler (1977) has observed (also see Hage, 1980). This model has also been called the bureaucratic model. One variation on this model labelled 'the mixed mechanical–organic' allowed for research departments and reflects the beginning of the growth of knowledge and its consequences for the economy (Landes, 1969) because these populations began to differentiate rather than consolidate. In contrast are the small high-tech organizations, where differentiation or a high founding rate is even higher. More emphasis is placed on human capital (Becker, 1964) than physical capital, the internal structure is an organic rather than a mechanical one, there are many specialists or market niches and product and process innovation are the major method for competition rather than productivity.

The Definition of an Organizational Population and Hypotheses about their Evolutionary Pathways

The Definition of an Organizational Population

Although these evolutionary pathways or processes are easy to describe and indeed appear to be quite generic, allowing us to predict a number of population or organizational characteristics, our definitions do not isolate the variables or factors that would anticipate whether consolidation or differentiation will unfold in any specific organizational population. To develop this theory, we should at first define our focus, namely organizational populations:

Organization Population$_{df}$ = the industrial sector with a similar technology and market[7]

In the economics literature, these are sometimes called technological regimes (Archibugi and Pianto, 1992; Breschi and Malerba, 1997; Guerreri and Tylecote, 1998; Kitschelt, 1991; Malerba and Orsenigo, 1993; 1997). A good first approx-imation are the various governmental codes of industrial sectors, for example, the seven-digit version in the United States. Meanwhile, the evidence for the necessity of analysing industrial sectors rather than the whole economy has been increasing (see Alter and Hage, 1993; Guerreri and Tylecote, 1998; Hage and Hollingsworth, 2000; Hollingsworth, 1991; Pavitt, 1984; van Waarden and Oosterwijk, 2006). In addition; the capital: human capital and R&D investments in these sectors vary considerably as does the speed with which inter-organizational networks are formed (Hagedoorn, 1993; Hage and Hollingsworth, 2000; National Science Foundation, 1996; O'Doherty, 1995; Powell and Brantley, 1992).

Assumptions of most Organizational and Management Theory

To develop an evolutionary theory about consolidation and differentiation, we need to examine the fundamental and somewhat hidden assumptions about technology–market nexi involved in Chandler's (1977) work and the many orga-nizational ecology studies (Baum, 1996). It would seem to me that there are basically three assumptions: one relates to the characteristics of the market, the second relates to the characteristics of the technology and the third describes the stability of the technology–market nexus. The first assumption is a single mass taste or market. The second and parallel assumption is that the technology and materials that one would exploit for the manufacturing of any specific product or the provision of any specific service is also standardized. Indeed, this assumption has given rise to an interesting literature on standard design (for a review see Utterback, 1994, and the empirical study of Anderson and Tushman, 1990). A third assumption is that both tastes and technology are relatively stable across time. This stability allows for long production runs and gains in productivity across time. Given this set of technology–market characteristics, then an organi-zational population within a country will move towards either a single company or an oligopoly of several firms or companies that are able to produce this prod-uct or provide this service most efficiently.

Examples of organizational populations with these technology–market charac-teristics from organizational ecological research are the studies of New York Life Insurance companies (Lehrman, 1994), banks (Banaszak-Holl, 1991), telephone companies (Barnett, 1990), hotels (Ingram and Baum, 1997) and credit unions (Barron *et al.*, 1994). And of course, the various industrial sectors that are involved in Chandler's (1977) analysis fit this pattern.

Furthermore, depending upon transportation costs, the standardized product can then be exported to other countries and a relatively small number of companies can become the prime producers for the entire world. Singer Sewing Machine was the first company to demonstrate how one firm could become a global monopoly in the middle of the nineteenth century (Chandler, 1977) – and long before the hue and cry over globalization – and Microsoft Windows software is a contemporary example.

Kinds of Technology–Market Nexi and Hypotheses about
Evolutionary Pathways

But none of these three assumptions pertain to all industrial sectors or technology–market nexi. First, for many products and services, customers have quite varying tastes and preferences. These tastes and preferences are influenced by such social characteristics within each country as age, sex, ethnicity, race, religion, urban versus rural location, region, income level, education, etc. Of these, probably the two most important factors are income level and education, which, as a long history of market research has demonstrated, have influenced the taste preferences in two important ways: (1) willingness to pay more money for quality or an interest in fashion or design; and (2) creation of alternative lifestyles that necessitate various products and services to demonstrate these styles. Tastes or preferences are also obviously even more impacted upon by cultural taste and historical antecedent differences between countries that interact in various ways with the social characteristics listed above.

Second, the availability of alternative materials and production technologies allows for income, education and culture to play an even greater role in the differentiation of the basic market into various niches that correspond to specific constellations of desired aspects of a product or service. Together, these two aspects, tastes and technology, reinforce each other, one reason why organizational populations or industrial sectors are best described as technology–market nexi.

Third, tastes can change across time, the meaning of fads and of course fashion. Similarly, technologies are not necessarily constant; they may also alter (Anderson and Tushman, 1990; Lynn *et al.*, 1996). Perhaps most critically organizational innovation generates new products some of which 'create' new tastes and necessitate new technologies to produce them (Hage and Powers, 1992). With this observation one can integrate the large literature on organizational innovation (Damanpour, 1991; Hage, 1965; 1980; 1999; Zammuto and O'Connor, 1992) into our discussion about alternative evolutionary pathways.

Each of these three ideas leads to a separate hypothesis about the relative pressure towards consolidation versus differentiation, as follows:

1 The greater the variety of tastes, the greater the differentiation of the organizational population at one time point.
2 The greater the variety of materials and production technologies, the greater the differentiation of the organizational population at one time point.
3 The greater the instability of tastes and technologies across time, the greater the differentiation of the organizational population across time.

Support for these ideas can be found in organizational ecology studies of savings and loan associations in California (Haveman, 1992), wineries in the same state (Delacroix and Swaminathan, 1991), as well as the American non-rubber footwear industry (Hage and Hadden, 2001).[8]

Although in this discussion I have implied that these variables co-vary, in fact they do not. Some technology–market nexi can have a great variety of tastes and production technologies but not much instability in either of these characteristics. Thus, one can describe various degrees of consolidation and of differentiation within a specific technology–market nexus depending upon the amount of variation in each of these three variables. In particular, in those sectors that are considered to be high-tech, the rate of change in tastes and technologies is much higher than in what might be called the traditional industries such as wineries and footwear, which leads to our point.

What is the role of knowledge relative to the processes of consolidation and differentiation? Although the topic of knowledge has recently emerged in the organizational literature (Brown and Duguid, 1998; Conner and Prahalad, 1996; Grant, 1996; Leonard and Sensiper, 1998; Nonaka and Takeuchi, 1995), if one ignores a much earlier literature on technology (Hage, 1980; Hage and Aiken, 1969; Perrow, 1967; Woodward, 1965), it has not been related to either the macro-institutional literature or the general changes associated with the new economy or knowledge society (Bell, 1973; Hage and Powers, 1992; Toffler, 1981). Instead the focus has been primarily on the problems of organizational learning (Cohen and Sproull, 1996) whether in the firm (Conner and Prahalad, 1996; Grant, 1996; Nonaka and Takeuchi, 1995) or in various inter-organizational networks (Kogut *et al.*, 1993; Oerlemans *et al.*, 1999). Yet, it is precisely as the knowledge level of society increases, the technology-market contexts of organizational populations also alter, indeed making organizational learning more critical; this is one reason why it has become a hot topic in the organizational literature.

The growth in the level of knowledge in a society can be defined by increases in its average education and average income and perhaps more to the point the greater *dispersion* in educational specialities and income levels, and thus more distinctive social categories and therefore tastes in the market place.[9] The role of knowledge or more specifically R&D in developing new materials and production technologies requires little explanation or elaboration because it is obvious. The most interesting contemporary example is nanotechnology, which has had and will have an impact on a large number of different industrial sectors. Finally, another well-established point is that with more and more R&D investments in any specific technology–market nexus, product lives are much shorter and tastes are hooked on technological advances as we have witnessed in the constant expansion of capability in computers and their software. In turn these investments are connected to the larger-societal investments in education and national R&D. Again, we have three hypotheses that help explain the tendency for organizational populations to differentiate across time rather than to consolidate:

4   The greater the growth in average education and income, the greater the variety of tastes within any specific organizational population across time.

5   The great the growth in investment in national R&D, the greater the variety of materials and production technologies within any specific organizational population across time.
6   The greater the growth in average education and income and national investment in R&D, the shorter the taste life and product life within any specific organizational population across time.

A major implication of these hypotheses is that *all* advanced industrial societies are involved in a historical shift away from a typical pattern of consolidation on which Chandler (1977) based much of his work with the proliferation of small organizations in many technology–market nexi. The most powerful proof of this is the movement towards differentiation in those technology–market nexi that had previously consolidated. Thus, we find micro-breweries, developing in the brewing industry, new speciality newspapers (Carroll, 1987) and magazines in publishing, new kinds of speciality stores in clothing and footwear, a proliferation of gourmet restaurants in the food service industry, etc. And in turn some of these firms are also consolidating into chains of various kinds.

These six hypotheses provide a partial explanation for the generic processes of consolidation and differentiation including the changes associated with the new economy or post-industrial society, but they do not explain the differences across societies except in a few circumstances. Some societies vary in whether a specific technology–market nexus has standardized or differentiated tastes, for example in brewing, wine making, clothes making, etc. But there is another set of factors that are more powerful for explaining differences between societies within the same technology–market nexus. The use of non-market modes of coordination affects the speed of consolidation and differentiation – our next topic.

Kinds of Macro-Institutional Governance Modes and Hypotheses about Evolutionary Pathways

All societies like to avoid competition if they can (which is one of the reasons why globalization has become a cause of demonstrations), but societies set limits on market governance or coordination in different ways. In recent years, there has been a growing macro-institutional literature about the use of non-market modes of governance within and across countries (Campbell *et al.*, 1991; Casper and Whitley, 2002; Hollingsworth and Boyer, 1997). In particular, in the Hollingsworth and Boyer (1997) reference there is an elaborate typology of the range of non-market governance modes as well as a discussion of their strengths and weaknesses. Dankbaar (1994) has compared sectorial governance in the automobile industry while Stråth (1994) has done the same for the shipbuilding industry.

Kinds of Institutional Governance Modes

In quite another literature on business systems (Whitley, 1992a; 1992b) or social systems of production (Hollingsworth, 1997) an attempt has been made to describe societies by their institutional arrangements including descriptions of various kinds of non-market modes of governance. Although this literature emphasizes the entire economy in contrast to a focus on specific technology–market nexi, which is our reference here, it is insightful especially for how specific kinds of non-market governance modes became dominant in society. From this perspective, perhaps the three most important themes in this literature are: (1) the obvious role of the state in countries as diverse as France (Cohen, 1992; Hage *et al.*, 1989; Suleiman, 1978), Japan (Gerlach, 1992; Whitley, 1992a; Womack *et al.*, 1990) and South Korea (Whitley, 1992a) to say nothing about China and the former Soviet Union, (2) associations of various kinds (industrial, professional or occupation, trade unions, etc., see Schneiberg and Hollingsworth, 1990) as in Italy (Lazeron, 1993; Piore and Sabel, 1984), Germany (Dankbaar, 1994; Herrigel, 1994; Streeck *et al.*, 1987), the Netherlands (Oerlemans *et al.*, 1998; Walton, 1987) and (3) inter-organizational networks of various kinds (joint ventures, alliances, family or clan business networks, etc.) in many countries, whether developed or developing (Aldrich and Sasaki, 1995; Alter and Hage, 1993; Doz and Hamel, 1998; Dussauge and Garrette, 1999; Gomes-Casseres, 1996; Hagedoorn, 1993; O'Doherty, 1995; Perry, 1999; Powell, 1998). Knowing which of these various kinds of non-market modes of coordination predominates in a specific country and technology–market nexus allows us to build in societal differences in the processes of consolidation and differentiation, remaining faithful to a sociological vision of historical time and social cultural space.

To appreciate the importance of these various non-market coordination modes, one also needs to know the many different ways in which organizational populations can be coordinated. In general the theory of markets has emphasized the importance of competition for coordinating prices. The role of the state in price and wage control is a well-known example of non-market coordination. But these mechanisms hardly exhaust the many aspects of an organizational population that can be coordinated, especially as they concentrate on narrow economic issues such as prices or costs and ignore some of the more fundamental social issues. Indeed, it is precisely as one broadens the perspective of what aspects of the technology–market nexus are being coordinated and especially a focus on the inputs such as labour, capital, technology and research investments rather than the out-puts that one begins to appreciate how important non-market modes of governance are.

Definition of Institutional Governance Coordination

Building upon this insight, the following kinds of intervention or coordination would appear to be fundamental:[10]

- The ease of entry into an organizational population;
- The ease of exit from an organizational population;
- The availability of various kinds of technical and managerial skills;
- The availability of credit, subsidies, or more generally capital of various kinds;
- The availability of research findings and ideas.

Clearly each of these aspects affects how easily new organizations can be founded because they deal with the various factors of production such as human capital,

capital and perhaps most critically, ideas for new products and services that are usually associated with the founding of new companies or the ability to compete in specific niches. They also deal with the relative competitiveness of firms in global markets or what might be called the comparative advantage following Porter's (1990) work. The ease of exit is an interesting issue because frequently the state intervenes to *prevent* large companies from failing as one mechanism for protecting employment and especially nowadays given globalization.

Within this intellectual framework on how the various factors of production can be coordinated, it requires only a small leap in thought to develop specific hypotheses about how non-market modes of coordination can affect the processes of consolidation and of differentiation. Since a number of hypotheses could be developed given the variety of intervention points, I will only concentrate on a few to illustrate how knowing the non-market coordination modes allows one to develop quite an interesting theory – at least for me – about societal differences not only in the pathways of evolution but more fundamentally in the different organizational population characteristics across countries. As argued above, if one knows whether a specific organization population or technology–market nexus unfolds with either consolidation or differentiation, one can predict a number of population characteristics and by extension, knowing how the non-market modes of coordination affect these evolutionary processes allows us to make forecasts about the differences in population characteristics between countries.

Hypotheses about Governance Mode and Evolutionary Pathway

North (1990) quite correctly emphasized the importance of the state in establishing the rules of competition or the framework in which the processes of economic development but he did not deal with the pathways of organizational evolution.[11] The state can tilt the pathway of evolution in a number of ways, in effect speeding up the processes of consolidation or differentiation. For example, the hypothesis that:

1   the more the state intervenes into a technology–market nexus to provide easy credit or subsidies or capital of various kinds to large organizations, the faster the process of consolidation.

One observes this kind of coordination most clearly in the French state policy of national champions (Cohen, 1992, which was quite explicit about believing that *one* large organization could compete better in global markets). South Korea is another example, where the policy of differential credit for the *chaebols* has allowed them to grow large and diversified at the expense of small organizations (Whitley, 1992a). Likewise, the Japanese state's policies of guided development helped the large *gruppen* to prosper even in times of sharp downturns (Gerlach, 1992; Stråth, 1994; Whitley, 1992a). And in the US, the supposed citadel of free markets, the state has allowed large corporations to buy failing ones, and then absorb their debt to reduce their income taxes on profits. Nor do I need to comment about the recent policy of tariffs to protect the US steel industry.

Although I have suggested above that knowledge creation typically favours the process of differentiation, a major exception to this is the nature of state policies regarding credits for investments in R&D. Japan has largely favoured the large companies with its industrial R&D policies (Aldrich and Sasaki, 1995). Or consider the industrial–military complex thesis in the United States in this context; this thesis is specifically about large companies and especially in certain industries such as aircraft production, ship building, electronics, tank construction, telecommunications, etc.

But states can also follow divergent policies in separate technology–market nexi, one reason why the analytical focus should be the organizational population:

2   The more the state intervenes into a technology–market nexus to provide easy credit or subsidies or capital of various kinds to small organizations, the faster the process of differentiation.

An interesting example of this is the recent successful Germany policy of attempting to jump-start a bio-tech organizational population (Casper, 2000; Casper and Whitley, 2002). A variety of policies were implemented in Germany to foster the process of differentiation; so it is important to recognize that creating new organizational populations is not just a matter of credit but may also mean the changing of other institutional pattern, whether laws or educational programs or industrial districts/parks (Cohen, 1992; Landes, 1969). In some countries, the state will provide start-up grants as have the Americans with their small business grants for minorities or the easy credit policies of the French for entrepreneurs.

Once one recognizes that state policies can have implicit subsidies involved in them as in American Corporate Tax Law cited above, it becomes possible to code the implications of various state policies relative to the ease of entry and thus the process of differentiation. An interesting example of this is the Italian exemption from most social security payments for businesses with less than ten workers (Lazeron, 1993). This policy not only encourages the formation of small organizations but also networks between them, the famous Italian model of industrial organization (Piore and Sabel, 1984). As a consequence, the Italian footwear, textile, ceramics, kitchen furniture and other technology–market nexi have remained far more differentiated than their American counterparts. I could continue with other examples but I think the point is clear: The state can easily facilitate the process of differentiation.

Associations of various kinds can also play multiple roles in the evolutionary processes depending on which aspects of a market framework they coordinate. Again, just as the state can intervene in the coordination of an organizational population in many ways, so can associations.[12] Some of the more interesting examples of the interventions by associations in the evolutionary pathway of organizational populations are the following:

3   The more the association limits the entry of new firms, the more that the process of differentiation is dampened.
4   The more the association coordinates technical and vocational education, the more that the process of differentiation is encouraged.

Associations in Europe typically control the entry of new firms and therefore dampen competitive processes and instead encourage more cooperation between firms as has been suggested in a large literature on this subject. But one consequence of this is that the lack of entry of new firms, which obviously reduces any tendency towards differentiation. However, given cooperation and the tendency to form cartels and other types of association that limit competition, consolidation is also paradoxically dampened. Thus, organizational populations in technology–market nexi coordinated by associations tend to have much more stability across time with both lower founding rates and lower failure rates.

Some associations, especially those in Germany, also have a considerable amount to say about the nature of technical and vocational education (Streeck *et al.*, 1987). As a consequence, this has encouraged a number of small and medium-size firms to compete successfully in the global market place by positioning themselves in the high-quality, high-technology segment of the market, namely encouraging the differentiation of markets into various niches that require specific kinds of skills and technical equipment (Prais and Steedman, 1986; Prais *et al.*, 1989; Steedman and Wagner, 1987; 1989).

Just as associations can be involved in the coordination of an organizational population in a variety of ways, so can inter-organizational networks. Furthermore, the range of these networks is quite large (Alter and Hage, 1993) including some very distinctive forms such as the Chinese family business found throughout Southeast Asia or the special variations found in South Korea (*chaebol*) (Whitley, 1992a) and Japan (*gruppen*) (Gerlach, 1992). Again, I will only discuss several kinds of interventions with their implications for the processes of consolidation and differentiation:

5   The more the inter-organizational network (family businesses, gruppen) emphasizes the sharing of credit or capital, the more that the process of consolidation is dampened.
6   The more the inter-organizational network (research consortia, joint venture, global alliance) emphasizes the coordination of R&D, the more that the process of differentiation is encouraged.

As is readily appreciated from these hypotheses, one must carefully specify not only what is coordinated but also observe the nature of the inter-organizational network. In hypothesis 5, the sharing of credit allows new businesses to be formed, dampening consolidation and more critically allowing old businesses to continue during periods of business contraction. Typically, for example, the Japanese would expand investments in machinery during down-cycles of economic activity in order to increase their productivity. In contrast, hypothesis 6 emphasizes the very special role that inter-organizational networks are now playing in the development of new products and services. A striking example is the role of the research consortia SEMATECH in the US, which saved the US semiconductor industry from disappearing or at least some of the major companies in this technology–market nexus (Browning *et al.*, 1995). More typically, joint ventures among small high-tech organizations or more typically between small and high-tech companies allow these small firms to survive. In other words, rather than the process of consolidation occurring as some firms became more productive, inter-organizational relationships allow for more innovation and quick time to market, and these become the basis of compensation.

Relevance for a Theory about Knowledge and Societal Change

Given the four essential components of our theory about evolutionary pathways in organizational populations – the distinction between consolidation versus differentiation as pathways; the properties of organizational populations; the ways in which non-market governance modes can intervene into organizational populations; and the distinctions between the state, associations and inter-organizational networks as examples of some non-market governance modes of coordination – we can now return to our basic theme of knowledge and societal change.

Ideally one would evaluate a new theory about societal change by examining a number of classical theoretical problems in the study of social change. Space prevents a long and considered analysis. Therefore, I propose to examine only a few issues, specifically the implications for management theory and for institutional theory. But before I do that, let me state the central thesis about knowledge as the basis for a new theory of societal change.

The central thesis is that increasingly organizational populations are differentiating rather than consolidating, that is the number of organizations in many but not all technology–market nexi are growing rather than diminishing. These processes of differentiation are being facilitated by the continued increases in investments in higher education and national R&D, two distinct ways in which knowledge in a society can be measured. Beyond this, two sets of hypotheses explain differential patterns of consolidation and differentiation between technology–market nexi and between national economies: hypotheses at the level of the technology/knowledge market and at the level of the institutional governance mode for the technology–market nexus. Thus, the proposed theory can explain not only comparative differences across society, a major theme in institutional analysis, but dynamic differences, something absent from most theories of societal change, as well. But what are the implications of this for management theory and institutional theory?

Implications for Management Theory

Management theory, organizational sociology, organizational ecology and industrial economics are based on the implicit assumptions outlined in the previous section that help explain why consolidation processes predominate, that is big is better and especially more productive. If in fact, the central thesis above is correct, then this classical model needs to be altered and in two directions, admittance that differentiation processes are becoming more predominate and the inclusion of the institutional governance mode.

Since knowledge is increasing now with more and more R&D investment in more technology–market nexi and especially in the developed countries, we are observing a historic shift in the generic processes of evolution. More and more technology–market nexi are following the generic model of differentiation.

Perhaps the most interesting implication is the emergence of new small companies and market niches in some organizational populations that have already experienced consolidation; examples include the micro-breweries, new kinds of gourmet restaurants, specialized travel agencies, etc. More typically one finds the emergence of new technology–market nexi such as biotechnology, software, dotcoms, etc., which are associated with considerable investments of R&D. Within these sectors, the processes of consolidation can still occur but they unfold in specific niches where there are standardized tastes and a standardized technology. Word and document processing is one example and the mobile telephone is another.

Perhaps most telling about the need to revise classical management theory are the many new areas of research that opened up within management theory and organizational sociology in the last decade: venture capital, management of knowledge, inter-organizational networks and the rising importance of innovation theory as reflected in the many new handbooks on the subject, etc. All of these are testimonials to the need for an expanded theory about knowledge and its implications for management theory.

The needed elements of this theory have been outlined in this essay. By knowing which variables at both the technology–market level and the institutional level are most important, then one can predict the relative amount of either consolidation or differentiation and beyond this to the various organizational population characteristics that were outlined in the first section.

One important implication of this is that this theory does not negate the existing theories that have been implicitedly built on processes of consolidation. Instead, these traditional models are contained as special cases and ones more dominant in the first phase of the industrial revolution. But rather than being bounded by this historical frame, the theory builds in the importance of knowledge and in a variety of ways and its implications for the processes of differentiation.

Models of consolidation and differentiation summarize the organizational ecology literature, generalizing it and combining it with the older contingency theory. In particular, the distinctions made about the variety of tastes and of technologies reconcile conflicting findings about the importance of organizational age and size. In addition, the theory of consolidation and of differentiation combines these literatures with the new ones on organizational knowledge and inter-organizational relationships as well as the older one on organizational innovation.

Another important implication is that this is a multi-level theory. Generally, organizational theory has ignored the role of institutions. In this theory, the interventions of the governance modes are explicitly built into the theory, an important step in developing a theory of social change because most of the previous theories have tended to focus on either the macro- or micro-level and ignored the meso-level of organizations.

Implications for Institutional Theory

Generally, institutional theory has largely ignored the topic of institutional change (for some new material on this subject see Hage and Meeus, 2006) and the organizational level of analysis. Processes of change have been built in by observing changes first in the nature of the knowledge investments of society, whether in higher education or in R&D and second in the nature of the interventions of the dominant institutional mode, and third as the processes of either consolidation or differentiation unfold within a specific technology–market nexus.

The processes of differentiation fit naturally into theory about the new economy such as endogenous theories of economic growth because this is what some of these theories have emphasized (Romer, 1986; 1990). What they have missed is the emergence of inter-organizational networks as a major mode of non-market governance and one that furthers the process of differentiation (Hage and Hollingsworth, 2000; Matthews, 1997; Perry, 1999; van Waarden and Oosterwijk, 2006). The growth in knowledge as represented by rising levels of investment in R&D and in higher education and the processes of differentiation that it produces mean a proliferation of many market niches corresponding to the divergence in income and education levels or thus tastes. This means the movement towards specialization and the many small organizations are an important component of the new economy. In turn, this has resulted in a movement away from vertical integration and towards inter-organizational networks. In other words, it helps explain the rapid growth in this new kind of non-market mode of coordination; it is becoming a dominant constraint on free market competition as understood in economics.

Given this differentiation, there are new set of problems that have begun to be analysied in another emerging institutional literature, the one on national systems of innovation (Edquist and Hommen, 1999; Lundvall, 1992; Nelson, 1993) because this literature has emphasized the similarities within societies even as they have expanded consideration of differences between society. But by including the organizational level and the many hypotheses as indicated above, variations within a country can be observed as well.

Beyond these literatures, there has been a recent interest in the nature of comparative business systems in which the argument is made that each country has its own distinctive form of organization. I am suggesting a modification of this perspective. While I agree that these countries vary in terms of their non-market coordination modes, I am also suggesting that the general processes of consolidation and differentiation if they have the same scores on the nature of the technology and the market that are also unfolding in the same specific technology– market nexi across these countries where these business systems are not as different as has been claimed.

Still another way of connecting organizational theory and institutional theory is that the central thesis of management theory, which is built upon the processes of consolidation, is particularly applicable in the liberal market economies because in them the dominant governance mode has the large company or vertical hierarchy, whereas in the coordinated market economies the pressures towards consolidation have been dampened (see Hage, 2006).

This reflects several ways of connecting the two levels and altering the dominant institutional theory, but these are not the only ones. Another and a more interesting one for the purposes of this book is the impact of knowledge specialization along the idea innovation chains (Hage and Hollingsworth, 2000). It is in this theory in particular, that one observes the impact of knowledge on processes of differentiation but in a much broader sense than the simple growth in the number of organizations. The specialization created by the growth in knowledge leads to the differentiation of basic research organizations, applied research organizations, organizations that specialized in product development, or the creation of pro-types, still others that are concerned with the development of the appropriate manufacturing processes and so forth. It is these processes of differentiation that create communication barriers to the continued development of industrial innovation – an important form of creativity. And the extent of this difficulty is the function of the kind of institutional mode that coordinates the technology–market nexus. To conclude, the increasing importance of differentiation across a number of technology–market nexi means that both management theory and institutional theory need to be altered to take into consideration these developments.

Endnotes

1 In an earlier version of this essay, additional topics including the welfare state, underdevelopment, stratification were treated but only in a superficial way. Therefore, they are not considered here and indeed would require a very long essay. I assert that this can be done because the real test is whether or not the theory can speak to the traditional problems within macro- and meso-sociology as well as future topics.

2 In community chains, the high value added such as R&D is maintained in the developed country while the low value addition such as labour costs are moved to the developing country. In this way jobs are not only exported but also lower living standards are maintained in the developing countries.

3 Hannan and Freeman (1989) and Aldrich (1999).

4 However, it should be noted that Hannan and Freeman (1989) do not report the importance of the technological revolution in brewing that caused this change.

5 Again, it should be observed that what organizational ecologists have attempted is to describe one generic pattern for all organizational populations, namely the assumption that there is first a period of rising legitimacy, and then a period of competition (see Hannan and Carroll, 1992). This is quite separate from the observation that there are different patterns of evolution in organizational populations.

6 The focus on the large chemical giants such as I. G. Farben and Imperial Chemical and the large electrical companies like General Electric and Phillips ignores the many other small and medium-size firms in a number of countries in these sectors, again explaining why the differentiation process has been missed.

7 Admittedly in practice, drawing the boundaries around the technology and market or ecological space is not easy but the seven digit codes represent a good first approximation.

8 It also should be noted, that not all the organizational ecology studies fit the patterns of consolidation and of differentiation as hypothesized here.

9 In my opinion, sociologists fail to focus enough on explaining and predicting dispersion rather than averages. This essay is an example where dispersion across both technology–market nexi and countries is explained.

10 This represents only a partial list. Consider various policies regarding the workforce or the availability of labour such as the right to form unions, the right to strike, the right for unions to participate in organizational decisionmaking, policies regarding immigration, etc. Societies vary enormously in the absence or presence of these institutional patterns as anyone familiar with Europe knows full well.

11 He does have the interesting idea of adaptive efficiency, which usually means the presence of rules that allow for greater economic growth. From this perspective encouraging consolidation during

the industrial revolution could be conceived as an example of adaptive efficiency in so far as it facilitated more rapid economic growth. This is one way of interpreting planned economies, the extreme in consolidation.

12 One of the very special kinds of intervention of associations is in the control of the labour process including strike activity.

References

Aldrich, H. (1999) *Organizations Evolving*. London: Sage.

Aldrich, H. and Sasaki, T. (1995) 'R & D Consortia in the United States and Japan', *Research Policy*, 24(2): 301–16.

Alter, C. and Hage, J. (1993) *Organizations Working Together*. Newbury Park, CA: Sage.

Anderson, P. and Tushman, M. (1990) 'Technological Discontinuities and Dominant Designs: A Cyclical Model of Technological Change', *Administrative Science Quarterly*, 35(4): 604–33.

Archibugi, D. and Pianto, M. (1992) *The Technological Specialization of Advanced Countries: A Report to the EEC on International Science and Technology Activities*. Boston, MA: Kluwer.

Banaszak-Holl, J. C. (1991) 'Incorporating Organizational Growth into Models of Organizational Dynamics: Manhattan Banks, 1791–1980'. PhD dissertation, Cornell University, Ithaca.

Barnett, W. P. (1990) 'The Organizational Ecology of a Technological System', *Administrative Science Quarterly*, 35(1): 31–60.

Barnett, W. P. (1997) 'The Dynamics of Competitive Intensity', *Administrative Science Quarterly*, 42(1): 128–60.

Barron, D. N., West, E. and Hannan, M. T. (1994) 'A Time to Grow and a Time to Die: Growth and Mortality of Credit Unions in New York City, 1914–1990', *American Journal of Sociology*, 100(2): 381–421.

Baum, J. A. C. (1996) 'Organizational Ecology', in S. Clegg, C. Hardy and W. Nord (eds), *Handbook of Organizational Sociology*. London: Sage, pp. 77–114.

Becker, G. (1964) *Human Capital*. New York: National Bureau of Economic Research.

Bell, D. (1973) *The Coming of Post-Industrial Society: A Venture in Social Forecasting*. New York: Basic Books.

Breschi, S. and Malerba, F. (1997) 'Sectoral Innovation Systems: Technological Regimes, Schumpeterian Dynamics, and Spatial Boundaries', in C. Edquist (ed.), *Systems of Innovation: Technologies, Institutions and Organizations*. London: Pinter, pp. 130–55.

Brown, J. S. and Duguid, P. (1998) 'Organizing Knowledge', *California Management Review*, 40(3): 90–112.

Browning, L., Beyer, J. and Shetler, J. (1995) 'Building Cooperation in a Competitive Industry: SEMATEC and the Semiconductor Industry', *Academy of Management Journal*, 38(1): 113–51.

Brüderl, J. and Schüssler, R. (1990) 'Organizational Mortality: The Liabilities of Newness and Adolescence', *Administrative Science Quarterly*, 35(3): 530–47.

Campbell, J., Hollingsworth, J. R. and Lindberg, L. (eds) (1991) *Governance of the American Economy*. New York: Cambridge University Press.

Carroll, G. R. (1987) *Publish and Perish: The Organizational Ecology of the Newspaper Industries*. Greenwich, CT: JAI Press.

Casper, C. and Whitley, R. (2002) 'Managing Competences in Entrepreneurial Technology Firms: A Comparative Institutional Analysis of Germany, Sweden and the UK', paper presented at the Takeda Foundation Symposium on Engineering Intellect and Knowledge, SCASSS, Uppsala, Sweden.

Casper, S. (2000) 'Institutional Adaptiveness, Technology Policy, and the Diffusion of the New Business Models: The Case of German Biotechnology', *Organization Studies*, 21(5): 887–914.

Chandler jr, A. (1962) *Strategy and Structure: Chapters in the History of Industrial Enterprise*. Cambridge, MA: MIT Press.

Chandler jr, A. (1977) *The Visible Hand: The Managerial Revolution in American Business*. Cambridge, MA: Belknap Press.

Child, J. (1972) 'Organizational Structure, Environment and Performance: The Role of Strategic Choice', *Sociology*, 6(1): 2–22.

Cohen, E. (1992) *Le colbertisme 'High Tech': Économie des Télécoms et du grand projet.* Paris: Hachette.

Cohen, M. D. and Sproull, L. S. (eds) (1996) *Organizational Learning.* London: Sage.

Conner, K. R. and Prahalad, C. K. (1996) 'A Resource-Based Theory of the Firm: Knowledge Versus Opportunism', *Organization Science*, 7(5): 477–501.

Damanpour, F. (1991) 'Organizational Innovation: A Meta-Analysis of Effects of Determinants and Moderators', *Academy of Management Journal*, 34(3): 555–90.

Dankbaar, B. (1994) 'Sectoral Governance in the Automobile Industries of Germany, Great Britain, and France', in J. R. Hollingsworth, P. C. Schmitter and W. Streeck (eds), *Governing Capitalist Economies: Performance and Control of Economic Sectors.* Oxford: Oxford University Press, pp. 156–82.

Delacroix, J. and Swaminathan, A. (1991) 'Cosmetic, Speculative, and Adaptive Organizational Change in the Wine Industry: A Longitudinal Study', *Administrative Science Quarterly*, 36(4): 631–61.

Doz, Y. L. and Hamel, G. (1998) *Alliance Advantage: The Art of Creating Value Through Partnering.* Boston, MA: Harvard Business School Press.

Dussauge, P. and Garrette, B. (1999) *Cooperative Strategy: Competing Successfully Through Strategic Alliances.* Chichester, NY: Wiley.

Edquist, C. and Hommen, L. (1999) 'Systems of Innovation: Theory and Policy for the Demand Side', *Technology in Society*, 21(1): 63–79.

European Commission (2004) *Towards a European Strategy for Nanotechnology.* Brussels: European Commission.

Gereffi, G. and Korzeniewicz, M. (eds) (1994) *Commodity Chains and Global Capitalism.* Westport, CN: Preager.

Gerlach, M. (1992) *Alliance Capitalism: The Social Organization of Japanese Business.* Berkeley, CA: University of California Press.

Gomes-Casseres, B. (1996) *The Alliance Revolution: The New Shape of Business Rivalry.* Cambridge, MA: Harvard University Press.

Grant, R. M. (1996) 'Prospering in Dynamically-Competitive Environments: Organizational Capability as Knowledge Integration', *Organization Science*, 7(4): 375–87.

Guerreri, P. and Tylecote, A. (1998) 'Interindustry Differences in Technical Change and National Patterns of Technological Accumulation', in C. Edquist (ed.), *Systems of Innovation: Technologies, Institutions and Organizations.* London: Pinter, pp. 108–29.

Hage, J. (1965) 'An Axiomatic Theory of Organizations', *Administrative Science Quarterly*, 10(3): 289–320.

Hage, J. (1980) *Theories of Organizations: Form, Process and Transformation.* New York: Wiley-Interscience.

Hage, J. (1999) 'Organizational Innovation and Organizational Change', *Annual Review of Sociology*, 25: 597–622.

Hage, J. (2006) 'Institutional Change and Societal Change: The Impact of Knowledge Transformations', in J. Hage and M. Meeus (eds), *Innovation, Science and Institutional Change.* Oxford: Oxford University Press, pp. 465–82.

Hage, J. and Aiken, M. (1969) 'Routine Technology, Social Structure and Organizational Goals', *Administrative Science Quarterly*, 14: 366–77.

Hage, J. and Alter, C. (1997) 'A Typology of Interorganizational Relationships and Networks', in J. R. Hollingsworth and R. Boyer (eds), *Contemporary Capitalism: The Embeddedness of Institutions.* Cambridge: Cambridge University Press, pp. 94–126.

Hage, J. and Hadden, W. C. (2001) 'The Many Meanings of Organizational Size and Age: Technology and Market Characteristics Provide Contextual Meaning', paper presented at the Society for the Advancement of Socio-Economics, Aix-en-Provence, France.

Hage, J. and Hollingsworth, J. R. (2000) 'A Strategy for Analysis of Idea Innovation Networks and Institutions', *Organization Studies*, 21(5): 971–1004.

Hage, J. and Meeus, M. (eds) (2006) *Innovation, Science and Institutional Change.* Oxford: Oxford University Press.

Hage, J. and Powers, C. H. (1992) *Post-Industrial Lives: Roles and Relationships in the 21ˢᵗ Century.* Newbury Park, CA: Sage.

Hage, J., Hanneman, R. and Gargan, E. T. (1989) *State Responsiveness and State Activism*. London: Unwin Hyman.

Hagedoorn, J. (1993) 'Strategic Technology Alliances and Modes of Cooperation in High-Technology Industries', in G. Grabher (ed.), *The Embedded Firm: On the Socioeconomics of Industrial Networks*. London: Routledge, pp. 116–38.

Hall, P. and Soskice, D. (eds) (2001) *Varieties of Capitalism*. Oxford: Oxford University Press.

Hannan, M. and Carroll, G. C. (1992) *Dynamics of Organizational Populations: Density, Legitimation, and Competition*. New York: Oxford University Press.

Hannan, M. and Freeman, J. (1989) *Organizational Ecology*. Cambridge, MA: Harvard University Press.

Hannan, M., Carroll, G. C., Dobreau, S. D. and Han, J. (1998a) 'Organizational Mortality in European and American Automobile Industries Part I: Revisiting the Effects of Age and Size', *European Journal of Sociology*, 14(3): 279–302.

Hannan, M., Carroll, G. C., Dobreau, S. D., Han J. and Torres, J. C. (1998b) 'Organizational Mortality in European and American Automobile Industries Part II: Coupled Clocks', *European Journal of Sociology*, 14(3): 302–13.

Harbison, J. R. and Pekar, P. P. (1998) *Smart Alliances: A Practical Guide to Repeatable Success*. San Francisco: Jossey Bass.

Haveman, H. (1992) 'Between a Rock and Hard Place: Organizational Change and Performance under Conditions of Fundamental Environmental Transformation', *Administrative Science Quarterly*, 37: 48–75.

Herrigel, G. (1994) 'Industry as a Form of Order: A Comparison of the Historical Development of the Machine Tool Industries in the United States and Germany', in J. R. Hollingsworth, P. C. Schmitter and W. Streeck (eds), *Governing Capitalist Economies: Performance and Control of Economic Sectors*. Oxford: Oxford University Press, pp. 97–128.

Hollingsworth, J. R. (1991) 'The Logic of Coordinating American Manufacturing Sectors', in J. L. Campbell, J. R. Hollingsworth and L. Lindberg (eds), *The Governance of the American Economy*. Cambridge/New York: Cambridge University Press, pp. 35–73.

Hollingsworth, J. R. (1997) 'Continuities and Changes in Social Systems of Production: The Cases of Japan, Germany, and the United States', in J. R. Hollingsworth and R. Boyer (eds), *Contemporary Capitalism: The Embeddedness of Institutions*. New York: Cambridge University Press, pp. 265–310.

Hollingsworth, J. R. and Boyer, R. (eds) (1997) *Contemporary Capitalism: The Embeddedness of Institutions*. New York: Cambridge University Press.

Ingram, P. and Baum, J. A. C. (1997) 'Chain Affiliation and the Failure of Manhattan Hotels, 1898–1980', *Administrative Science Quarterly*, 42(1): 68–102.

Kitschelt, H. (1991) 'Industrial Governance Structures, Innovation Strategies, and the Case of Japan: Sectoral or Cross-National Comparative Analysis?', *International Organization*, 45(4): 453–93.

Kline, S. and Rosenberg, N. (1986) 'An Overview of Innovation', in R. Landau and N. Rosenberg (eds), *The Positive Sum Strategy*. Washington, DC: National Academy Press, pp. 227–305.

Kogut, B., Shan, W. and Walker, G. (1993) 'Knowledge in the Network and the Network as Knowledge: The Structuring of New Industries', in G. Grabher (ed.), *The Embedded Firm: On the Socioeconomics of Industrial Networks*. London: Routledge, pp. 67–94.

Korzeniewicz, M. (1994) 'Commodity Chains and Marketing Strategies: Nike and the Global Athletic Footwear Industry', in G. Gereffi and M. Korzeniewicz (eds), *Commodity Chains and Global Capitalism*. Westport, CN: Preager, pp. 247–66.

Korzeniewicz, R. and Martin, W. (1994) 'The Global Distribution of Commodity Chains', in G. Gereffi and M. Korzeniewicz (eds), *Commodity Chains and Global Capitalism*. Westport, CN: Preager, pp. 67–92.

Landes, D. (1969) *Unbound Prometheus*. Cambridge: Cambridge University Press.

Lawrence, P. and Lorsch, J. (1967) *Organization and Environment: Managing Differentiation and Integration*. Cambridge, MA: Harvard Graduate School of Business.

Lazerson, M. (1993) 'Factory or Putting-Out? Knitting Networks in Modena', in G. Grabher (ed.), *The Embedded Firm: On the Socioeconomics of Industrial Networks*. London: Routledge, pp. 203–26.

Lehrman, W. G. (1994) 'Diversity in Decline: Institutional Environment and Organizational Failure in the American Life Insurance Industry', *Social Forces*, 73(2): 605–35.

Leonard, D. and Sensiper, S. (1998) 'The Role of Tacit Knowledge in Group Innovation', *California Management Review*, 40(3): 112–32.

Lundvall, B.-A. (1992) *National Systems of Innovation: Towards a Theory of Innovation and Interactive Learning*. London: Pinter.

Lynn, G. S., Morone, J. G. and Paulson, A. S. (1996) 'Marketing and Discontinuous Innovation: The Probe and Learn Process', *California Management Review*, 38(3): 8–38.

Malerba, F. and Orsenigo, L. (1993) 'Technological Regimes and Firm Behavior', *Industrial and Corporate Change*, 2(1): 45–71.

Malerba, F. and Orsenigo, L. (1997) 'Technological Regimes and Sectoral Patterns of Innovative Activities', *Industrial and Corporate Change*, 6(1): 83–117.

Matthews, J. A. (1997) 'A Silicon Valley of the East: Creating Taiwan's Semiconductor Industry', *California Management Review*, 39(4): 26–55.

Mockler, R. J. (1999) *Multinational Strategic Alliances*. Chichester, NY: Wiley.

Mohrman, S. and Monge, P. (2005) *Network attributes impacting the eneration and flow of knowledge within and from the basic science community*. Technical report contract 84882. The Center for Effective Organizations, University of Southern California.

Mohrman, S., Galbraith, J. and Monge, P. (2006) 'Network Attributes Impacting the Generation and Flow of Knowledge within and from the Basic Science Community', in J. Hage and M. Meeus (eds), *Innovation, Science, and Institutional Change*. Oxford: Oxford University Press, 196–216.

National Science Foundation (1996) *National Science and Engineering Indicators*. Washington, DC: Government Printing Office.

Nelson, R. R. (ed.) (1993) *National Innovations Systems: A Comparative Study*. Oxford: Oxford University Press.

Nelson, R. R. and Winter, S. G. (1982) *An Evolutionary Theory of Economic Change*. Cambridge, MA: The Belknap Press of Harvard University Press.

Nonaka, I. And Takeuchi, H. (1995) *The Knowledge Creating Company*. Oxford: Oxford University Press.

North, D. C. (1990) *Institution, Institutional Change, and Economic Performance*. New York: Cambridge University Press.

O'Doherty, D. (ed.) (1995) *Globalisation, Networking, and Small Firm Innovation*. London: Graham and Trotman.

Oerlemans, L., Meeus, M. and Boekema, F. (1998) 'Do Networks Matter for Innovation? The Usefulness of the Economic Network Approach in Analyzing Innovation', *Journal of Social and Economic Geography*, 89(3): 298–309.

Oerlemans, L., Meeus, M. and Boekema, F. (1999) 'Interactive Learning within a Regional System of Innovation: A Case Study in a Dutch Region'. Unpublished paper. Eindhoven Centre for Innovation Studies, Faculty of Technology Management, Eindhoven University of Technology, Eindhoven, The Netherlands.

Pavitt, K. (1984) 'Sectorial Patterns of Technical Change: Towards a Taxonomy and a Theory', *Research Policy*, 13(3): 343–73.

Perrow, C. H. (1967) 'A Framework for the Comparative Analysis of Organizations', *American Sociological Review*, 32(2): 184–208.

Perry, M. (1999) *Small Firms and Network Economies*. London: Routledge.

Piore, M. and Sabel, C. (1984) *The Second Industrial Divide: Possibilities for Prosperity*. New York: Basic Books.

Porter, M. (1990) *The Comparative Advantage of Nations*. New York: Free Press.

Powell, W. W. (1998) 'Learning from Collaboration: Knowledge and Networks in the Biotechnology and Pharmaceutical Industries', *California Management Review*, 40(3): 228–40.

Powell, W. W. and Brantley, P. (1992) 'Competitive Cooperation in Biotechnology: Learning through Networks', in N. Nohria and R. Eccles (eds), *Networks and Organizations*. Cambridge, MA: Harvard Business School Press, pp. 366–94.

Prais, S. J. and Steedman, H. (1986) 'Vocational Training in France and Britain in the Building Trades', *National Institute Economic Review*, 116: 45–56.

Prais, S. J., Karvis, V. and Wagner, K. (1989) 'Productivity and Vocational Skills Services in Britain and Germany: Hotels', *National Institute Economic Review*, 130: 52–74.

Romer, P. (1986) 'Increasing Returns and Long-Run Growth', *Journal of Political Economy*, 94(5): 1002–37.

Romer, P. (1990) 'Endogenous Technological Change', *Journal of Political Economy*, 98(5): 71–102.

Schneiberg, M. and Hollingsworth, J. R. (1990) 'Can Transaction Costs Economics Explain Trade Associations?', in M. Aoki, B. Gustafsson and O. Williamson (eds), *The Firm as a Nexus of Treaties*. Newbury Park, CA: Sage, pp. 320–46.

Steedman, H. and Wagner, K. (1987) 'A Second Look at Productivity, Machinery and Skills in Britain and Germany', *National Institute Economic Review*, 122: 84–95.

Steedman, H. and Wagner, K. (1989) 'Productivity, Machinery and Skills: Clothing Manufacture in Britain and Germany', *National Institute Economic Review*, 128: 40–57.

Stråth, B. (1994) 'Modes of Governance in the Shipbuilding Sector in Germany, Sweden, and Japan', in J. R. Hollingsworth, P. C. Schmitter and W. Streeck (eds), *Governing Capitalist Economies: Performance and Control of Economic Sectors*. Oxford: Oxford University Press, pp. 72–96.

Streeck, W., Hilbert, J., van Kevelaer, K.-H., Maier, F. and Weber, H. (1987) *Steuerung und Regulierung der beruflichen Bildung: Die Rolle der Sozialpartner in der Ausbildung und beruflichen Weiterbildung in der BR Deutschland*. Berlin: Sigma.

Suleiman, E. (1978) *Elites in Society: The Politics of Survival*. Princeton, NJ: Princeton University Press.

Toffler, A. (1981) *The Third Wave*. New York: Bantam.

Utterback, J. (1994) *Mastering the Dynamics of Innovation: How Companies Can Seize Opportunities in the Face of Technological Change*. Boston, MA: Harvard Business School Press.

van Waarden, F. and Oosterwijk, H. (2006) 'Turning Tracks? Path Dependence, Technological Paradigm Shifts, and Organizational and Institutional Change', in J. Hage and M. Meeus (eds), *Innovation, Science and Institutional Change*. Oxford: Oxford University Press, 443–64.

Walton, R. (1987) *Innovating to Compete: Lessons for Diffusing and Managing Change in the Workplace*. San Francisco, CA: Jossey-Bass.

Whitley, R. (1992a) *Business Systems in East Asia: Firms, Markets and Societies*. London: Sage.

Whitley, R. (1992b) *European Business Systems: Firms and Markets in their National Context*. London: Sage.

Womack, J., Jones, D. and Ross, D. (1990) *The Machine that Changed the World*. New York: Rawson Associates.

Woodward, J. (1965) *Industrial Organizations: Theory and Practice*. Oxford: Oxford University Press.

Zammuto, R. and O'Connor, E. (1992) 'Gaining Advanced Manufacturing Technologies Benefits: The Role of Organizational Design and Culture', *Academy of Management Review*, 17: 701–28.

Section Three

New Information Technologies and Communication, Communities and Public Sphere

4

Mobilities, Networks and Communities

By John Urry

Mobile Spaces and their Other

The past decade or so has seen a remarkable series of changes in both travel and communications. There are 760 million legal international journeys each year, a figure soon to pass 1 billion. There are 600 million or so cars, a figure expected to rise within a few decades to 1 billion. The Internet has grown faster than any previous technology, with soon 1 billion users across the globe. Foreign exchange dealings each day are worth $1.4 trillion, 60 times greater than the flows of world trade. Communications 'on the move' are being transformed with new mobile phones more common than land-line phones. It is thought that 3 billion people receiving the same income as the richest, mobile 300. Globally branded companies employ staff from around the world with budgets greater than those of individual countries. Images of the blue earth from space or the golden arches of McDonalds are ubiquitous across the world and on the billion or so TV screens.[1]

In analysing these various new mobile technologies there is rather little examination of the 'other' to these technologies, what it is that is transformed by them. Whether these technologies are utopic or a dystopic, the pre-virtual is presumed to be a knowable and taken-for-granted other that is transformed by new forms of a mobile existence. There have been various attempts to formulate such transformations in connections 'at-a-distance': a 'death of distance' (Cairncross, 1997), a 'liquid modernity' (Bauman, 2000), an 'internet galaxy' (Castells, 2001), the 'global transformations' of economic, social and political life (Held *et al.*, 1999) and 'global complexity' (Urry, 2003). All these presuppose something knowable about life before what we might term the electronic and mobile 'big bang'.

Normally this knowable other is characterized as 'real', as opposed to the airy, fragile and virtual relationships of the electronic. And the real is normally taken to involve the concept of 'community'. Real life is seen to comprise enduring, face-to-face, communitarian connections, while the virtual world is made up of fragile, mobile, airy and inchoate connections. Examining the consequences of the various new technologies rests upon a series of overlapping dichotomies: real/unreal, face-to-face/life-on-the-screen, immobile/mobile, community/virtual and presence/absence.

I argue against such dichotomies. In part this is because all relationships in all societies have always involved diverse 'connections'. Such connections are more or less 'at a distance', more or less intense, more or less mobile and more or less machinic. Social relations are not fixed or located in place but are constituted through various '*circulating* entities' (Latour, 1999: 17). There are many circulating entities that bring about relationality at multiple and varied *distances*. Circulating entities result in multiple 'connections' that cannot be conceptualized in terms of the dichotomies above. All social relationships involve complex patterns of immediate presence and intermittent absence at-a-distance.

However, sociology, like other social sciences, has overly focused upon ongoing, more or less face-to-face social interactions between peoples and within social groups. Sociology has taken connections to be most importantly face-to-face, characterized by social interactions with those who are immediately present. But there are many connections with peoples and social groupings at a distance, not based upon regular face-to-face interactions. There are many forms of 'imagined presence' through diverse objects and images that carry connections across, and into, multiple kinds of social space, even within the same 'organization'.

Also on occasions and for specific periods, face-to-face connections are made, but generally resulting from one or more modes of corporeal movement. People travel on occasions to connect, but how and why some travel takes place for some connections has not been much examined. It has not taken such face-to-faceness as itself needing explanation (see Urry, 2002).

What thus is missing is the more general nature of networked connections, especially how these are formed and reformed through various kinds of 'circulating entities', including patterns of travel and various machines that on occasions result in co-presence. Intermittent mobility we can say is central to the way in which people live in an increasingly 'networked society' and especially within the kinds of networking seen as essential to the knowledge-economy (Castells, 1996).

There are five highly interdependent 'mobilities' that form and re-form diverse networks within contemporary social, and organizational life:

- *corporeal* travel of people for work, leisure, family life, pleasure, migration and escape;
- physical movement of *objects* delivered to producers, consumers and retailers;
- *imaginative* travel elsewhere through images of places and peoples upon TV;
- *virtual* travel often in real time on the Internet so transcending geographical and social distance; as Microsoft asks: 'Where do you want to go today?';
- *communicative* travel through person-to-person messages via letters, telephone, fax, PDA and mobile.

Most social research focuses upon one or the other of these separate mobilities, such as passenger transport or the Internet. This chapter examines the profoundly important interconnections between these mobilities that are all central to making and maintaining complex connections in a 'networked' knowledge-based society. I consider first some notions of 'community'. I then examine some ways in which virtual connections are significantly remaking the notions of presence and absence, but these remakings are not the simple replacement of the continuously present by the electronically absent. Physical co-presence is still highly significant. Finally I consider various 'mobile machines' that involve transformations in the very nature of humans.

Communities

It is useful to distinguish between three different senses of 'community' (Bell and Newby, 1976). First, there is community in a topographical sense. This refers to settlement based upon close geographical *propinquity*, but where there is no implication of the quality of the social relationships found in such settlements of intense co-presence. Second, there is the sense of community as the *local* social system in which there is a localized, relatively bounded set of systemic interrelationships of social groups and local institutions. Third, there is *communion*, a human association that is characterized by close personal ties, belongingness and warmth between its members. The last of these is what is conventionally meant by the idea of 'community' relationships (and see Putnam, 2000).

Bell and Newby (1976) show that communion is not necessarily produced by any particular settlement type and can be generated even where those involved do not dwell in close physical proximity. Geographical propinquity also does not necessitate a local social system, nor does localness necessarily generate communion. Moreover, there are many ways of reaffirming a sense of community through *movement* within boundaries, such as travelling along well-worn paths or roads. And places are also always interconnected beyond boundaries, to many other places through real and imagined travel. Thus Raymond Williams in the *Border Country* is 'fascinated by the networks men and women set up, the trails and territorial structures they make as they move across a region, and the ways these interact or interfere with each other' (quoted by Pinkney, 1991: 49; Williams, 1988). Massey similarly argues that the identity of a place is derived in large part from its interchanges with other places that may on occasions be progressive (1994: 180). Travel, we might say, is central to communities, even those characterized by relatively high levels of propinquity and communion.

However, there are many forms of communication between people, including the personal messenger, letter, telegram, telephone, email, text messaging, radio, TV and video conferencing (the last of these is said to have increased post-9/11). Thus travel only happens on occasions and this can best be explained through the concept of the 'compulsion to proximity', that people travel in order to be physically co-present with others for particular moments of time (see the classic Boden and Molotch, 1994; as well as Urry, 2002).

Through travel people are physically co-present with workmates, business colleagues, friends, partner, or family, or they bodily encounter some particular landscape or townscape, or are physically present at a particular live event. What I call corporeal travel results in the anticipation of, and the realization of, intermittent periods of physical proximity to particular peoples, places or events. Such proximity is felt to be obligatory, appropriate or desirable, not a matter of choice. Especially in order to sustain particular relationships with friend or family or work colleague that is 'in the mind', that person has intermittently to be seen, sensed, through physical co-presence.

BT (British Telecom) says 'it is good to talk' but it is especially good to talk through co-presence, through rich, multi-layered and dense conversations even within business organizations (Boden and Molotch, 1994). These involve not just words, but indexical expressions, facial gestures, body language, status, voice intonation, pregnant silences, past histories, anticipated conversations and actions, turn-taking practices and so on. Co-presence affords access to the eyes. Eye contact enables the establishment of intimacy and trust, as well as insincerity and fear, and power and control. Simmel considers that the eye is a unique 'sociological achievement' since looking at one another is what effects the connections and interactions of individuals (1997: 111). This is the most direct and the 'purest' interaction. It is the look between people which produces moments of intimacy since: 'One cannot take through the eye without at the same time giving'; this produces the 'most complete reciprocity' of person to person, face to face (Simmel, 1997: 112). The look is returned and trust can get established and reproduced. Face-to-face conversations enable the talking-through of problems, especially the unmediated telling of 'troubles'. In such conversations topics can come and go, misunderstandings can be corrected, and commitment and sincerity can be directly assessed. Also physical co-presence can demonstrate the lack of trust, that someone is not to be believed and the deal should not be done, the relationship ended.

Co-present bodies are actively involved in turn-taking within conversations, a tilt of the head indicating a willingness to receive an utterance. Likewise co-present people can touch each other, with a rich, complex and culturally variable vocabulary of touch. The embodied character of conversation is 'a managed physical action as well as "brain work"' (Boden and Molotch, 1994: 262).

Participants travel to meet together at work and in many other contexts. People commit themselves to remain there for the duration of the interaction, and each uses and handles the timing of utterances and silences to 'talk'. There is an expectation of mutual attentiveness and this is especially the case within 'meetings'. Such meetings are often multi-functional, for making decisions, seeing how one is heard, executing standard procedures and duties, distributing rewards, status and blame, reinforcing friendship as well as distance, judging commitment, having an enjoyable time and so on. They are typically information-rich encounters (Schwartzman, 1989; Urry, 2002).

Research shows that managers in the United States spend up to half of their time in face-to-face meetings and much of their time lies in working with and evaluating colleagues through extensive physical co-presence (Boden and Molotch, 1994: 272). This reflects the apparent shift within how organizations work, from the 'individual work ethic' to the 'collective team ethic' in which face-to-face social and leadership skills are especially valued (Evans and Wurstler, 2000: 107–09). This seems especially important within creative and knowledge-based organizations. And the higher the position in an organizational hierarchy the more significant is establishing and nurturing 'complex networks', where unwritten and informal co-presence is especially salient, as Boden shows in *The Business of Talk* (1994).

Such networks also facilitate the 'inadvertent' meetings that occur because people from similar social networks are informally encountered in certain parts of towns or cities, on golf courses, campuses, cafes, bars, parties, book launches, conferences and so on (see Watts, 1999, on the mathematical properties of the 'it's a small world' phenomenon). Where people live geographically distant from each other, then sites of 'informal co-presence' are regularly visited. Research on the city of London in particular also shows how its intense communicative role has if anything been enhanced, with those working in financial services regularly travelling to meet up especially in informal 'thirdspaces' for intense moments of quality time (see Boden, 2000; Thrift, 1996).

Given then these arguments about the complex interweaving of presence, imagined presence and intermittent absence, I turn to the nature of connections within generic electronic spaces.

Virtual 'Communities'

It is often claimed that so-called virtual communities are not real communities (Jones, 1995: 24; Sardar, 1996). Virtual communities involve more and more connections but these connections are said to 'grow more fragile, airy, and ephemeral', as electronic space is said to supplant the rich complex diversity of pre-existing social space (Heim, 1991: 74). Virtual communities are thought to lack the substance of 'real communities' providing only a life on the screen (Turkle, 1996).

However, intermittent co-presence is important even within electronic spaces (Baym, 1995: 157). People meet up from time to time, dwelling together in a shared place for periods. This 'compulsion to proximity' is said to reinforce the 'magical, intensely personal, deeply emotional bonds that the medium had enabled them to forge among themselves' (Rheingold, 1994: 237). Thus even electronic spaces seem to depend upon moments of face-to-face co-presence for developing trustful relationships.

Indeed new electronic or virtual communities may presuppose an enhanced corporeal mobility of people (as well as the extensive use of phone conversations). Or to put the argument the other way round: an IT executive argues that the 'daily information and entertainment needs of a traveller are typically multitudes greater than those of the average residential customer' (quoted by Graham and Marvin, 1996: 199). The more people travel corporeally, the more they seem to connect in cyberspace.

Thus there is not a fixed amount of travel that has to be met in one way or another, and that there could be the straightforward 'substitution' of virtual travel for corporeal travel. It seems that both virtual and physical travel transform the very nature and need for co-presence. Koku *et al.* argue on the basis of research on research scholars that '[f]requent contact on the Internet is a complement to frequent face-to-face contact, not a substitute for it' (quoted by Putnam, 2000: 179). Other research suggests that those who are online are those most active in voluntary and political work within their immediate neighbourhood (Wellman, 2001: 10). Their range of contacts may be predominantly local but significantly broader than those who are not online. Virtual connections would thus seem to promote more extensive local connections, *contra* Putnam, and hence more and not less corporeal travel.

But further broader changes seem to be occurring in what we mean by 'community' such that people increasingly interact and form 'communities' or 'small worlds' with those who are geographically distant (see Lodge's account of academic 'small worlds', 1983). This changing nature of community life can be seen within diasporic cultures. The proliferation of such diasporas has extended the range, extent and significance of all forms of travel for far-flung families and households. Clifford summarizes the importance of travel:

> dispersed peoples, once separated from homelands by vast oceans and political barriers, increasingly find themselves in border relations with the old country thanks to a to-and-fro made possible by modern technologies of transport, communication, and labour migration. Airplanes, telephones, tape cassettes, camcorders, and mobile job markets reduce distances and facilitate two-way traffic, legal and illegal, between the world's places.

(Clifford, 1997: 247; Cohen, 1997)

In the case of Trinidad Miller and Slater argue that one can really only be 'Trini' by going abroad, with about 60 per cent of nuclear families having at least one member living abroad (2000: 12 and 36). But at the same time, using the Internet is becoming central to being a real 'Trini'. The use of the Internet in Trinidad 'has permeated all sectors of society' as hot, stylish, and fashionable (Miller and Slater, 2000: 27).

Miller and Slater (2000) go on to argue that as virtual travel thus becomes part of everyday life so it transforms what we think of as near and far, present and absent. It changes the character of co-presence, even where the computer is resolutely fixed in place. Thus we should regard: 'Internet media as continuous with and embedded in other social spaces, that they happen within mundane social structures and relations that they may transform but that they cannot escape into a self-enclosed cyberian apartness' (Miller and Slater, 2000: 5). Thus the very distinction between online and offline gradually dissolves since 'many community ties are complex dances of face-to-face encounters, scheduled get-togethers, dyadic telephone class, emails to one person or several and broader online discussions among those sharing interests' (Wellman, 2001: 11).

Thus networked ties exist in and across both physical space and cyberspace. Virtual proximities involve multiple networks, where people can switch from one to the other, using connections from one network as a resource within another. Virtual travel offers various social affordances as cyberspace is transformed into multiple cyberplaces (see Wellman, 2001). Thus electronic spaces are 'incontrovertibly social spaces in which people still meet face-to-face, but under new conditions of both "meet" and "face", of changing kinds of connections at-a-distance' (Stone, 1991: 85).

Mobile Machines

More generally, various technical means of communications are increasingly combined with humans, forming new material worlds. There are new modes of present and absent 'strangerness' (Bogard, 2000). These machinic hybrids involve

a contradiction between nearness and remoteness, or mobility and fixation [...].
Cyberspace communications, in a word, are strange – at the push of a button, territories
dissolve, oppositions of distant and close, motion and stasis, inside and out, collapse;
identities are marginalized and simulated, and collectivities lose their borders.

(Bogard, 2000: 28)

Indeed, more generally, there are now almost always 'strangers' in our midst – on
multiple screens not only in the workplace or home but also in cars, airports,
shopping centres, post offices, stores, garages, trains, aircraft and so on (see
McCarthy, 2001, on the widespread growth of such 'ambient television'). There
is a curious 'flickering' combination of presence and absence. Bogard characterizes
such a collapse of distance as an impure or indeterminate relationship, neither one
nor two, as a fractal space: 'This blurring of boundaries between the monad and
the dyad is an excellent image of the rapidly evolving symbiosis of bodies and
computers, groups and communications networks, societies and cybernetic
systems' (2000: 40). Connections are simultaneously private and public, intimate
and distant. We could describe these as new fractal social spaces, as each realm
folds over, under, through and beyond each other in striking new social topologies.
These are oscillatory, flickering, both here-and-there and inside and outside, like
a Mobius strip.

The blurring of the boundaries between presence and absence is especially
marked with those newer communication devices that are small, mobile and
embedded within, or part of, the very means of mobility. These involve what one
might call a simulated co-presence, with PDAs, laptops, wireless connections,
palmtops, computer connections on trains and aircraft, cars as 'portals' to the net,
the 'mobile Internet' and so on. There is convergence between new modes of
transport and communication and this further 'mobilizes' the characteristics of
co-presence.

Indeed the twenty-first century would be the century of 'inhabited machines',
machines inhabited by individuals or very small groups of individuals. It is
through the inhabiting of such machines that humans will come to 'life'. Further,
machines only function because they are so inhabited; they are machines only
when one or more humans come to inhabit them. These inhabited machines are
miniaturized, privatized, digitized and mobilized. They include walkmans, mobile
phones, the individual TV, the networked computer/Internet, the individualized
smart car/bike, virtual reality 'travel', tele-immersion sites, helicopters and smart
small aircraft and other micro-mobiles yet to emerge. Such machines are desired
for their style, smallness, lightness and demonstrate a physical form often closely
interwoven with the corporeal (see Bull, 2000 and du Gay *et al.*, 1997, on the
Sony Walkman). Mobile phone users often describe them as prosthetic, as physically
co-terminous with their body (Hulme and Peters, 2001).

These machines depend upon *digital* power that is substantially separate from
material form or presence and involves exceptional levels of miniaturization and
portability. They serve to constitute what Makimoto and Manners term 'digital
nomads' (1997). These machines re-order Euclidean time–space relations, bending,
stretching and compressing time–space. Such machines mean that inhabiting
them is to be connected to, or to be at home with, 'sites' across the world – while

simultaneously such sites can monitor, observe and trace each inhabited machine. These machines are producing a 'liquid modernity' of interdependent flows of text, messages, people, information and images (see Bauman, 2000).

Conclusion

Such mobile machines thus reconfigure humans as physically moving bodies and as bits of mobile information and image, as individuals exist both through, and beyond, their mobile bodies. These inhabiting machines enable people to be more readily mobile through space, or to stay in one place, because of the capacity for 'self-retrieval' of personal information at other times or spaces. People inhabit networks of information, image and movement through such machines. 'Persons' thus occur as various nodes in these multiple machines of inhabitation and mobility. Such machines are inhabited, not just used and not just enabling or constraining. The machines only work when they are inhabited and especially when they are on the move. And in their inhabitation of such machines connections are crucially transformed, with others being uncannily present *and* absent, here and there, near and distant, home and away, and proximate and distant (Bogard, 2000).

And those inhabiting machines do intermittently on occasions come together to connect through physical co-presence. And we might indeed hypothesize that the greater the hybridized mobility such as in knowledge industries, the more intense the need for moments of quality co-presence (as Boden, 2000, argues with financial traders). Even so, the arrangements about such face-to-face meetings will be increasingly made flexible, and 'on the move'. Thus the dichotomies of real/unreal, face-to-face/life-on-the-screen, immobile/mobile, community/virtual and presence/absence need to be dispensed with.

Moreover, those mobilities always depend upon multiple stabilities. The complex character of such systems stems from the multiple time–space fixities or moorings that enable the fluidities of liquid modernity to be realized. Thus 'mobile machines', such as mobile-phones, cars, aircraft, trains and computer connections, all presume varied time–space immobilities (see Graham and Marvin, 2001).

This relationality between mobilites and immobilities is a typical characteristic of complexity theorizing. There is no linear increase in fluidity without extensive systems of immobilities. Thus the so-far-most-powerful mobile machine, the aeroplane, requires the largest and most extensive immobility, of the airport–city employing tens of thousands of workers (see Pascoe, 2001, on the complex nature of such multiple 'airspaces').

There are specialized *periods* and *places* involving machines in temporary rest, storage, infra-structural immobility, disposal and immobile zones. How, when and where these materialize is of immense systemic consequence, relating to the organizing of time–space. The intersections of these periods and places facilitate or preclude the apparently seamless mobilities of people, information, objects and equipment across time–space. Overall it is these moorings that produce movement. And it is the dialectic of mobility/moorings that generates complexity. If all relationality were mobile or 'liquid', if systems really were entirely fluid, then there would be no complexity in emergent global systems. Complexity stems from the dialectic of mobility and moorings, whereby systems are neither anarchic nor ordered, neither exhibiting free will nor determinism, neither total presence nor complete absence. Systems are strangely ordered on the edge of chaos as Prigogine famously describes (1997; see Urry, 2003: chapter 7, for developments of this 'complexity' argument).

Endnote

1 This essay is a substantially edited version of Urry (2004), related to the other material in this issue.

References

Bauman, Z. (2000) *Liquid Modernity*. Cambridge: Polity.
Baym, K. (1995) 'The Emergence of Community in Computer-Mediated Communication', in S. Jones (ed.), *Cybersociety*. London: Sage, pp. 138–63.
Bell, C. and Newby, H. (1976) 'Communion, Communalism, Class and Community Action: The Sources of New Urban Politics', in D. Herbert and R. Johnston (eds), *Social Areas in Cities*. Vol. 2. Chichester: Wiley, pp. 189–207.
Boden, D. (1994) *The Business of Talk*. Cambridge: Polity.
Boden, D. (2000) 'Worlds in Action: Information, Instantaneity and Global Futures Trading', in B. Adam, U. Beck and J. van Loon (eds), *The Risk Society and Beyond*. London: Sage, pp. 183–97.
Boden, D. and Molotch, H. (1994) 'The Compulsion to Proximity', in R. Friedland and D. Boden (eds), *Nowhere: Space, Time and Modernity*. Berkeley, CA: University of California Press, pp. 257–86.
Bogard, W. (2000) 'Simmel in Cyberspace: Strangeness and Distance in Postmodern Communications', *Space and Culture*, 4/5: 23–46.
Bull, M. (2000) *Sounding Out the City*. Oxford: Berg.
Cairncross, F. (1997) *The Death of Distance*. London: Orion.
Castells, M. (1996) *The Rise of the Network Society*. Oxford: Blackwell Publishers.
Castells, M. (2001) *The Internet Galaxy*. Oxford: Oxford University Press.
Clifford, J. (1997) *Routes*. Cambridge, MA: Harvard University Press.
Cohen, R. (1997) *Global Diasporas*. London: University College London Press.
du Gay, P., Hall, S., Janes, L., Mackay, H. and Negus, K. (1997) *Doing Cultural Studies: The Story of Sony Walkman*. London: Sage.
Evans, P. and Wurstler, T. (2000) *Blown to Bits: How the New Economics of Information Transforms Strategy*. Boston, MA: Harvard Business School Press.
Graham, S. and Marvin, S. (1996) *Telecommunications and the City*. London: Routledge.
Graham, S. and Marvin, S. (2001) *Splintering Urbanism: Network Infrastructures, Technological Mobilities and the Urban Condition*. London: Routledge.
Heim, M. (1991) 'The Erotic Ontology of Cyberspace', in M. Benedikt (ed.), *Cyberspace*. Cambridge, MA: MIT Press, pp. 59–80.
Held, D., McGrew, A., Goldblatt, D. and Perraton, J. (1999) *Global Transformations*. Cambridge: Polity.
Hulme, M. and Peters, S. (2001) *Me, My Phone and I: The Role of the Mobile Phone*. Lancaster: Teleconomy Group PLC/Lancaster University Management School.
Jones, S. (1995) 'Understanding Community in the Information Age', in S. Jones (ed.), *Cybersociety*. London: Sage, pp. 10–35.
Latour, B. (1999) 'On Recalling ANT', in J. Law and J. Hassard (eds), *Actor Network Theory and After*. Oxford: Blackwell/Sociological Review, pp. 15–25.
Lodge, D. (1983) *Small World*. Harmondsworth: Penguin.
Makimoto, T. and Manners, D. (1997) *Digital Nomad*. Chichester: John Wiley.
Massey, D. (1994) *Space, Class and Gender*. Cambridge: Polity.

McCarthy, A. (2001) *Ambient Television*. Durham/London: Duke University Press.

Miller, D. and Slater, D. (2000) *The Internet*. London: Berg.

Pascoe, D. (2001) *Airspaces*. London: Reaktion.

Pinkney, T. (1991) *Raymond Williams*. Bridgend: Seren Books.

Prigogine, I. (1997) *The End of Certainty*. New York: The Free Press.

Putnam, R. (2000) *Bowling Alone*. New York: Simon and Schuster.

Rheingold, L. (1994) *The Virtual Community*. London: Secker and Warburg.

Sardar, Z. (1996) 'alt.civilizations.faq: Cyberspace as the Darker Side of the West', in Z. Sardar and J. Ravetz (eds), *Cyberfutures*. London: Pluto, pp. 14–41.

Schwartzman, H. (1989) *The Meeting*. New York: Plenum Press.

Simmel, G. (1997) *Simmel on Culture*. London: Sage.

Stone, A. (1991) 'Will the Real Body Please Stand Up? Boundary Stories about Virtual Cultures', in M. Benedikt (ed.), *Cyberspace*. Cambridge, MA: MIT Press, pp. 81–118.

Thrift, N. (1996) *Spatial Formations*. London: Sage.

Turkle, S. (1996) *Life on the Screen*. London: Weidenfeld and Nicolson.

Urry, J. (2002) 'Mobility and Proximity', *Sociology*, 36(2): 255–74.

Urry, J. (2003) *Global Complexity*. Cambridge: Polity.

Urry, J. (2004) 'Connections', *Environment and Planning D: Society and Space*, 22(1): 27–38.

Watts, D. (1999) *Small Worlds*. Princeton, NJ: Princeton University Press.

Wellman, B. (2001) 'Physical Place and Cyber Place: The Rise of Networked Individualism', *International Journal of Urban and Regional Research*, 25(2): 227–52.

Williams, R. (1988) *Border Country*. London: Hogarth Press.

5

Information Technology and the International Public Sphere[1]

By Craig Calhoun

Information technology (IT) and globalization have each been the objects of enormous hope and considerable disappointment. So too is their combination in the notion of an international public sphere supported by the Internet and other communications media. This is basic to the dream of international civil society that has flourished since the early 1990s after the collapse of communism and opening of capitalist markets. And indeed, such an international public sphere clearly already exists. Equally clearly, however, it has not yet provided the basis for cosmopolitan democracy that its advocates have hoped.

The task of this essay is to outline something of the stakes of thinking about an international public sphere, the role that IT can play in it, and some of the challenges that lie in the way of realizing its potential. I will discuss IT and the international public sphere against the background of globalization and shifting bases of in order for the production and dissemination of knowledge. I will not attempt to review the empirical specifics of where and how and by whom the Internet is used, or how public communication based on one technology compares to that based on others. While this would be useful and there are beginning to be interesting case studies to complement the usual journalistic anecdotes, social science research on the Internet has barely started.[2] The present essay does not offer findings so much as attempt to orient questions.

Globalization

Information technology has of course been an important basis for globalization. This did not start with the Internet, despite its hype. From the sextant to the map to the invention of calculus, the development of early modern navigation was centrally a matter of IT – and the ships circulated information as well as goods and helped to link the globe in networks of exchange and control. Telegraphs, radio and television; trains, cars and aeroplanes all helped to establish links across space and shorten the time-lags to action at a distance. The development of national and international highway infrastructures paved the way to flows of information long before the 'information superhighway'. Colonial empires were pioneers in IT from at least the sixteenth century. They developed bureaucracies, accounting systems, file-management hardware and software and both open and secret networks of communication. They also remind us that new forms of war figure centrally in the story of modern globalization – with new weaponry, certainly, but also military reliance on ever-more complex systems of control and coordination managed by technologies that evolved quickly from carrier pigeons to coded telegraph messages to satellite transmissions. As the last suggests, too, globalization has all along included an element of surveillance, which has always been a matter of data management and analysis as much as observation, and which has benefited from technologies to improve each.

Old though some of the trends are, recent innovations in computer and communications technologies have also been powerful. Modern financial markets are inconceivable without computer-mediated communication – and action. Not only are there nearly instant flows of money through global networks, ever-more complex forms of derivatives are driven by algorithms that their 'owners' never know, and trading is done indirectly by software 'robots' programmed by their human 'supervisors'. Satellite transmissions and electronic filing of stories speeds up the flow of information through broadcast and print media. New Internet media complement older forms of circulation of public (and sometimes not so public) information. Migrants maintain global diasporic cultures and translocal communities partly by email and websites. The Internet is an important support also for global social movements and for local social movements seeking global attention or support. It is important, though, not to imagine that with electronic help popular forces can easily get the jump on more centralized or elite powers – whether economic or political. For all the energy and innovation of global activism challenging neoliberalism or inequality, at least as much and a good deal more resources are deployed in support of global capitalism. NGOs focus not just on human rights or the environment but on accountancy standards, corporate advocacy and arbitration between firms. And IT is employed intensively in organizing global production processes as well as global markets. It makes possible not only just-in-time shipping but centralized control of manufacturing facilities that are physically dispersed throughout the world. What distinguishes the past 30 years or so, as Manuel Castells puts it, is the creation of 'an economy with the capacity to work as a unit in real time on a planetary scale'. (1996: 92) This is a 'global' rather than merely a 'world' economy. It is also the basis for Castells' metaphor of the 'network society', which refers not simply to the fact of global connections but also the adaptive advantage of flexible, network-based forms of organization in relation to dynamic, global capitalism.

Global interconnections still include war, of course, which itself is transformed by the rise of flexible, network organizations (Kaldor, 1999; 2002). This is covered by nearly instantaneous press reports and often carefully managed visual images that make it a broadcast spectacle. In three senses it is appropriate to speak of IT contributing to the emergence of 'virtual war'. First, there is the conversion of warfare into a media spectacle woven into the same fabric as Hollywood war movies. Second, there is the blurred line between war games and automated strategic response as Pentagon planners rely on computer models (Der Derian, 2002). Third, there is the waging of air wars that keep casualities all but invisible – for those in the planes or back at the missile bases. In this second sense, war may be 'virtual' for the United States with its enormous technological superiority and military strategy premised on the notion that American casualities cannot be tolerated even while it is all too 'real' for those suffering on the ground. The Persian Gulf War inaugurated this new asymmetrical virtuality; it was honed in Kosovo and deployed effectively in Afghanistan. But virtual war is not the whole story. New forms of war increasingly involve non-state actors – famously, the terrorist network Al Qaeda. These sometimes rely heavily on the Internet to maintain organization and plan action while dispersed. They also use both broadcast and computer-mediated communications to disseminate their message and recruit new adherents. While 'virtual war' sanitizes killing by technological mediation and keeps bloody violence at a distance, terrorists rely on exactly the opposite use of technology. Violence is not simply a way to accomplish military objectives for terrorist networks, it is one of their objectives in itself. Footage of the World Trade Centre attacks offered Al Qaeda and similar groups one of the world's greatest recruiting videos. And part of the message was that technology could be a double-edged sword, one that those who considered themselves oppressed could master and use against its creators.

So far, cyberterrorism has been minimal and largely symbolic – as for example Indians and Pakistanis flooded several sites in each other's countries, demonstrating not only enmity but also the capacity to penetrate security systems. This capacity is relatively widespread, but still unevenly so. Distribution of skill may be one reason for the low prominence of cyberterrorism. While few if any discontented populations lack members with the skills to hack into websites, organizing a major destabilizing of social systems by means of attacking a technological system is more complex than merely hacking in. More important, perhaps, is that while cyberterrorism has begun to figure in science fiction it has not yet lent itself to spectacular representation. A key feature of the World Trade Centre attacks is that they both imitated film and made good film. They followed a template for a spectacular public devastation that was more widely available and thus easier to publicly conceptualize and communicate about than cyberterrorism. While an attack on a computer system might be a more effective way to bring parts of the global financial system to crisis than an attack on buildings, it wouldn't be equally capable of immediate, clearly interpretable global representation. It would in important senses be a private attack on the public world, not a public attack.

It is also important to note the extent to which global discussions of IT and its regulation have come to be embedded in security concerns. Especially since 9/11 attacks, security (and military, intelligence and police cooperation) has moved to the forefront of the agenda among those organizing interstate connections. This is likely to have long-term implications for the development of IT use, which is contingent in important ways on the legal regulatory infrastructure created. This involves issues about security and surveillance as well as property rights which are seldom openly debated in the public sphere.

Alongside war, and partly spread by war, disease also figures prominently in the 'dark side' of globalization. This is not just a matter of possible bioterrorism. More people die daily of AIDS than those died in the World Trade Centre attacks. And if the spread of deadly viruses from the less well-developed (and thus less healthy and less vaccinated) world is a source of anxiety in rich countries, it is nonetheless the poor who suffer disproportionately from nearly all diseases. And disparities in access to treatment become one of the most dramatic faces of global inequality. Here too IT matters, though what we see most is the weakness of the global public sphere in spurring effective action. We see also the power of Western and especially American media. These portrayed AIDS largely as a gay disease, thus adding a stigma to the difficulties of fighting it in the rest of the world – where homosexual contact is a minor vector compared to heterosexual transmission, drug use and unsafe blood supplies – and as more or less 'handled' by drugs available only at a cost prohibitive to much of the world.

In this context, it is worth noting that the most influential of electronic media is not yet the Internet or any form of computer-mediated communication, but it is still the television. Even its reach is not altogether global, but it comes close. Access to and use of the Internet are still much more uneven, and although usage of the Internet grows it is less basic to shaping the broad 'information background' to all public discourse. The different technologies are mutually intertwined, of course, not only with Internet sites run by TV broadcasters but with news reports gathered by Internet. Just as TV often alerts people to stories they will read in newspapers, so an email message can tell someone to turn on the TV, or a TV show can send someone to the web for more detail.[3] Aside from inequalities of access, there may be even more telling inequalities in production of content for various media. Though access to the Internet is uneven, it does allow for point-to-point communication, dispersed access to common information resources, and relatively inexpensive posting of new content. Broadcast media remain almost completely one-directional, with broadcasters determining the form in which content appears and with the costs of competitive entry high. On the other hand, while more and more information is available on the Internet there is a wealth of globally significant knowledge still accessible only in the libraries and computer data centres of rich countries. The results of most social science research on the world's less-developed countries, for example, are accessible only in the knowledge centres of the rich countries. Moreover, commercial sites tend to drown out non-profit ones oriented to the public good; search engines not only miss much of the web but generally relegate small-scale sites to their back pages.

Global news media are heavily controlled by a small number of Western corporations and public broadcasters of a few Western governments.[4] This is mitigated somewhat by the prevalence of national broadcasters, though without their own substantial news-gathering operations the global content these can provide is limited to what they can acquire from the major global providers. One of the interesting sidebars to the post-9/11 'war on terrorism' was the emergence of Al Jazeera as an important global media player. This Arabic network not only broadcast throughout the Arabic-speaking world but it also became a key source of content for the major American networks and European broadcasters. Much Western commentary initially treated Al Jazeera with suspicion, viewing it as 'an Arab voice' while the Western media were treated as neutral or universal. That Al Jazeera became a conduit for the messages of Osama bin Laden fuelled this perception, but it may be more apt to see Al Jazeera as part of the emergence of a transnational Arabic-speaking public sphere.

All the electronic media, like books, newspapers and the International Postal Union before them play a crucial role in extending communication beyond local, face-to-face contexts. They thus underwrite globalization. Again, though, there is a tendency in some of the speculative literature of early enthusiasts to imagine that the new media turn the tables on traditional inequality of access to information and effectiveness of communication more than they do. It is certainly true that international activism of indigenous peoples, environmentalists and opponents of the WTO have been organized in new ways and with greater efficacy because of the Internet. It is equally certainly not the case that such use yet rivals the efficacy of information control by transnational corporations. Both the corporate control of much public content provision and the corporate use of IT to manage internal production and private financial transactions so far considerably outstrip insurgent and activist uses of the new technologies. This doesn't make the latter unimportant, but it should encourage a certain realism. As with other technologies, the ability to use IT varies not just with the potential of the technology but with the resources different users can invest.

The very ubiquity of IT has another curious effect on the global public sphere. It is part of a construction of globalization as an inevitable result of technological progress. From different national vantage points, the question is commonly posed not as whether to join in this globalization but how to adapt to it. Challenges to the dominant Western – indeed American – neoliberal, capitalist forms appear simply as backward-looking traditionalism. This was perhaps especially true during the economic boom of the late 1990s; how visions of the future and struggle over capitalism will fare in less soaring economic times is unclear. But IT continues to plan a double role – as the visible face of high technology and as part of the technical underpinning of a greater awareness of global trends.

In many countries around the world, the response is to try to adopt new technology as rapidly as possible, while simultaneously trying to protect 'traditional' culture. Contemporary Indian politicians thus project their country as a potential IT superpower at the same time that they encourage a renewal of studying the Vedas and a more or less fundamentalist embrace of Hinduism. It is precisely the most culturally conservative party to lead the country in its modern history that announces the most high-tech economic plans – as part of its 'Vision 2020' proposals. The very phrase 'Vision 2020' is not uniquely Indian, however, having been employed in Malaysia and elsewhere. The common rhetoric pairs technology-grounded progress with protection or renewal of cultural traditions. The formula is old, being something of an update of the nineteenth-century Chinese response to the West: 'Western learning for material progress, Eastern learning for spiritual values' (a phrase commonly summarized by the syllables *ti-yong*). But as the Qing emperors learned, it was hard to import railways and telegraphs without bringing Western values along. China's communist leaders worried about the same issue in the 1980s, and both their successors and some contributors to China's popular websites worry about the same thing today.[5] Even Canadian politicians echo the same theme, showing that anxiety about local identity has as much to do with American – that is, United States – power as with a clash between the West and the rest. As government officials told *Financial Times* reporters, 'the country wants to become a lean global competitor while maintaining traditional local values' (Morrison and Warn, 2001: 1).

Politicians presenting globalization as an irresistible force commonly embrace neoliberal policies as the necessary response. Global economic competition demands, citizens are told, that public sector jobs be cut, taxes lowered, state-owned resources be privatized. The same IT that potentially makes possible a more vigorous public sphere is cited as an example of global pressures before which public opinion should bow down; it is used to squelch dissent. Ironically perhaps, the IT industry itself often backs this neoliberal rhetoric, focusing on the image of freedom and seeing states and bureaucracies only as possible fetters on innovation (rather than also embodiments of social achievements such as public education or health care). The result is to reduce the chances of the socially trans-formative and publicly engaged use of IT, while encouraging its domination and domestication by commercial interests.

Nonetheless, IT use does escape being harnessed entirely by capitalism. Some of this depends on slipping out of the net of property rights in order to enter the World Wide Web. In India, by some estimates, the majority of people make access to the Internet illegally, from informal sector Internet vendors who establish hidden or black market access to the system's backbone or trunk lines.[6] Without this – and a variety of other shady but creative adaptations around the world – IT access would be even more asymmetrically distributed than it is. But the solution is only partial. It enables email and bulletin boards and access to public information. But it does not speak to the extent to which the provision of content on the Web is itself ever more commercialized.

Both the flow of information and the financial value of Internet communications put IT on the agenda of government and multilateral regulators. Information flows on the Internet raise concerns about security, manipulation and crises of unintended consequences (such as the financial flows that were central to the East-Asian fiscal crisis of 1997). So far, there has been relatively little public discourse about the nature of this regulation. Indeed, non-governmental advocates for the public interest have largely been excluded from the discussion. When the G-7 powers established a working group on Internet policies in 2000, for example, they determined that each government would have one representative and that there would be a representative of each national private business estab-lishment. Only under pressure did they agree to 'observers' from less-developed countries. Efforts to secure representation for the non-profit sectors in the different countries failed. This brings up the basic issue of whether there is an effective way for non-business civil-society interests to be heard. The open-source software movement has made remarkable strides, but advocates for this sort of vision of large-scale cooperation in the creative process, and of a more demo-cratic approach to developing a technological infrastructure are not significantly represented in core discussions of legal and political regulation. National public spheres and the nascent international public sphere alike are sharply challenged by the partnership of corporate powers and national governments, backed up by international agencies serving that partnership and a global culture heavily shaped by neoliberalism.

To the extent that there is a direct response to self-organized public communication, it comes mostly from nation-states. Though businesses are susceptible to campaigns focused on their public image (famously pioneered by the Nestle boycott), they are much less directly attentive to public opinion when it is expressed in non-financial terms. It is the translation of opinion into either consumer purchasing patterns or capital investment patterns or occasionally the willingness of other firms to work cooperatively that matters. Likewise, multilateral organizations like the World Bank, the IMF and the WTO can be challenged by public outcry, but are governed largely by states and operated along technocratic lines, with expertise conceived mainly within the terms of neoliberal ideology. Accordingly, it is a mistake for democrats to accept too readily the idea that the growth of a global civil society makes states unimportant. States still matter, they still wield considerable power, and this is at least in part a good thing, not least because they are the main locus for democracy.

It is common to speak of globalization as though the fact of worldwide interconnections meant that there was really a single, seamless whole.[7] I have done this to some extent here, but it can be misleading. Globalization looks different from different regions and localities in the world. It is both an opportunity for the EU and a pressure behind European unification. The implications are more ambiguous in much of Africa, where access to the benefits of globalization has been minimal and the legacy of colonialism and other ills have in some cases been exacerbated by it. Instead of wondering whether states will lose their familiar power, for example, many Africans must wonder instead whether states will become strong enough to manage public services and unite countries. Likewise, senders and receivers of migrants must view migration differently. And while unequal access to IT is an issue everywhere, the inequality is between countries as well as regions within them. And the term 'access' can be misleading, since even countries that are in a good position to make access to the web may not be in a strong position to become suppliers of global information resources.

To a large extent, the notion of a single, uniform global culture or economy is an illusion encouraged by the way dominant Western media presents information about the world. From other vantage points, the divergences are readily visible. Globalization is made up of a variety of different projects that clash with each other in varying degree and combine in different ways in different places. Western dominance is contested. This is not to say that what happens elsewhere is simply survival or response to West-initiated trends; it is rather the other, creative development of alternative modernities (Gaonkar, 2001). This is something of what has been at stake in clashes between Islamists and the West in recent years – not tradition versus modernity so much as struggle over whether Western trends can control the whole of the modern. Is the freedom to make pornography predominate in the content available on the Web inherent to modernity, or a contingent choice the West has made in constructing modernity – not only in terms of sex but in terms of minimally restricted commercialization. Moreover, Western-dominated globalization is not all of a piece – the WTO and the anti-WTO protests have both been West-dominated. Neither is there simply a tension between the West and the rest, as though the latter were uniform. Regional and local differences still matter, along with religious, cultural, class and other differences that cut cross regions. Even nationalism is commonly a response to globalization, not simply something old and passing.

Globalization is a heterogeneous process, in short, which produces multiple and overlapping layers of interconnection. It is a matter of enmities and rivalries as well as interdependence. Moreover, the other side of connectivity is exclusion. The more densely certain networks are woven together, the more difficult it is for outliers to find their way in.

International civil society has grown as part of globalization, but its enthusiasts must be careful not to overstate its strength. It is sometimes suggested that IT is a great equalizer, but as we have noted IT is used by corporations at least as effectively as protesters (if not a good deal more so). Describing the surge of global protest over capitalist hegemony, unequal development and the environment some writers seem almost to imply that the protesters outside the WTO meeting in Seattle came close to overpowering the global elite within. In fact, of course, they were able to get a message heard and to create a disruption but not to assume significant organizational power.

IT plays an important role, finally, in making it possible for globalization to combine decentralization and dispersal of activity with concentration of power (Calhoun, 1992b). As Saskia Sassen (1996) notes, much of what official statistics present as global trade among seemingly independent nations is in fact coordinated production within individual global corporations. Carburettors may seem to be sold from Mexico to the US, but this is just one link in Ford's new global assembly line, with computer-assisted control systems and financial management as important as computer-assisted design or robotics.

Networks and Knowledge

IT is powerful, but not all powerful. It is introduced into a world of existing social relations, culture, capitalism and inequalities. These shape what will be made of IT. So does the creativity of engineers, designers and users. So too, potentially, can the creative work of artists and others for whom the Internet provides a new medium for both production and circulation of work. Indeed, the aesthetic potential of IT is both important in itself, and potentially part of the contribution of IT to the public sphere. The latter is never simply a matter of rational–critical argument but also of cultural creativity, the reimagining of the nature of social relations can be as important as debate in the life of the public sphere. Through most of the twentieth century, for example, the public sphere joined an aesthetic and a distributive critique of capitalism, a bohemian discourse with the socialist, hopes for a more beautiful world with hopes for a more egalitarian world. To a considerable extent this combination came unstuck in the 1990s (see the useful discussion in Boltanski and Chapiello, 1999). Egalitarian ideals were tarred with the brush of defunct Soviet-style bureaucratization and notions that government regulation was excessive even in the West. Conversely, capitalism appeared often in the aesthetically appealing guise of the high-tech corporate campus rather than the polluting factory. For a time, at least, its paradigmatic occupation became website designer and not only its economic but its aesthetic potentials seemed unlimited. There was more artistic freedom offered by the dotcoms than by government (and even universities looked awfully stodgy). How much of the changed attitude will survive the dotcom crash is unclear, but the example nonetheless illustrates the ways in which the revision of cultural images is important to the construction of public opinion. And of course, it was not an accident. The hybridization of Madison Avenue and Bellevue, Washington was central to the dotcom era, and focused precisely on the revision of public opinion by aesthetic means.

Attempts by states and others to regulate the Internet and similar technologies may reflect purely bureaucratic concerns or may respond to such public discourse. A significant gap in this process, so far, is that IT has been the object of a great deal of speculation – often utopian but sometimes dystopian – and not much serious social research. Such research will advance best if there are more researchers with serious knowledge of both IT and social science. Such 'cross-training' is not encouraged in contemporary universities, but is not impossible. In any case, for the public to make informed choices about the development and deployment of IT – and perhaps about remedying inequalities in access or impacts – knowledge is crucial.

Perhaps ironically, at the same time that more and better knowledge is needed about the social changes in which IT plays a central role, the traditional institutions of knowledge production, storage and distribution – like universities – are undergoing an unannounced structural transformation partly based on IT. This can serve as an example for issues in the study of IT. Various commentators have wondered what the implications of new technologies might be. Optimists have pointed to the capacity to reach new students in dispersed settings, to bring currently centralized resources like libraries to learners and researchers in remote places, to put and give students more chances to control their own pace and directions of study, and to make institutions more efficient. Pessimists have worried that 'efficiency' will be used only to cut costs not to expand offerings, that personal contact will be reduced, that knowledge work (and curricula) will become more standardized, that this might be linked to more reliance on standardized testing, or that social benefits associated with campus communities will be lost if students are isolated from each other. All of these good and bad possibilities are realistic. Two problems stand between speculation and useful knowledge, however. First, there is little research, especially research showing not just whether any of these things are happening someplace, but which of them are happening where and in association with what else. Second, we must overcome the tendency to try to figure out the impact of IT in isolation from broader social patterns of which it is part. In this case, the role of IT is currently secondary, but growing, within large-scale structural transformation of higher education that has gone largely unannounced and unexamined – at least within the United States.

Sticking only to the American example (though versions of this process are widespread), several different changes are intertwined and are fundamentally changing the character of higher education. The changes are not evenly distributed, to be sure. Most especially, wealthy institutions have more capacity to shape their own futures – and to maintain attractive features of their current character. Thus it is not likely that Harvard University or Williams College will employ IT simply to cut costs, reduce faculty, or teach students online. They may use their 'brand names' to offer profitable distance-education programs, but their endowments and social status will enable them to continue to serve a privileged segment of the student population with residential programs that reach far beyond the formal curricula and that include face-to-face relations among students and between them and the faculty. The options open to less well-endowed institutions are different, and so too the pressures shaping them. One reason we know less about the overall transformation of higher education is that researchers tend to be drawn from the upper tier of schools and reflect mainly on what has gone on in the institutions in which they were educated or worked. But higher education in the United States is a highly differentiated system in which schools have different missions, student bodies, places in academic labour markets and resources.

Some of the most noticed innovations in higher education have come with the rise of for-profit schools. These are disproportionately (but not exclusively) distributed in the less-selective segments of the higher education market. It is no surprise that DeVry Institute of Technology competes more with community colleges than with Stanford (or that the institutions acquired worldwide by Sylvan International Universities are primarily in the market for first-generation university students wanting to study applied fields). It is also significant that providing technical education – much related to IT – has been a mainstay of the new institutions. The older higher-education system has been slower to develop needed offerings. But if this is partly simply conservatism, it is also partly a question about the nature of education. Colleges and universities have commonly maintained that even technical education was best pursued in the context of broader liberal arts and sciences; that it was important to train citizens as well as technicians, and that students needed to develop critical thinking skills for both roles. In relation to IT, many have pointed out the difference between mastering a specific software package or hardware configuration, both of which are likely to change quickly, and mastering the underlying principles that will enable students and workers to learn about new systems in the future. Absenting a much greater social investment, though, this broader vision of higher education is inevitably somewhat elitist; it speaks less well to students worried about choosing the fastest, surest course to a good job.

Traditional colleges and universities are expensive – and are under challenge from 'rationalizers' – not only because they are inefficient, but because they bundle together a number of different activities and functions. They house libraries and sometimes publishing companies, counselling services and sports teams, computer centres and hospitals. They provide entertainment, housing and at least implicitly dating services. One of the basic questions today is which can – or should – maintain this bundling together of disparate activities. Perhaps most basically, the ideal of the university will combine the production and dissemination of knowledge, and research and teaching. Some efficiency can be gained through unbundling these, which is now happening. Like many of the changes, it is happening within traditional institutions as well as in a redistribution of activities among institutions. Some faculty are able to negotiate privileged reductions in their teaching loads because of their research productivity; others make up the difference. The most extreme dimension of this is the rise in employment of temporary and part-time teachers, usually with low salaries, minimal benefits and marginal status within the institutions. Though transformations in higher education are often described in terms of 'privatization', this shift appears in public institutions as well, and market pressures are felt throughout the system.[8]

Indeed, profit and non-profit orientations are being intermingled. Not-for-profit universities have established for-profit corporations to try to make money from online offerings. University presses long-subsidized because of the academic value of their publications are being asked to pay their way as businesses. Charges for some library resources, especially those provided electronically, are becoming more widespread. The primary products of scholarly research – journal articles and books – are increasingly accessible only for a price. The institutions most immune from pressure are in fact not the public universities but the very well-endowed private ones. MIT and Princeton, thus, have made their online offerings free – both seeing them as more valuable for public relations and alumni loyalty than to be seen as profit centres, and suggesting that there may not be as much profit in this kind of offering as is sometimes thought. On the other hand, such well-endowed institutions are also operated partly as for-profit businesses, not least when they get into joint ventures based on the inventions and innovations of their faculty.

In this as in other areas where IT is part of a larger change, inequalities are growing but masked. Not only individuals but institutions also become unequal when facing technological innovation. Around the world, privatization of higher education is part of the more general process of reducing state support of social goods. This is encouraged by the neoliberal ideology dominant in contemporary globalization (Bourdieu, 1998; 2001a[9]).But it means that states – the institutions best placed to defend the gains, workers and other popular forces have made in their previous struggles – are instead abandoning them. Some of those struggles – such as for low-cost, equitably or perhaps meritocratically distributed public education – have been waged in part through the public sphere, with material pressures complemented by shifts in public opinion. The supporters of neoliberal capitalism have effectively dominated elite public opinion, including the ways in which the most powerful states perceive the implications of globalization. This means that debate in the broader public sphere is an important test for the capacity of civil society to resist the imperatives of capitalism. The debate influences not only current state actions but the availability of knowledge for future public discourse.

The Internet will always be a supplement to but not a replacement for other connections. Those who already have power can make more effective immediate use of the technology – so those with less power have to work harder to make it effective on their side. The Internet makes it easier to find things out, thus, but often harder to find out what we don't know. I don't mean simply that it adds to volume and creates new demands for ability to discriminate and evaluate sources, though this is certainly true. I mean also that it makes new forms of surveillance possible that are inherently hard to and for ordinary people to observe and which may nonetheless dramatically enhance the control others have over their lives. Despite the fact that privacy issues have received more research and public attention than almost any other dimension of IT, surprisingly little public outcry has greeted US government proposals – and actions – to reduce restrictions on such surveillance. People still seem to think mainly in terms of new information being gathered rather than recognizing the immense detail of information already produced as byproducts of computer use but (usually) not linked across data sets. The label privacy is partly misleading, thus, since the issues involve not just 'exposure' but control.

Control is also important in another way. It is often obscure to users who do the editorial shaping of content available on what are seemingly open and public websites. China, for example, has a range of extremely lively web-based discussions about issues from international affairs to government corruption. Content that offends the government usually disappears quickly, however, and there is presumably also a good deal of self-censorship. The result is that sites apparently offering a glimpse of public opinion are skewed representations. Unlike a newspaper that can be read in certain ways based on the assumption that it is censored and its content controlled, websites give the impression of consisting simply of the spontaneous postings of the public. This doesn't mean that the web doesn't bring a gain in sharing information. Indeed, journalists on official Chinese newspapers have been known to anonymously post to the web stories which censors would otherwise stop them from publishing – and these get some airing even if they are quickly censored. And, to complicate the matter further, the government sometimes tolerates web content that it would censor from print publication. The reason seems to be that it assumes that the Internet reaches a relatively elite part of the population within which the government is willing to see issues aired. This may offer a kind of safety valve; it may be monitored by the government to see what its more publicly informed and vocal citizens think; it has the advantage that it doesn't seem as official as what appears in government-owned publications. Perhaps most basically, the government may simply recognize that it cannot effectively restrict all information from reaching this elite – but still wish to restrict what reaches the broader population. In the information age, it may be all but impossible to stop information flows – including across borders – but it may be more possible to keep them relatively elite. In other settings, censorship may ultimately be less of a factor in determining the accessibility of information on the web than invisibility (because of the limits of search engines, the extent to which commercial sites push public ones to the margin, and the costs of advertising or maintaining links).

One argument has been that web-based 'communities' are effective organizational counterparts to corporations, governments and other more formally organized structures of power and action. There is some truth to this – organization is always crucial to making otherwise dispersed popular voices heard. Electronic communication is extremely effective at facilitating links among strangers – for example facilitating both widely distributed protests and participation from widely distributed groups in demonstrations or other shared events. It is a useful vehicle for sharing information which can either motivate or inform action. At the same time, we need to note the ambiguity of the language of community in this regard. Writers seem to refer without clear distinction to (a) dense networks of personal ties, (b) broad but loosely linked categories of people linked by shared information and (c) IT users who derive their social connections from some other basis (say, trade-union membership) but then communicate partly online. If we mean the first of these, the most sociologically specific use of 'community', then communities are effective only on relatively small scales; density of connections – everyone knowing (and potentially trusting) everyone else necessarily declines with scale. Precisely because social life began to be organized on ever-larger scales in the modern era, community could organize proportionately less of it. States, markets and other kinds of connections among people came to organize more – even when people still valued community a great deal. Much of what IT facilitates is linkage among relative strangers – the second and third usages above, though I would hesitate to use the term community with its connotations of dense social networks. The term community is misleading, moreover, because it implies that collectivities formed in web-based discourse are somehow equivalent to local communities grounded in face-to-face relationships (Calhoun, 1998). Here too the reality is that the Internet is most effective as a complement to face-to-face communication not a replacement for it. It empowers local activists who would otherwise find it harder to reach others with similar concerns in remote locations. It enables both lateral sharing of information and better access to information controlled by centralized providers (including government agencies). Here it is worth noting that how effective the technology is in this regard depends a great deal on institutional arrangements over which there can be political struggle. For example, are government agencies required to make all their data effectively accessible? What laws and regulations govern public provision of data by other actors?

More generally, 'community' is a misleading term for thinking about the Internet's role in social solidarity. It may be true, as William Mitchell (1998) puts it, that his keyboard is his café. Internet communications provide many of the functions that coffee houses (and newspapers) played in Habermas's model of the eighteenth-century public sphere. At the same time, neither is necessarily best understood through the notion of community. Part of what Habermas described as important to coffee-house society was precisely that it provided a setting for interactions among strangers, for discussions among those who were not knit to each other by communal ties. The same goes for various sorts of multi-user domains (MUDs) and is part of the basis for the creative identity-work that Sherry Turkle (1997) has described. MUDs may evoke a sense of community for participants, and may be given metaphorical topographies complete with 'neighbourhoods'. But it is also misleading to apply the warm, fuzzy language of the local without regard to scale. There is a crucial difference among MUDs that provide occasions for strangers to fantasize, LISTSERVs and websites that enable political organization among strangers, and web resources that provide supplemental communication channels for people also joined in directly interpersonal relationships. The three (and other variants) can shade into each other, but are distinct not just in conception but in implications. A particularly important part of the distinction comes with the difference between categorical identifications (categories of people with similar interests or identities) and network ties (more or less dense webs of actual relationships, especially multiplex ones) (Calhoun, 1992b; 2002; White, 1992). The latter join more or less 'whole' people; the former tend to join people one issue or identity at a time. The former, however, transcend locality much more easily.

The point is not that one mode of interconnection is better or worse than the other, but that they have different implications. The Internet can make local community less isolated or it can lead people to substitute online ties to relative strangers for interaction with neighbours. It can promote both enclaves and connectivity, nations and cosmopolitanism. Heavy reliance on the term 'community' to describe computer-mediated groupings borrows from the warm and fuzzy connotations that the idea of community has in everyday life and especially in nostalgia. But it also obscures one of the most important potential roles for electronic communication which is enhancing public discourse – a form of discourse that joins strangers and enables large collectivities to make informed choices about their institutions and their future.

The Idea of the Public Sphere

To say that a public exists is mainly to say that there is more or less open, self-organized communication among strangers. There are settings in which such public communication is minimal, in which strangers feel sharply constrained in what they can or should say to each other, or in which external regimentation of who may speak to whom or what may be the topics of communication prohibits self-organization of publics. So this minimal sense of publicness says a good deal.[10] It does not, however, give an adequate sense of the stakes of the idea of the public sphere. These focus not simply on the general existence of public communication, but on its capacity to guide social life.

The most famous study of the public sphere, Jürgen Habermas's *Structural Transformation of the Public Sphere* (1989), focuses on the emergence in the eighteenth century of a widespread ideal – and partially successful actual practice – of open debate concerning questions about the public good and policies for pursuing it.[11] This debate was conducted by individuals with autonomous bases in civil society – that is, with their own sources of income and identity – but the debate achieved rationality to the extent that the wealth and identities of the individuals did not intrude on argument itself. The public sphere was thus crucial to the capacity of civil society to influence the state; it was political, but not part of the state. Habermas describes the development of this political public sphere out of an earlier literary one, in which the formation of opinion about works of literature was elevated by rational–critical discourse. He also points to the importance of institutional supports for public communication, notably the newspaper and the coffee house.[12]

In Habermas' analysis, however, the ideal of the public sphere was shown to mask a contradiction. It aspired equally to openness – in manner of communication and in entrance to the discourse itself – and to the critical use of reason to form opinion. Its successive structural transformations, however, reflected the extent to which expanding the scale of the public sphere led to a degeneration in the processes of opinion formation. Instead of individuals debating, public communication became increasingly a matter of organized interest groups – corporations, trade unions, political parties – using the techniques of advertising and mass communications. Opinion was formed less rationally on the basis of manipulation. The advent of opinion polls did nothing to arrest this, since they simply asked the opinion of discrete individuals without providing an occasion for different individuals to inform each other through discussion. Such opinions were less likely, therefore, to be based on knowledge. Indeed, opinion polls simply gave better information on people to those who would seek to influence or control them – treating them as 'objects' – rather than enabling them to become better subjects of public discourse.

Behind both Habermas' optimistic account of the eighteenth century and his pessimistic account of subsequent transformations lie the same issues. Can public communication be a means of forming opinions based on reason and improved by critical discourse? Can these opinions then inform the creation or operation of social institutions and more generally the constitution of social life?[13] In other words, can ordinary people use their faculties for reason and communication to choose the nature of their lives together – even on a relatively large scale in which most are strangers to each other – rather than have this imposed on them by inherited tradition, political power, or economic wealth? For Habermas, the main issue was whether citizens could guide a state, which helps to explain why 'the public sphere' appears as singular – it is the sum of the ways in which the open, rational–critical discourse of citizens at large can inform the (singular) state. The same broader questions can be asked of international public discourse, however, and with regard to influencing a multiplicity of states, of multilateral organizations, of quasi- or non-governmental bodies, and indeed, of business corporations.

Communication among strangers in the public sphere thus appears as one of the various mechanisms by which social integration is achieved and social institutions shaped and guided. Shared participation in public life, itself, can be a form of social solidarity, joining people in relations to each other and to the public projects they debate – even when they disagree about specifics. Among the various forms of social integration, public communication is distinctive because more than any of the others it offers the possibility of ordering collective life on the basis of reasoned choice. People are joined together by functional interdependence, as in markets, by subjection to political power, and by commonalities of culture. The public sphere has the potential to shape each of these other forms of connection, as well as offering a kind of connection of its own. It complements, the realms of directly interpersonal relationships – family, friendship, neighbourhood.

These are open in varying degree to choice and to construction through interpersonal communication. But they can join only modest numbers of people; they cannot organize relations among strangers. Moreover, when they steer affairs of state this is usually the illegitimate influence of one part of a polity over the rest. The public sphere distinctively offers the chance for the whole citizenry – or at least a large part of it – to participate in guiding the state, thus conferring legitimacy on it. This of course implies that legitimacy is based on the will of the people. While this is a predominant conception in the modern world, it is not the only possibility. Other approaches to legitimacy base it on divine will, on inheritance, or on the formal excellence of institutional arrangements. When legitimacy is based on the will of the people, a key question must be how that will is formed. Is it a matter of inheritance or of a tradition that should be above question – as some proponents of ethnic nationalism would argue? Is it a matter of manipulation by those who can draw power from control over the media, or over jobs, or over the members of self-interested organizations? Or is this will of the people formed through discussion and debate among the people?

This is not the place to pursue questions of political theory like how to balance unity and diversity, the sense of common commitment implied by the phrase 'will of the people' and the need for tolerance and mutual engagement across lines of difference required by liberal democracy. But it is crucial to see that these questions are made pressing by any appeal to the public sphere as a basis for organizing life together. Take simply the relationship to nation as an example. Nationalist ideology commonly presents individuals as joined directly and identically to a common whole; differentiation appears as a threat to national unity. Such an ideology can have popular appeal and can be supported by masses of public communication – messages posted to both American and Chinese websites during the spy-plane crisis of 2000 demonstrated this. But this sort of public demonstration of unity and identity is different from public discourse in which rational–critical debate improves the quality of opinions, educates the participants and forms a collective understanding of issues that advances beyond pre-existing definitions of interests or identities.[14] Among other things, the mass version of popular nationalism is eminently open to manipulation by demagogues, the government and other forces. Recall, indeed, that democracy can mean mass rule but not protection for rights and that publicity and expansion of the media can be tactics in mobilizing such masses (and not just in Nazi Germany or Maoist China).

More or less open, self-organized public communication among strangers is evident in both mass nationalism and more rational–critical public discourse. The minimal definition of the public sphere does not adequately make the distinction (though to the extent that mass nationalism is manipulated by the state or others it is not 'self-organized'). It is recognizing the deeper stakes of the question of the public sphere that makes the tension between these two 'ideal types' of public communication evident and important. And yet, it should not be imagined that the realities to which they refer are completely distinct. There is no communication that is not also participation in the production or reproduction of culture. Even in the most rational–critical of public debates, thus, organized by the fairest rules of procedure and pursued in the least self-interested spirit, are thus conditioned by the cultural idioms in which they are conducted and contribute to the formation of common culture (as well as the recognition of cultural differences) among participants. Moreover, common culture is important to the commitment of participants to each other and to the process of public discourse. To recognize the difference between simple affirmation of commonality and differentiated public debate should not lead us to imagine that the ideal of reasoned discourse is sufficient in itself to account for what goes on in any public sphere or how and why it survives and exerts its influence. Conversely, we should see also that popular nationalism (and other cultural or political traditions) is not immune from rational–critical discourse. It can be shaped and reshaped both by the culture-forming and the rational–critical dimensions of public discourse. Even when ideologues assert that there is one true and correct way to be American or Chinese or any other nationality, they tend always to offer distinct visions of that one and true way. This opens up the possibility of debate even in the midst of affirmations of unity. And different nationalisms may incorporate greater recognition of internal diversity, of the importance of reason, or of debate as part of the self-understanding of the nation.

The existence of public communication, vital as it is, does not answer the questions we need to ask about public spheres. We need to know not only how active the communication is and how inclusive and open participation is, but what the qualities of the communication are. We need to attend to the processes by which culture is produced and reproduced in public, not treat it as mere inheritance or private product of individuals or small groups. We need to ask how responsive public opinion is to reasoned argument, how well any public sphere benefits from the potential for self-correction and collective education implicit in the possibilities of rational–critical discourse. And we need to inquire how committed participants are to the processes of public discourse and through it to each other. Finally, and not least of all, we need to ask how effectively the public opinion formed can in fact influence social institutions and wielders of economic, political or indeed cultural power.

These questions should all be basic to inquiry into the implications of new information technology for public life and democracy. Various technologies have the potential to constrain or facilitate openness, reason, cultural creativity, self-organization and solidarity. This is as true internationally as domestically. Moreover, questions of unequal access, cultural diversity and perhaps most basically, the multiplicity of agents of power and potential objects of public influence loom even larger in the global arena.

Conclusion

The implications of IT for the global public sphere are still being determined. Whether it will be put to use in ways that open and encourage public communication as much as in ways that facilitate commerce and control is an open question. If not, then web-based resistance to power – viruses, hacking, site-flooding and other IT and web-based strategies for attacking corporations, states, other users – may become more prominent. There is no perfect 'firewall' between systems of public communication and infrastructural systems. Accordingly, the stakes are high should cyberterrorism become more prominent. At the same time, opportunities for democratic choice about how socio-technical systems are organized are limited. And it is often the sense of being excluded from choices about the future that fans the flames of discontent.

Prospects for democratization of the global order depend crucially on the development of a global public sphere, as well as on attention to global inequities within the public discourse of individual societies. There are opportunities for activism. This need not always involve a leap to the truly global, but may involve the building of transnational communications networks on a regional scale – as has happened to some extent around Latin America and South Asia. It will be important for those who would open up the public sphere to figure out how to work within organizations (including corporations and states) not just against them or in seemingly separate and autonomous 'communities'. It may also be possible to *choose* at least some aspects of the transformation of colleges and universities instead of just letting it happen, and thus to choose to have stronger bases for producing and sharing knowledge to inform the public. In this regard, one of the most important actions may be is to do real research to help replace the contest of anecdotes and speculations with a reasoned debate in the public sphere.

Endnotes

1 Presented to the International Sociological Association, Brisbane, Australia, 11 July, 2002. An earlier version of this essay was presented to Directions and Implications of Advanced Computing 2000, Computer Professionals for Social Responsibility, Seattle, 20 May, 2000.

2 See Dimaggio *et al.* (2001) for a useful review (though an overwhelmingly North American one). Even where there is serious research on the Internet, it is more likely to address the behaviour of individual users than social processes or public communication as such, and it is commonly contained within national contexts (and within the global North). See Wellman (1999); Wellman and Haythornthwaite (2003) for a useful account of research, though this remains heavily oriented to the processes of sociability. Important as this is, it is distinct from reorganization of power, the construction of more or less autopoetic systems, and the problems of design of complex technical infrastructures.

3 It is important to recognize, though, the extent to which broadcast media subsidize the provision of news by Internet – because the latter is not yet autonomously profitable.

4 The literature on media concentration is huge; see, among the best examples (but still heavily US focused), McChesney (1999) and Compaine and Gomery (2000).

5 For more on China's web-based public discourse and especially the interpenetration of domestic and international themes, see Yang (2003).

6 I am informed here by the work of Ravi Sundaram and colleagues in Serai, a research institute on IT at the Centre for the Study of Developing Societies in New Delhi.

7 Interestingly, it is an illusion that informs critics as well as celebrants. In their influential book, *Empire*, Michael Hardt and Antonio Negri (2000) present a picture of a fully sutured and self-sufficient dominant world order, one that lacks the internal contradictions to generate immanent transformation.

8 Privatization may be a more precise term for discussing changes in higher education in some other countries. In many of these cases, it is more closely correlated with a for-profit orientation than in the United States which has a long history of private, but not-for-profit higher education. And in many of these cases, neoliberal states' policies are leading to efforts not just to found new private institutions but to reduce public support for existing institutions.

9 A translation of 'Uniting to Better Dominate' appears in Bourdieu (2001b).

10 Warner (2002) offers a more elaborated version of this minimal definition:

- A public is self-organizing;
- A public is a relation among strangers;
- The address of public speech is both personal and impersonal;
- A public is the social space created by the circulation of discourse;
- Publics exist historically according to the temporality of their circulation.

For more history of the concept see Calhoun (2001a; 2001b).
11 For several critical analyses of the issues Habermas raises, see Calhoun (1992a).
12 A website imaginatively devoted to coffee includes Markman Ellis (2001).
13 Habermas focuses mainly on political life and assumes the existence of a state to be influenced. Writing slightly earlier, Hannah Arendt (1958) emphasized the broader process of creating social institutions and also the moments of creation of states in acts of founding and revolutions.
14 For a recent study that addresses the interrelationships of the two dimensions, see Rajogopal (2001).

References

Arendt, H. (1958) *The Human Condition*. Chicago, IL: University of Chicago Press.
Boltanski, L. and Chapiello, E. (1999) *Le nouvel esprit du capitalisme*. Paris: Gallimard.
Bourdieu, P. (1998) *Acts of Resistance*. New York: New Press.
Bourdieu, P. (2001a) *Contre-feux II*. Paris: Raisons d'Agir.
Bourdieu, P. (2001b) 'Uniting to Better Dominate', *Items and Issues*, 2(3–4): 1–6. Available at: www.ssrc.org.
Calhoun, C. (ed.) (1992a) *Habermas and the Public Sphere*. Cambridge, MA: MIT Press.
Calhoun, C. (1992b) 'The Infrastructure of Modernity: Indirect Relationships, Information Technology, and Social Integration', in H. Haferkamp and N. J. Smelser (eds), *Social Change and Modernity*. Berkeley, CA: University of California Press, pp. 205–36.
Calhoun, C. (1998) 'Community without Propinquity Revisited: Communications Technology and the Transformation of the Urban Public Sphere', *Sociological Inquiry*, 68(3): 373–97.
Calhoun, C. (2001a) 'Civil Society/Public Sphere: History of the Concepts', *International Encyclopedia of the Social and Behavioral Sciences*. Amsterdam: Elsevier, pp. 1897–903.
Calhoun, C. (2001b) 'Public Sphere: 19th and 20th Century History', *International Encyclopedia of the Social and Behavioral Sciences*. Amsterdam: Elsevier, pp. 12595–99.
Calhoun, C. (2002) 'Imagining Solidarity: Cosmopolitanism, Constitutional Patriotism, and the Public Sphere', *Public Culture*, 14(1): 147–72.
Castells, M. (1996) *The Information Age*. Vol. 1, *The Rise of the Network Society*. Cambridge, MA: Blackwell.
Compaine, B. M. and Gomery, D. (2000) *Who Owns the Media: Competition and Concentration in the Mass Media Industry*. 3rd edition. Indianapolis, IN: Erlbaum.
Der Derian, J. (2002) '9.11: Before, after and in between', in C. Calhoun, P. Price and A. Timmer (eds), *Understanding September 11*. New York: New Press, pp. 177–90.
DiMaggio, P., Hargittai, E., Neuman, W. R. and Robinson, J. P. (2001) 'Social Implications of the Internet', *Annual Review of Sociology*, 27: 307–55.
Ellis, M. (2001) 'Habermas, the coffee houses and the public sphere', at www.qmw.ac.uk/~english/personal/Coffeehome.html.
Gaonkar, D. P. (ed.) (2001) *Alternative Modernities*. Durham, NC: Duke University Press.
Habermas, J. (1989) *The Structural Transformation of the Public Sphere*. Cambridge, MA: MIT Press.
Hardt, M. and Negri, A. (2000) *Empire*. Cambridge, MA: Harvard University Press.
Kaldor, M. (1999) *New Wars and Old*. Stanford, CA: Stanford University Press.
Kaldor, M. (2002) 'Beyond Militarism, Arms Races, and Arms Control', in C. Calhoun, P. Price and A. Timmer (eds), *Understanding September 11*. New York: New Press, pp. 159–76.
McChesney, R. (1999) *Rich Media, Poor Democracy*. Urbana, IL: University of Illinois Press.
Mitchell, W. (1998) *City of Bits*. Cambridge, MA: MIT Press.

Morrison, S. and Warn, K. (2001) 'Liberals Strive to Sharpen Competitive Edge', *Financial Times*, 11 June, 'Canada Survey', pp. 1–2.

Rajogopal, A. (2001) *Politics after Television: Religious Nationalism and the Reshaping of the Indian Public*. Cambridge: Cambridge University Press.

Sassen, S. (1996) *Losing Control?* New York: Columbia University Press.

Turkle, S. (1997) *Life on the Screen*. New York: Touchstone.

Warner, M. (2002) *Publics and Counterpublics*. Cambridge, MA: Zone Books.

Wellman, B. (ed.) (1999) *Networks in the Global Village*. Boulder, CO: Westview Press.

Wellman, B. and Haythornthwaite, C. (eds) (2003) *The Internet in Everyday Life*. Cambridge, MA: Blackwell.

White, H. (1992) *Identity and Control*. Princeton, NJ: Princeton University Press.

Yang, G. (2003) 'The Internet and the Rise of a Transnational Chinese Cultural Sphere', *Media, Culture & Society*, 25(4): 469–90.

6

Creativity in an Orwellian Key: A Sceptic's Guide to the Post-Sociological Imaginary

By Steve Fuller

Introduction: The Rise of Knowledge Society Newspeak

Over the past few years I have come to believe that an Orwellian regime of Newspeak is colonizing our understanding of social life – to such an extent that it threatens to erase the intuitions that originally made compelling the idea of the social sciences as a body of knowledge distinct from both the humanities and the natural sciences (Fuller, 2006). The alleged uniqueness of the contemporary world as a 'knowledge society', or even just an 'information society', epitomizes this Newspeak. It has bred a speciality called 'knowledge management', an oxymoron in earlier times but now a field that promises to teach universities – formerly the centres of societal knowledge production – how to collectivize their intelligence 'effectively' as, say, a fast-food franchise routinely does (Fuller, 2002: chapter 1). Like other totalitarian ideologies, from Nazism to Maoism, this one involves a radical reversal of values, typically a subordination of the elites to the vulgar through the complicity of disenfranchised members of the elite. Thus, academic researchers on short-term contracts and hence with tenuous loyalties to universities are in the forefront of ushering this new era of knowledge management by levelling the distinction between academic knowledge and other cognitively adaptive responses to the environment.

Perhaps the best display of knowledge society Newspeak in all its glory appears in the 'Glossary' to *The New Production of Knowledge* (Gibbons *et al.*, 1994), the single-most influential academic work in European science policy circles since the end of the Cold War. This book provides the most wide-ranging legitimation of the 'postmodern condition' first identified in that great anti-university tract of our times, Lyotard (1983). The notoriety of Gibbons *et al.* (1994) and the follow-up work, Nowotny *et al.* (2000), come largely from having introduced the world to the distinction between 'Mode 1' and 'Mode 2' knowledge production as a roughly two-stage process which marks the transition from knowledge being driven by 'internal' to 'external' mechanisms. *Prima facie* the distinction captures the difference between inquiry governed by strictly academic interests and by more socially relevant interests. But in practice, the scope of 'Mode 1' is much narrower than the university – closer to a Kuhnian paradigm – and 'Mode 2' is much more diffuse than 'relevance' normally connotes – closer to a market attractor (Fuller, 2000b: chapter 8). As a result, the university is reduced from a Humboldtian concept with the aim of unifying knowledge to a convenient physical space that enables the 'communication' of various knowledge interests. Here 'communication' doubly resonates of a Habermasian 'ideal speech situation' for establishing consensus and a Hayekian 'clearing house' for setting prices (see Delanty, 2001). In Table 6.1, I have listed the major terms in 'Modespeak', along-side their *prima facie* innocent meanings ('Not this...') and their more sinister practical ones ('But that...').

The overall impression the reader should receive from this tableau is that some recognizably capitalist, and even pre-capitalist, forms of domination are masked by a rhetoric of pluralism that disperses power and responsibility. Indicative of the workings of Modespeak is the translation effected in the first row of Table 6.1: 'codified/tacit knowledge'. What academics routinely cele-brate as our capacity 'to know more than we can tell' appears as a nightmare to managers trying to maintain the corporate knowledge base in the face of mobile workers in a flexible economy. Not surprisingly, then, when academics advise managers that our competence is not reducible to our performances, managers conclude that they must find ways of replacing that competence with a more reliable source of performances that can be made a permanent feature of corporate memory, or what Marx would have called 'fixed capital'. In that case,

Table 6.1   *'Modespeak': Knowledge society newspeak*

MODESPEAK	NOT THIS...	BUT THAT...
'Codified/Tacit Knowledge' (Conversion Principle)	Performance/Competence (Creativity)	Fixed/Variable Capital (Knowledge Management)
'Context of Application'	Applied Research	Client-Centred Research
'Globalization'	Universalization	Specialization
'Heterogeneity'	Anti-Homogeneity	Anti-Autonomy
'Hybrid Agora/Forum' (University Redefined)	Knowledge Unifier	Knowledge Advertiser
'Informatization of Society'	Knowledge Mediates Social Relations	Knowledge Alienated From Individuals
'Knowledge Industries'	University Privileged	University De-Privileged
'Massification of Higher Education'	Knowledge Adds Value	Knowledge Devalued
'Pluralization of Elites'	Knowledge Workers Respected	Knowledge Workers Modularized
'Reflexivity'	Critical of Context	Adaptive to Context
'Social Capital'	Public Good	Corporate Property
'Social Distribution of Knowledge'	Integrated Unit (Institution)	Dispersed Network (Interaction)
'Socially Robust Knowledge'	Universally Resilient Knowledge (Science)	Locally Plastic Knowledge (Culture)
'Technology Transfer'	Academia Legitimates Industry (19th century)	Academia Services Industry (21st century)
'Transdisciplinarity'	Interdisciplinarity	Antidisciplinarity

employees are best regarded as transient sources of knowledge – or 'variable capital' – that need to be 'captured' while they are still on site. Towards this end, computerized expert systems have offered much promise to a business world that, for the most part, has historically succeeded by modelling the human mind on a need-to-know basis (Nonaka and Takeuchi, 1995; see Fuller, 2002: chapter 3).

The Orwellian Turn in Sociology: Post-Sociological Newspeak

Modespeak has also infiltrated sociology more specifically. My critique will concentrate on two key terms in the 'post-sociological' mindset – *mobility* and *innovation* – and the corresponding downgrading of *institution* and upgrading of *community* as supporting concepts. Historically the terms 'mobility' and 'innovation' have had a progressive ring. One thinks of 'upward social mobility' as an aspiration of the working classes, as well as the geographical mobility that enables people and artefacts to transform host cultures, typically by introducing innovations from which everyone ultimately benefits. In this context, 'order' and 'tradition' suggested at the very least conservatism and perhaps even stagnation and repression. However, in our brave new world, the key terms have shifted their meanings. In particular, their teleological connotations have disappeared. Thus, mobility and innovation are valorized *as such*, without regard to the consequences. Moreover, in keeping with the deconstructive sensibilities of these postmodern times, there is a tendency to argue that the very distinction between tradition and innovation is bogus, since there are traditions of innovation and all innovations recover earlier traditions. And in light of chaos and complexity theory, we can even say that different kinds of order are simply patterned mobilities (Urry, 2000: chapter 5), thereby conferring new meaning on the maxim, 'The more things change, the more they stay the same'.

Lost in these semantic manoeuvres is the idea that there may be better or worse innovations and better or worse ways of diffusing them. Judgments of this sort presuppose a standard external to the process under investigation. Such a standard would be typically manifested in the investigator's adoption of a fixed standpoint – what used to be called a theoretical framework – in terms of which some of the phenomena under investigation would appear normal and others deviant. Whether the standpoint is treated as 'normative' or 'empirical' depended on whether its resistance to the phenomena is treated as grounds for disciplining the phenomena or altering the standpoint. In practice, science usually negotiated a settlement between the two extremes.

In Orwell's *1984*, this erasure of standpoint was accomplished by the continual rewriting of history to make the present appear as the realization of current state policy. The records department of the Ministry of Truth, where *1984*'s protagonist Winston Smith worked, was thus dedicated to the implementation of the Hegelian motto, 'The real [in the sense of 'actual'] is rational and the rational is real. Smith's society was one whose grounding norm was the reduction of cognitive dissonance, specifically through what social psychologists call 'adaptive preference formation'. In short, one strives to achieve a state of mind in which one wants what one is likely to receive – to be sure, a perverse reading of socialism's aspirations to leave no human needs unmet. The political theorist Jon Elster (1983) has spoken of 'sour grapes' and 'sweet lemons' in this context, as ways by which people find the hidden good in *prima facie* bad outcomes. The formation of adaptive preferences is facilitated by the elimination of reminders of previous goals, or at least the promotion of ambiguity through the compressed expression of those goals. Thus, in *1984*, copies of newspapers stating old government policies were placed in 'memory holes', pneumatic tubes that sent the documents to a fiery end.

Of course, the systematic destruction of documents by itself could not erase the memories potentially triggered by the continued use of words appearing in those documents. Consequently, *1984*'s official language, Newspeak, tended towards neologisms that shortened words so as to minimize the time needed for thought before a response is elicited. These words, coined in the name of efficiency and convenience, provided a surface continuity that masked what were often radical shifts in policy import. However, it would be a mistake to regard Newspeak as the product of linguistic prescription in the sense of a standardized grammar and diction that in the name of national unity is legislated against the wills of many, if not most, native speakers. On the contrary, Newspeak's diabolical character lies in its ability to capitalize on the default tendency of linguistic forms to become condensed at the lexical, syntactic and semantic levels through repeated use (Fuller, 1988: part II). This tendency has been more effectively exploited in cap-italist than socialist societies through the subliminal component of advertising, whereby a familiar phrase or slogan is given a new twist to stimulate consumer demand (Packard, 1957).

What's in a Name? Part One: 'Mobility'

The loss of a distinctly sociological standpoint is perhaps most straightfor-wardly illustrated in the case of 'mobility', a popular topic among sociologists of the post-classical generation, notably Pitirim Sorokin, whose work is conspicuous by its absence from more recent discussions (e.g. Urry, 2000; 2002). Sorokin (1928: 747–52) would regard today's tendency to assimilate 'mobility' to the sheer statistical drift of individuals across regions or categories as 'pre-sociological', in that no judgment is made about the benefit or harm caused to either the mobile individuals or the host societies. Rather, the sheer persistence or increase in a tendency – 'survival' in its extended sense – is presumed to establish an emergent norm. This is very much how an evolution-ary biologist or an epidemiologist sees matters. It has also gained increasing currency among social scientists who look to genetics for objective traces of large-scale, long–term, socio-cultural mobility (e.g. Cavalli-Sforza, 2000). Nevertheless, the sociologist's professional task would not be complete without considering what else needs to change to enable the emergence of certain patterns of mobility.

Whereas Sorokin himself pointed to the dissolution of traditional social bonds as a potential casualty of mobility, the US historian Christopher Lasch (1995: chapter 3) has focused on the trade-offs that have resulted from the elision of mobility and *opportunity*. For example, the drive to upward social mobility presupposes that membership in the working class – as either a mode of production or consumption – is not inherently respectable. To achieve respect, and hence to realize their full potential as people, the working class has been urged to engage in substantial mobility of some sort. This implies that there is no *prima facie* value attached to who they already are, what they already do, or where they already do it. A more distant, but no less real, consequence of this elision of mobility and opportunity is a devaluation of politics in the conventional sense of party membership, voting and public service: Why go through the trouble of constructing an identity around a social position like 'working class' that other groups in your society largely regard as unfortunate and undesirable? More broadly, why struggle to redress injustices at home, when given the opportunity to emigrate to a more hospitable land? Thus, the decline of state-based citizenship has ushered an era of 'lifestyle politics' that is relatively indifferent to the location of its pursuit (Urry, 2000: chapter 7).

Of course, the preceding remarks are not meant to belittle the plight of asylum seekers through the ages. But as the chequered but overall progressive history of democratic politics illustrates, long-lasting purposeful social change has typically required the mounting of organized resistance to dominant tendencies in the *domestic* environment. The result has been the construction of corporate persons – originally *universitates* in Roman Law – whose aims transcend those of its constituent members and whose perpetuation occurs by means other than hereditary succession. This category includes chartered cities, states, churches, universities and – starting in the nineteenth century – business enterprises. The construction of these entities has involved the redistribution of powers and properties across a wide range of otherwise conflicting or indifferent groups of individuals by a procedure that Max Weber would have recognized as 'legal–rational' (Fuller, 2006). In short, it has been the establishment of institutions – not the facilitation of immigration – that has enabled *homo sapiens* to overcome its animal origins, thereby making it a fit object for sociological inquiry. In this context, much more needs to be made sociologically of the role that returning exiles have played in revolutionizing their native societies.

Not surprisingly, the meltdown of institutions into mobilities has been accompanied by a renascent interest in the pre-institutionalized forms of social life epitomized in the word 'community', now understood more positively than in classical sociology. Here the German word, *Gemeinschaft*, stood for the residual structures of pre-modern world. These structures set biological and geographical parameters on the meaning of human existence, such that kinship ties provided the grounding ontology for face-to-face interactions, which were in turn regarded as the most authentic form of social life. In this context, Ferdinand Tönnies originally spoke of *Gemeinschaft* as 'racial' rather than strictly 'political' in its social basis. Tönnies wrote in the 1880s, when the unification of Germany was within living memory and the emerging German superstate clearly had imperial ambitions outside Europe that would entail the reorganization and integration of racially diverse peoples. In this context, *gemeinschaftlich* bonds placed obstacles in the way of what Norbert Elias has called, with respect to Europe itself, the 'civilizing process'. However, today's conceptually face-lifted version of 'community' does not require literal bio-geographical embeddedness. Its phenomenologically distinctive features may be preserved – or 'virtualized' – by the increasing immediacy afforded by the emergent information and communication technologies (Urry, 2002). Thus, the proliferation of mobile videophones puts paid to the alleged opposition between 'mobility' and 'community' – yet both terms remain resolutely anti-institutional in their focus.

The knock-on effects of this anti-institutionalism are subtle but pervasive. For example, the concept of *race*, whose exclusionary character always haunted classical sociological depictions of 'community', is beginning to receive a more acceptable face, one inflected with the idea of mobility. Fortified by the marriage of Mendelian genetics and Darwinian evolutionary theory, Cavalli-Sforza (2000) has revitalized the old ideal of 'racial purity' in the guise of 'genetic diversity' that needs to be maintained, especially against the various threats of homogenization and assimilation faced by so-called indigenous peoples. Evidence for human genetic diversity is tracked – just as the early-nineteenth-century German philologists had tracked racial purity – in terms of linguistic diffusion. To be sure, Cavalli-Sforza treats racism as an arbitrary form of discrimination, since any two individuals, while genetically identical in almost all respects, will display genetic differences at some level of resolution. Nevertheless, from this acknowledged arbitrariness, he concludes that one should target culturally salient genetic discriminations for preservation (also known as segregation). Not surprisingly, this conclusion leads him to follow the movements of peoples across times and places, resulting in an endorsement of scientifically updated versions of theses prevalent in late-nineteenth-century anthropology. Thus, after asserting that political units such as the state are analogical extensions of the family, Cavalli-Sforza says: 'Cultural transmission is easier, faster, and more efficient when a powerful authoritarian chief forces the acceptance of an innovation' (2000: 182). His examples are the Pope and Mussolini. Sociology's hard-won insight from the law – that institutional perpetuation can fruitfully cut across hereditary modes of succession – is alien to this line of thought.

If Cavalli-Sforza's co-valorization of authority and mobility appears strange to contemporary readers, then it is worth recalling that before Hannah Arendt firmly established the 'totalitarian' credentials of Nazi Germany in the minds of social scientists, close observers both pro and con the regime regarded fascism as quite a flexible corporate actor. It was more Behemoth than Leviathan, to quote Franz Neumann's (1944) famous invocation of Hobbes' distinction in rule by weakly bounded factions versus a strongly bounded sovereign. Were it not for strictures of political correctness, we would now regard the regime as an especially supple 'actor-network' (Fuller, 2000b: chapter 7). The secret of Nazi Germany's flexible fascism lay in its studied anti-institutionalism, which enabled local authorities to enforce the Führer's will however they saw fit, suspending rule of law in order to tackle more effectively the contextually specific ways in which the regime was subject to external threat (Scheuerman, 1994). Not surprisingly, in these historically amnesic times, we find that the jurist who did the most in his day to provide intellectual respectability to this policy, Carl Schmitt, is now rehabilitated as a deconstructionist *avant la lettre* – of course, laundered of his painfully obvious Nazi associations (Latour, 2002; see Lilla, 2001: chapter 2).

What's in a Name? Part Two: 'Innovation'

Innovation is the first global policy craze of the twenty-first century. One could be forgiven for thinking that 'fostering', 'seeding' and 'nurturing' innovation are the most popular pastimes of public and private sector decision-makers *outside* the United States. The exclusion of the United States from this generalization suggests that one innovates mainly to catch up in the world political–economic arena. In this context, innovation is presented as the key to competitiveness. Of course, the United States realizes that it too must remain competitive to maintain its premiere position in the global marketplace. However, the United States relies on such distinctly uninnovative activities as erecting foreign-trade barriers, subsidizing domestic industries and investing in controversial overseas political adventures. Without defending American policies, which have been criticized almost to the point of banality, I wish to question the contemporary fascination with innovation in the rest of the world. The most that can be said in favour of innovation as a normative economic strategy is that it is the prerogative of losers, as set out in the unjustly neglected thesis of the 'relative advantage of backwardness' (Fuller, 1997: chapter 5; Gerschenkron, 1962).

In the UK and its overseas emulators, universities are increasingly urged to measure their worth in terms of the number of patents generated, perhaps the most facile indicator of corporate innovativeness, yet the indicator that is most easily met by academics trained to realize the fruits of their labour in a refereed piece of analytical writing. To be sure, if policymakers were serious about converting universities into 'engines of economic growth', they would simply provide incentives to have academics seconded to industry in aid of implementing the ideas behind the patent essays (Granstrand, 1999: chapter 6). Interestingly, despite a greater tolerance for academics volunteering their services to industry as consultants, there is no general policy encouraging the tendency. The reason has probably less to do with the objections of academic purists than the policy-makers' own exposure to risk. After all, bringing an innovation to market, like any other trial-and-error process, typically requires significant prior investment before any payoff is delivered. The formal secondment of academics to industry, while increasing the likelihood that an innovation will pay off, would at the same time draw attention to any failure that might result. In contrast, the perpetually promissory character of innovation for its own sake – as measured by the endless generation of patents – would seem to square the policy circle, while incidentally pacifying academics who typically find writing a new kind of text (a patent) more palatable than interacting with a new kind of person (an industrialist).

Thorstein Veblen (1904) would have recognized what is going on here. In his terms, the imperative to innovate characterizes the dominance of 'business' over 'industry'. Veblen was one of the last political economists who tried to uphold Adam Smith's normative ideals in a time (roughly, a century ago) that had already left them far behind. Before what we now call the 'Industrial Revolution', Smith held, people bound to the land by birth were restricted from applying themselves freely to satisfy the needs of their fellows. Writing over a hundred years after Smith, Veblen saw society suffering from the opposite problem of *hyper-mobility*, as in the idea that markets should be regularly 'creatively destroyed' by self-styled innovators seeking to replace producers who might be already adequately satisfying consumer needs (Fuller, 2002: 51–52). Whereas in the eighteenth century, the landed aristocracy was the parasitic class inhibiting industry, in the twentieth century the corporate marketing division – the business class – turned out to be new parasites, or more precisely cancers that metastasize industrial effort.

In short, the business class manufactured new wants in the course of claiming that the new products satisfy old wants (see Jacques, 1996: chapter 7). In this way, adaptive preference formation became institutionalized in the economy without explicit government intervention – except to allow business to grow to unprecedented proportions. Thus, once everyone had a car, advertisers insisted that one's entire automotive experience would be compromised without the possession of an air-conditioned, four-wheel drive car. (Compare the marketing techniques nowadays for upgraded software packages.) These observations received their most influential elaboration from John Kenneth Galbraith (1967), whose concept of the 'new industrial state' epitomized advanced capitalist nations in the middle-third of the twentieth century, when marketing came to overtake manufacturing as the focus of corporate enterprise.

Whence comes this endless drive to innovation? One may be initially tempted to draw on contemporary evolutionary psychology, which updates much perennial philosophical speculation about 'human nature': To be human is to be capable of genuine novelty. Unfortunately, this criterion suffers from obvious anthropomorphism: Might not the detectability of 'genuine novelty' be related to the perceiver's ability to find meaningful differences? (Of course, a Chomskyan who regards the 'generative' capacity of language as unique to *homo sapiens* would see nothing problematic here, since a native listener's ability to make sense of a novel utterance is precisely the criterion used to establish genuine novelty.) If, instead, one were to apply to humans the criterion normally imposed on animals – that is, to check whether apparent novelties significantly alter behavioural patterns outside the immediate context of utterance – then many of our own innovations would appear as so many contextually explicable local deviations that leave the basic patterns undisturbed. Here one would need to resist the lazy rhetoric of 'building on the past', which assumes that every innovation – especially if published and stored – remains indefinitely part of the living memory of at least some humans. One wonders how this 'building' might occur (except by some subliminal or genetic means), given two tendencies: the diminishing half-life of the average article cited in the scientific literature and the strengthening of the boundary between historical and contemporary scholarship in each scientific discipline (Fuller, 2000a: chapter 5). It is more likely that our sense of recurrent novelty is somehow tied to a systematic forgetting, and hence modified reinvention, of the past. I shall have more to say about this Orwellian point below.

Moving from species-general to more historically specific explanations of the drive to innovate, while Joseph Schumpeter (1934) may well be right that the creative destruction of markets constitutes the lifeblood of capitalism, the tightness of fit between innovation and capitalism comes from the tendency of innovation to involve 'capitalization' – that is, the conversion of non-capital into capital. This was certainly the spirit of Werner Sombart's coinage of 'capitalism' in 1902, to capture how traditionally non-commercial aspects of social status come to be spontaneously generated in market transactions (Grundmann and Stehr, 2001). At the most general level, 'capitalism' in this sense carried into the human realm the translation of physical substances into mathematical functions that had characterized the Scientific Revolution (Cassirer, 1910/1923). The relevant function in this case is the law of supply and demand. This shift in ontological sensibility is also captured in the memorable definition of the logician Quine: 'To be is to be the value of a bound variable'. At the level of our psychic economy, this principle implied that objects are valuable solely in relation to the desires they satisfy – or, in the language of political economy, a particular good has no value other than the cost of its replacement in supplying a particular demand, where demand is presumed to be elastic (Smith, 1994: chapters 8–10).

According to this logic, the innovator thinks about existing goods as placeholders for demands that may be met by several competing goods, especially new ones that meet the demands more efficiently. Goods are what John Dewey called 'instrumentalities' – that is, ends whose value rests on being means towards still other ends. Thus, Carl Menger, Eugen von Böhm-Bawerk, and the Austrian school of economics from which Schumpeter descended famously countered Marx's labour-based theory of value by arguing that labour, like all other forms of capital, constitutes a market for second-order goods, whose values are determined in a competitive field, which may include *inter alia* automated technology. In this respect, factory owners are consumers of labour power only because that is the most efficient means to produce the goods they need to sell. But this is a contingent fact of history that may be overturned by innovation in the future, not a necessary fact about the composition of the goods or the social relations governing them. One can also shift the focus from the factory owner to the customer and apply a similar strategy. Thus, when American institutionalist economists like Veblen and Galbraith wrote derisively of 'business', they meant those who innovate by manufacturing demand. Specifically, market researchers determine the various demands served by a good currently on the market and then develop goods that can meet each of these demands more efficiently, thereby multiplying the level of demand and hence the potential for sales.

To be sure, innovation works somewhat differently in the Austrian and American cases, though both share the Schumpeterian awareness of innovation as creative destruction. In the Austrian case, the consumer comes to accept a new product as worth the cost of replacing the old product. Thus, what might be lost in the details of craftsmanship is more than made up in the product's timely completion and delivery to market: At least this would be one reason for preferring automated technology to human labour. In making this judgement, the consumer – in this case, a factory owner – is trading off against competing desires that are satisfied to varying degrees by the human and the machine. In the American case, by contrast, the consumer comes to regard an old product as simultaneously satisfying several desires, each of which would be better satisfied with new products. Thus, rather than forcing trade-offs where previously there were none, the consumer – in this case, regarded as someone not directly involved in production – is led by the power of advertising to regard a heretofore satisfactory product as suboptimal along several dimensions, each of which needs to be addressed separately.

In both the Austrian and American accounts of innovation, 'creative destruction' does not cancel itself out, as its oxymoronic name might suggest. Rather, it exacts an additional cost of its own. That cost was adumbrated in our discussion of Lasch in the previous section: *Innovation is correlated with a devaluation of what things have been in favour of what they might become.* Thus, people, products and research are not valued in themselves but as means to still greater ends. At first glance, this places innovation in defiance of the 'discounting principle' in welfare economics, which, for example, justifies redistributive taxation on the grounds that, without coercion, people tend to prefer the gratification of baser desires in the present to nobler desires in the future (Price, 1993). However, the welfare economists had not anticipated that people might discount the past *in order to discount the future.* After all, the discounting principle stipulates that the future needs to be regarded in a certain way to avoid being 'discounted'. Not only must the future be seen as consequences of earlier people, things and events, but these consequences must also be seen as enjoying their own autonomy, and not simply reflecting whatever we would now wish them to be. Unfortunately, the innovative mentality makes forsaking the past attractive by discounting the future's autonomy from the present in just this sense. In short, the past may be set in stone but the innovator believes that the future may be made in his/her own image. Thus, the innovator reduces the future to a mode of experiencing the present and hence a potential source of immediate gratification, as exemplified by the much advertised joys of risk-taking (which may be ultimately commodified in 'virtual reality' machines).

An important consequence of the innovative mentality's discounting of the future is that the mystique surrounding innovation – especially the alleged genius of entrepreneurship – is tied to the ease with which precursors are forgotten as mere means for satisfying the ends defined by the current generation. Indeed, the shortened half-life of current achievements may be much more than an indicator of a very innovative society: *It may be that the shortening of collective memory itself motivates people to innovate and enables them to recognize achievements as innovative.* This impetus to innovation may be seen as the positive side of the phenomenon of adaptive preference formation.

It may also help resolve a conundrum that Karl Popper (1957) famously raised about the prospect of planning scientific progress – namely, if scientific progress consists of genuinely new discoveries, then if these discoveries can be predicted, then they must be already known and hence not genuinely new. This paradoxical conclusion stands as long as we assume that the 'new discoveries' are indeed truly new and not simply modified reinventions of a half-forgotten past. I say '*half-forgotten*' because we need to explain, despite famous examples to the contrary, how allegedly genuine novelties so often manage to diffuse *so quickly*: Why are they not more often the source of more general cataclysms in thought and taste, if not regarded with indifference or incomprehension? Rather than investing entrepreneurship with preternatural powers of genius, it might make more sense to credit innovators with repackaging – by design or accident – a past with which consumers are already dimly (also known as 'subliminally') familiar. All that is required is that, as a matter of fact, a society's collective memory is never as finalized as the sales figures on corporate spreadsheets or the logical outcomes of truth tables would suggest: What fails to sell may still affect consumer behaviour, and what fails to be valid may still affect scientific inquiry. In other words, there is always room for a 'return of the repressed', as long as the past has not been completely segmented from the present in a self-contained market called 'history' (Fuller, 2003a: chapter 9).

In light of the preceding discussion, two complementary conclusions may be reached about the nature of innovation. First, what is normally called 'the past' is the repository of lost futures. Put less paradoxically, the achievements consigned to history are normally ones that, had they remained in living memory, would have taken us to a different present. Their counterfactual character is signified by labels like 'false', 'remaindered' and 'ignored'. However, as long as the boundary between the past and the present is porous, these lost futures may be reactivated as 'innovations'. The ultimate model for this conceptualization of innovation is Plato's *Meno*, in which all learning is portrayed as a form of reminiscence (Polanyi, 1957). But whereas Plato himself seems to have thought that in education worked by tapping into a genetic or racial memory, it is possible to update his theory of 'anamnesis' in a less metaphysically forbidding way by supposing that innovation – as a society-wide learning process – occurs through non-standard contact with such external memory stores as libraries and databanks. Some innovators may even see themselves as agencies of justice, championing ideas that had been previously discarded because they were 'before their time'.

The second complementary conclusion is that a highly innovative society wastes its potential by making poor use of its past. A charge of this sort is most familiar as a characterization of natural selection, regarded from a strictly economic viewpoint. Perhaps the strongest Neo-Darwinian argument against the existence of a divine creator is the amount of genetic wastage at various stages in the life cycle. For this reason, the kind of 'selection' that nature metaphorically performs is regarded as 'blind' (Hardin, 1959). That the market is not also normally seen as completely sightless has to do with capitalism's historic coupling of the alleviation of human misery and the manufacture of surplus wants. While the latter may involve an unnecessary expenditure of human effort, the former has been necessary for promoting and maintaining our general sense of humanity. However, as Schumpeter (1942) perhaps first saw clearly, capitalism's blind eye can interfere with its sighted one. The intensified expectations and disappointments generated by the boom and bust phases in the business cycles of the modern period – he was especially thinking about the 1920s – were due to an uncritical belief in the value of innovation.

In that case, socialism may be understood as an attempt to rationalize this situation by ensuring that more of the past is made more available to more of society. The sheer impulse to innovate would thus not interfere with the effective diffusion of innovations. Admittedly, this level of planning would destroy the mystique surrounding entrepreneurship, reducing it to a kind of social experimentation. But very much like the other great economic sociologist, Max Weber, Joseph Schumpeter regarded such 'disenchantment' as a fair price to pay for a more stable and just social order. Socialism would extend the mandate of social science from the empirical to the normative realm: Whereas positivistic social science had demystified theological ideas of Grace and Providence, socialism would purge the last vestige of theology in secular social thought – capitalism's invisible hand (Milbank, 1990). Of course, the second half of the twentieth century has itself witnessed a demystification of the promise of socialism, which has landed us in a situation not so different from the one for which Schumpeter thought socialism would provide a solution. However, as befits an Orwellian turn in the historical cycle, the term 'Neo-Schumpeterian' today is normally invoked by science-policy theorists who stress the creative rather than the destructive side of Schumpeter's definition of innovation in terms of the market's creative destruction.

Conclusion: Steps towards the Reinstitutionalization of Sociology

Is there a way back to sociology from the emerging post-sociological order? I believe that our very sense of humanity depends on an affirmative answer to this question (Fuller, 2006). However, it would be a mistake to imagine that the decline of the sociological imagination is entirely due either to successful external replacements from the humanities and the natural sciences (as suggested by, for example, Wallerstein, 1996) or, as a reader of this essay might conclude, the perverse redeployment of the sociological vocabulary. Rather, the seeds of sociology's self-destruction were sown at the outset. This general nature of this problem is unavoidable in a discipline that aspires to universality, yet has no choice but to be formulated in particular times and places: It is the Achilles Heel of any science. Nevertheless, the diagnosis of specific failures should prove instructive to the reinstitutionalization of sociology. A useful frame of reference is the *Gemeinschaft–Gesellschaft* distinction (community *versus* society) on which Tönnies founded sociology as an academic discipline.

The basic mistake made by sociology's founders was to include all market relations – from medieval trade fairs to transnational business firms – in the category of *Gesellschaft*. In retrospect, it is easy to see how this was done: The corporate character of modern business was assimilated to that of the state and other traditional corporations. However, business is perhaps the latest arrival to the legal form of the corporation. Until the nineteenth century, most business activity could be understood within the two recognized categories in Roman Law prior to the twelfth-century innovation of the *universitas*: On the one hand, the firm was an extension of the household, with both ownership and control transmitted along hereditary lines (i.e. *via gens*). On the other, trade that cut across hereditary lines was conducted on perhaps a regular but temporary basis in centrally located market towns or overseas joint-stock ventures, in which the traders were presumed to act on behalf of their own or other households, to which they would return once the goods have cleared the market or the venture has achieved its promised goals (i.e. *via socius*). It was only when the state saw its own nation-building ambitions enhanced by scaled-up business enterprise that firms received the legal protection that enabled them to expand their markets overseas with relative impunity and distribute their ownership and control in ways that subverted hereditary succession. Academic sociology's founders flourished as this transformation was taking place, and they understandably projected it backward as the hidden potential of all market relations. As a result, the market is made to look like the harbinger of all distinctly modern social relations.

The conceptual cost of this instance of syncretism is considerable. Sociologists have been blindsided by evolutionary psychologists who invoke concepts like 'kin selection', 'reciprocal altruism' and 'indirect reciprocity' to capture what they allege to be the biological bases of all social behaviour (Barkow *et al.*, 1992). This invariably involves a reduction of sociology to a genetically programmed version of rational choice economics. To be sure, there have been several worthy attempts to undermine this strategy (Archer and Tritter, 2000; Rose and Rose, 2000). Nevertheless, sociology is itself largely to blame for keeping the door open to sophisticated forms of biological reductionism by blurring the pre-modern and modern forms of market relations. Even within economics, a pre-modern sensibility of the market remains in the Austrian school (though, to his credit, not Schumpeter). Thus, one finds evolutionary psychologists today postulating 'modules' for 'social accounting' in the brain that suspiciously look like the competence that Friedrich Hayek (1948) attributed to traders in the sort of market that Adam Smith could still envisage in the late eighteenth century. Not surprisingly, a nebulous pseudo-*gemeinschaftlich* concept like 'trust' is then made to bear the burden of providing the ontological glue that links interpersonal transactions at the trade fair to the impersonal dealings that are most emblematic of modern social life. From this standpoint, the prospect that people's default behavioural tendencies might be constructively channelled through normative strictures – changes in the selection environment, if you will – is ridiculed as the 'standard social science model', from which even sociologists have begun to distance themselves.

But suppose, in contrast, we took seriously that the socially significant behaviours we call 'innovations' did not emerge spontaneously from the most biologically salient forms of social life but have required planned collective effort aimed at producing benefits for humanity that may not be fully realized by those engaged in them. Here we would have a sociological sensibility that breaks decisively with biology, which I believe was what sociology's founders intended. In that case, the value of innovation would lie primarily in the destructive side of Schumpeter's creative destruction, that is, the lifting of barriers on human potential. The state would then have an obligation to seed innovation – in the form of publicly financed education – as an extension of its trans-generational stewardship over part of that potential. That only a relative few so supported turn out to be genuine innovators, yet others manage to benefit quickly through the diffusion process, would no longer be regarded as a paradox but rather evidence for the relative equality of humans, rendering issues of priority a matter of luck, and hence grounds for regarding society is a very modern *gesellschaftlich* fashion as a whole much greater than the sum of its parts (Fuller, 2003b).

References

Archer, M. and Tritter, J. (eds) (2000) *Rational Choice Theory: Resisting Colonization*. London: Routledge.

Barkow, J., Cosmides, L. and Tooby, J. (eds) (1992) *The Adapted Mind: Evolutionary Psychology and the Generation of Culture*. Oxford: Oxford University Press.

Cassirer, E. (1910/1923) *Substance and Function*. La Salle, IL: Open Court.

Cavalli-Sforza, L. (2000) *Genes, Peoples, and Languages*. New York: Farrar, Straus and Giroux.

Delanty, G. (2001) *Challenging Knowledge: The University in the Knowledge Society*. Milton Keynes: Open University Press.

Elster, J. (1983) *Sour Grapes*. Cambridge: Cambridge University Press.

Fuller, S. (1988) *Social Epistemology*. Bloomington, IN: Indiana University Press.

Fuller, S. (1997) *Science*. Milton Keynes: Open University Press.

Fuller, S. (2000a) *The Governance of Science*. Milton Keynes: Open University Press.

Fuller, S. (2000b) *Thomas Kuhn: A Philosophical History for Our Times*. Chicago, IL: University of Chicago Press.

Fuller, S. (2002) *Knowledge Management Foundations*. Woburn, MA: Butterworth-Heinemann.

Fuller, S. (2003a) *Kuhn vs Popper: The Struggle for the Soul of Science*. Cambridge: Iconbooks.

Fuller, S. (2003b) 'In Search of Vehicles for Knowledge Governance: On the Need for Institutions that Creatively Destroy Social Capital', in N. Stehr (ed.), *The Governance of Knowledge*. New Brunswick: Transaction, pp. 41–76.

Fuller, S. (2006) *The New Sociological Imagination*. London: Sage.

Galbraith, J. K. (1967) *The New Industrial State*. Boston, MA: Houghton Mifflin.

Gerschenkron, A. (1962) *Economic Backwardness in Historical Perspective*. Cambridge, MA: Harvard University Press.

Gibbons, M., Limoges, C., Nowotny, H., Schwartzmann, S., Scott, P. and Trow, M. (1994) *The New Production of Knowledge*. London: Sage.

Granstrand, O. (1999) *The Economics and Management of Intellectual Property*. Cheltenham: Edward Elgar.

Grundmann, R. and Stehr, N. (2001) 'Why is Werner Sombart not Part of the Core of Classical Sociology?', *Journal of Classical Sociology*, 1(2): 257–87.

Hardin, G. (1959) *Nature and Man's Fate*. New York: New American Library.

Hayek, F. (1948) *Individualism and Economic Order*. Chicago, IL: University of Chicago Press.

Jacques, R. (1996) *Manufacturing the Employee*. London: Sage.

Lasch, C. (1995) *The Revolt of the Elites and the Betrayal of Democracy*. New York: Norton.

Latour, B. (2002) *War of the Worlds: How about Peace?* Chicago, IL: Prickly Paradigm Press.

Lilla, M. (2001) *The Reckless Mind: Intellectuals in Politics*. New York: New York Review of Books.

Lyotard, J.-F. (1983) *The Postmodern Condition*. Minneapolis: University of Minnesota Press.

Milbank, J. (1990) *Theology and Social Theory*. Oxford: Blackwell.

Neumann, F. (1944) *Behemoth: The Structure and Practice of National Socialism: 1933–1944*. Oxford: Oxford University Press.

Nonaka, I. and Takeuchi, H. (1995) *The Knowledge-Creating Company*. Oxford: Oxford University Press.

Nowotny, H., Scott, P. and Gibbons, M. (2000) *Re-Thinking Science*. Oxford: Polity.

Packard, V. (1957) *Hidden Persuaders*. New York: Pocket Books.

Polanyi, M. (1957) *Personal Knowledge*. Chicago, IL: University of Chicago Press.

Popper, K. (1957) *The Poverty of Historicism*. New York: Harper and Row.

Price, C. (1993) *Time, Discounting, and Value*. Oxford: Blackwell.

Rose, H. and Rose, S. (eds) (2000) *Alas, Poor Darwin: Arguments against Evolutionary Psychology*. London: Jonathan Cape.

Scheuerman, W. (1994) *Between the Norm and the Exception*. Cambridge, MA: MIT Press.

Schumpeter, J. (1934) *The Theory of Economic Development*. Cambridge, MA: Harvard University Press.

Schumpeter, J. (1942) *Capitalism, Socialism, and Democracy*. New York: Harper and Row.

Smith, B. (1994) *Austrian Philosophy: The Legacy of Franz Brentano*. La Salle, IL: Open Court Press.

Sorokin, P. (1928) *Contemporary Sociological Theories*. New York: Harper and Row.

Urry, J. (2000) *Sociology beyond Societies*. London: Routledge.

Urry, J. (2002) 'Mobility and Proximity', *Sociology*, 36(2): 255–74.

Veblen, T. (1904) *The Theory of Business Enterprise*. New York: Scribners.

Wallerstein, I. (1996) *Open the Social Sciences*. Cambridge: Cambridge University Press.

Section Four

Creativity and Communication in the Production of Knowledge

7

Between Science and Rhetoric: A Recurrent Debate on the Role of Communication and Creativity in the Definition of Knowledge

By Philippe Breton

Any hypothesis on the close links between knowledge, communication and creativity seems to depend, among other factors, on the way the first of the three terms is defined. This very question is the subject of a recurrent debate, which is not independent from the social context in which it takes place. What place is given, in the field of knowledge, to scientific knowledge and what place is given to opinion and thus to rhetoric? Must science be seen as a particular kind of opinion or must emphasis be laid upon the difference between science and opinion? Is it right, for example, to favour a type of knowledge over another and to see opinion just as an 'ill-formed' type of knowledge? The answers to these questions determine an evaluation of the role of communication processes, networking and relation to an audience on the concrete conditions of creativity.

The purpose of this chapter is first to show the age and even the permanence of this debate in the history of thought. These questions were first formulated by Aristotle in his *Organon* (1990) where he forges the distinction between analytics, the set made up of dialectics and rhetoric and poetics. From this point of view, the history of the reception of Aristotle's *Rhetoric* (1967) is an interesting guideline. This historical review will help to make it clear that the interplay between the status given to the statement of truth, scientific in particular, in relation to the rhetorical statement (opinion) is at the core of the debate.

This field once cleared, I will formulate two hypotheses. First, the question must be raised whether the role given to the audience and the communication processes in the production of knowledge is not a central element in the discussion on the definition of knowledge. Then, there is the question of knowing if the status given to opinion or scientific statement is not partly determined by the nature of the society in which they occur and are granted, from time to time, a dominant character. Or, in other words, is not the variability of the definition of knowledge *in fine* a social variability?

Between these two hypotheses, I will suggest an interpretative framework for the debate on the status of knowledge. Three major positions, clearly opposed one to the other – an objectivist point of view, a representation of all knowledge as opinion, a principle of symmetry between science and opinion – can be identified to allow a better understanding of the current debate on these questions.

An Old Debate

Any interrogation of the status of knowledge demands frequent comings and goings between Antiquity, the Renaissance and the Contemporary periods. Unless one assumes that the history of thought is completely impervious to social contexts, and I certainly do not support this assumption here, such an enterprise must be tackled with modesty because it is a limited approach. The context of Greek and Roman Antiquity is obviously not the same as today's and it seems quite bold to bridge the gap between so widely diverging periods. This context is marked by at least three major differences from the modern and contemporary period, which produce a clear effect on the topic discussed here.

First, science was much less advanced in many directions (a scholar like Aristotle has probably been the first and the last, despite what is said of the humanists in the Renaissance, to be able to provide a comprehensive view of all the fields of knowledge of his time). Then, the nature of social relationships – even though it can prevail itself, at least from the threshold of the Empire onwards, of a major reference to democracy as an institution and to its republican corollary – was not 'individualistic' in the modern sense of the term.[1] This has obvious consequences on the conceptions about the production of knowledge. Finally, and as a result from the above comments, the social practices of the Greek and Roman Antiquity have disappeared.

Yet, despite this important proviso – which is worth, in a way, for any inquiry into the status of knowledge in the Renaissance –, it is highly interesting for an analytical purpose to approach the evolution of the status of knowledge since Aristotle as a single block. A great part of today's debates have actually their origin in Antiquity and the variability of positions within this specific debate must be linked to the evolution of Western societies – and of Jewish and Arabic societies – during the period under consideration.

While doing so, I am consciously introducing an assumption in this chapter through the deliberate use of the word 'knowledge' to refer at the same time to scientific knowledge and to knowledge which takes the form of opinion. It would even be necessary to enlarge the scope of this term to 'poetic' knowledge – in Aristotle's sense of poetics. In that regard, one can mention the insistence of Paul Ricoeur (1981) to see in the 'metaphorical statement' a process 'by which speech liberates the power of certain pieces of fiction to redescribe reality', which is, as he himself concedes, an echo of Max Black (1962)'s association of metaphor in art and model in science.

The Importance of Ancient Sources

Aristotle was the first to systematize a classification of knowledge which was based on a distinction between demonstrative science (analytics), reasoning from probable premises (dialectics and rhetoric) and lastly production of fiction (poetics).

This effort of systematization definitively broke up with myth, which totalized in a single and same set of beliefs and the knowledge of ancient societies. There was no longer one single knowledge, regulated by the same rules of production and usage (within a given society), but different kinds of knowledge, which came under particular heuristics and thus divided reality into distinct epistemological areas. Are the effects of this original diffraction and its consequences on today's thinking fully taken into account? What is sure is that the very words of the debate have been there since the fourth century BC.

The foundations of this diffraction which inaugurated three distinct types of knowledge are first a typically Greek thinking on being. As Evencio Beltran suggests:

> It is known that Aristotle takes as a principle that the question of logos must be solved from a reflection on being. To say what is strictly and absolutely necessary comes under analytics, which is the science of demonstrative reasoning based on certain premises. To say what is but might have been else comes under Topics: which means on the one hand dialectics which is the art of argumentation from probable premises, accepted by most people; and on the other hand rhetoric which is the art of persuasive argumentation. Finally, poetics – fiction – takes in charge what is not, but might have been nonetheless.

> (Beltran, 1998: 161)

But the consequences go far beyond a simple speculative reflection on being. This diffraction in the order of knowledge opens up a space for scientific thinking and allows its development. It is immediately provided by Aristotle with two essential tools for the production of knowledge: deductive reasoning and inductive reasoning.

The first concrete effect of this diffraction is to found a differentiated heuristics. The working of metaphor constitutes the specific heuristics of fiction. Rhetoric and dialectics, the sciences of plausible knowledge, are also given specific tools: enthymeme (a syllogism based on probable premises) and example. Thanks to Aristotle, the intellectual game on opinion, inaugurated by sophists, becomes a real form of reasoning which calls for method and rigour. There is an essential rupture here which grants opinion a status of knowledge. In his own words:

> until today, those who have compiled the techniques of speech have only given a small part of them; for only proofs are techniques; everything else is incidental. Actually, our authors do not say anything of enthymemes, and yet these are the substance of proof; they devote most of their treaties to questions which are outside their very subject; because suspicion, pity, anger and other passions of the soul do not relate to the topic.

> (Aristotle, 1967: Book I, 1354a)

The *logos*, cleared from the constraint of emotions, always suspect in a democracy, but framed by pathos and ethos, which are its necessary, but secondary, supportive forces, has a central place in Aristotle's rhetorical thinking. Beyond the new tripartite status of knowledge (analytics, dialectics and rhetoric and poetics), there is an underlying division of the real (of being) into different areas according to the relevance of each type of knowledge.

But the matter is not that simple, for, under the influence of Platonic philosophers (with whom Aristotle had broken when he chose, as he himself confesses in *Nicomachean Ethics*, 1997, to prefer 'truth over friendship'), many authors have tried to inflect Aristotle's symmetry between the three orders of knowledge, by constantly underrating the status of opinion, and thus of rhetoric. The debate started from this very point and it is still going on 2,300 years later.

Evolution of the Status of Opinion

This attempt either to minor or to heighten the status of opinion, particularly by some authors from the humanist tradition, is still going on today and it is one of the essential driving forces of the debate on the status of knowledge. The purpose here is not to give an accurate picture of all that is at stake in this debate; the reception of the text of Aristotle's *Rhetoric*, particularly in the Renaissance, provides a very good analyser of the extremely differing statuses given to opinion and to the discipline which is in charge of its production.

Aristotle's legacy is actually not linear and the interpretations of this particular part of his work are extremely varied. As Peter Mack puts it:

> the transmission and use of Aristotle's rhetoric is of great importance for all historians of rhetoric. To modern readers Aristotle's rhetoric is practically the most important text of rhetorical tradition, but the history of its reception prior to the eighteenth century is rather slight and is only now beginning to be understood.

(Mack, 1998: 299)

Without getting into further detail,[2] let us summarize what is at stake. Aristotle wrote two texts on the question of opinion: *Topics* (1990), where he presents the dialectic method, and *Rhetoric* (1967). The interpretation of the relations between dialectics and rhetoric has helped fill an incredible number of pages until today. Dialectics is a method of argumentation devoted to contradictory debate, among peers in a way, and it is at the same time a heuristics to find out arguments and thus produce additional knowledge on a given opinion. Argumentation is a method to convince within the frame of public debate, epidictic, legal, or political. In a sense, dialectics participates in the formation of opinions and rhetoric in the art of convincing of already conceived opinions.

The text of *Rhetoric* disappeared for a long time and was rediscovered in the West (Black, 1990), via its Arabic version (Al-Farabi's text), in 1256 through a Latin translation by Hermann the German. Until the eighteenth century, rhetoric had been reduced in the Middle Ages to its meaning as *trivium*, essentially an epistolary art.

The rediscovery of this text caused a lot of discussions which, all things being equal, are reminders of some contemporary developments of the debate on the status of knowledge. Just where Aristotle had clearly linked dialectics and rhetoric in a common relation to opinion, many authors from the eighteenth century onwards have attempted to present rhetoric, either as a subsection of analytics, aimed at the vulgar, or as a set of figures of a quasi-literary nature. Some have thus distinguished rhetoric from dialectics, giving the latter a noble position, though inferior to that of demonstration, and categorizing rhetoric as a merely poetic device.

Opinion, through the status of rhetoric, is constantly tossed about, either reduced to a subdivision of logic, or classified in the fields of poetics. In the process, it loses its status as proper knowledge. From this moment on, there has been a tradition of the 'two cultures', literary and scientific, which still exists today as a system of representation of knowledge and which Snow (1959/1993) has clearly shown in the 1960s (a position itself criticized, by Leavis,

1963, in particular). Caught up between these two cultures, rhetoric has obviously no status, just as opinion.

But other authors have attempted to remain faithful to Aristotle's tripartite division, like Philipp Melanchton (1497–1560), for whom, as Kees Meerhoff points out, 'the fundamental bound between dialectics and rhetoric is a recurrent motif' (1998: 323), or Jean de Jandun (1285–1328), who supports the view, according to Evencio Beltran

> that 'rhetoric is the replica of dialectics' and that it is part of it in some respects. This conception is in perfect accordance with Aristotle's great intuition, which established the connexion between the dialectic concept of plausibility and the rhetorical concept of persuasion. In dialectics, oratory art is strongly linked to philosophy as a whole and acquires a dimension much richer and more complex than the one it has been reduced to in later catalogues of simple 'figures'.
>
> (Beltran, 1998: 161)

Beyond this debate, which seems very technical, on the reception of Aristotle's *Rhetoric* or on the difference between dialectics and rhetoric looms the fundamental debate which has animated the history of thinking on knowledge since Antiquity: is there, between the quest for truth for its own sake and the domain of pure fiction which exalts passions, a place for opinion as knowledge appropriate to public affairs? One must admit that the most common answer to that question has been negative. One either proves, with a scientific demonstration, or one comments, in the literary sense of the word.

The distinction of scientific truth from theological truth – both of them still being intimately linked until the Renaissance – did not alter much the destiny of opinion, which had difficulties in being recognized as knowledge in itself, specific, and legitimate. As will be made clear at the end of this chapter, the epistemological status of opinion as knowledge is not independent from its social status as an operator of public action.

An Interpretative Framework: Three Positions on the Status of Knowledge

From the point of view of the debate on the status of knowledge, the contemporary period is characterized by the fact that many disciplines, having an interest in a better understanding of the conditions of production and invention of scientific ideas and of knowledge in general, have now tackled this question explicitly. One can mention, among other, epistemology, history of science, heuristics, cognitive science, philosophy, sociology of science and even sociology of communication, which constitutes the conceptual framework of this chapter in regard of the close links between knowledge and communication.

Although cautiousness is required concerning such a complex question, and it is easy to slip into oversimplification, in this chapter, I suggest to divide the different documented points of view into three distinct positions, which transcend academic distinctions and are three different combinations of two major components of human knowledge: scientific statement and opinion. In that regard, the contemporary debate is in direct continuity with the interrogations born in ancient Greece.

An Objectivist Point of View

The first position articulates scientific statement and opinion along a continuum and organizes them according to a strict hierarchy. Opinion is a mode of knowledge but its epistemological status is inferior to that of scientific statement.

Opinion would be a degraded version of knowledge, which could achieve a higher level of accuracy through the use of scientific method. In this conception, one might believe that opinion, such an 'impure' approach of reality, would be thrown out of the scope of knowledge and would not even deserve attention. Yet, there is a 'solidarity' between these two modalities of knowledge: one climbs over the shoulder of the other, the giant needs the dwarf to exist.

One of the fiercest advocates of this position might well be Gaston Bachelard, whose notion of 'epistemological obstacle' to the formation of the scientific spirit has inspired a great part of contemporary thinking on science since 1945. He claims, for instance, that

> science, in its need of being carried out as well as in its principle, must absolutely be opposed to opinion [...]. Opinion does not think well; it does not think: it points to a want of knowledge. Nothing can be founded on opinion: it must first be destroyed. It is the first obstacle to overcome. It would not be enough for instance, to rectify it on particular points, and maintain, as a sort of temporary morals, a temporary, vulgar knowledge. The scientific spirit forbids to form opinions on questions we do not understand, on questions we cannot formulate clearly. The first thing is to know how to pose the problem. And, whatever one might say, in scientific life, problems are not posed by themselves. It is precisely the sense of the problem which is the mark of the true scientific spirit. For a scientific spirit, all knowledge is the answer to a question. If there has not been a question, there cannot be scientific knowledge. Nothing is given. Everything is constructed.
>
> (Bachelard, 1977: 14)

This radicality of epistemology towards opinion is paradoxically a sign of the very necessity of the latter. As a matter of fact, Bachelard (1977: 13–14) clearly says that 'it is in terms of an obstacle that the problem of scientific knowledge must be posed' and disputes, in that respect, 'the idea that one must start from zero to found and grow one's good'. The obstacle is necessary, if it is to be overcome. Without an obstacle, without a first thought that one must destroy to progress, there is no scientific statement. In the ashes of opinion lie the remains of science's fire.

This position might well be termed as 'objectivist', because it constructs itself against the subjectivity, prejudice and empiricism of opinion, against the constraint of need, and aims at reaching 'abstract', objective positions. It is not totally devoid of a form of contempt towards all the situations when the construction of scientific statements is not possible by nature or because the amount of work already done is not sufficient. This is why the objectivist point of view regards some social sciences as being able, at most, to produce such 'degraded' knowledge. In the same way, knowledge produced in the field of politics to conduct human actions is considered as an inferior or 'irrational' matter. The whole hope of cybernetics was condensed in this criticism and in the possibility of introducing rationality and objectivity into the affairs of the polis, by limiting, through appropriate methods, the extension of opinion, particularly in human sciences (Lafontaine, 2003).

Science as Opinion

A second position has appeared recently. But its newness might be misleading. It also consists in considering that there is a continuum between scientific statement and opinion, but it claims, just as radically, that the production of scientific statement, its rules of validation and recognition, has the same status as the production of opinion. Social practices contributing to the production of scientific statement would obey, in this frame of mind, the same rules and regulations as social practices contributing to the production of opinion. And if rhetoric as 'the art of persuasion' can be said to be the 'science' of the production of opinion, it brings about a better understanding of scientific statement itself.

Epistemology should then be re-founded on the basis of rhetoric and rehabilitate figures (like analogy) or practices encouraging the approval of the audience. The first works by Bruno Latour and Steve Woolgar (1986) consisted in looking into the detail of scientific production in laboratories, to show that rhetoric played an essential part in it and that everything else was only an almost theological smokescreen, aiming at an 'objectivity of science' which could indeed never exist.

What is at stake, in order to highlight the rhetorical dimension of scientific discourse, is a reversal, as Vincent de Coorebyter says it, of a conception of history which would be marked by 'the successive elimination of its rhetorical remains, through a constant purifying of the forms and rules of learned textuality, whose constitutive norms seem to be inspired from an ideal of dehumanization and self-generation of discourse' (1994: 1).

There is no distinction to be made between the scientific and the non-scientific, between objective fact and opinion, because both of them are part of knowledge and knowledge is built on the bases of dialectics and rhetoric.

George Thinès went as far as claiming, using as an example the theory of evolution, that rhetoric plays here [in the field of science] a similar role to that it has always assumed in court or in the pulpit. The examples are so numerous that one can wonder whether fundamental discoveries do not tend, through the very movement of their development, to seek general approval, rather than a purely technical validation, of their possible exactness. Scientific truths regarded as definitive are ultimately those that can be turned into opinions (or doxical sets) without risking losing their essential scientific range (Thinès, 1994: 124).

Authors following this line of thinking have then tried to rehabilitate the role of a number of figures of thought, analogy, or metaphor for instance, just as Gerald Holton (1986) in a research on the role of this last figure in the history of physics. In other contexts, scientific activity can be perceived in terms of power relationships (Bourdieu, 2004) and as a social construct (Knorr-Cetina, 1981).

Symmetry between Science and Opinion

Facing these two positions which combine, each in its own way, the relationship between scientific statement and opinion, one can find, though it is more difficult to trace, the point of view according to which there is a 'symmetry' between science and opinion, and that, simply, their fields of application are different.

Scientific statement would be valid only for the domains investigated by natural sciences, whereas opinion would be the knowledge, legitimate and perfect in a way, valid for the domains covered by human affairs. As Chaïm Perelman, Belgian philosopher and jurist, clearly and profoundly says: 'it is because the domain of action is that of contingency, which cannot be governed by scientific truths, that the role of dialectic reasoning and rhetoric discourse is inevitable to introduce some measure of rationality in the exercise of individual and collective willpower' (1977: 171).

This new epistemology (only seemingly new as we shall see) could be strongly supported by a sociology of communication which would include and modernize the rhetorical tradition. Other advocates of these positions are to be found in the field of social sciences: they are convinced that the knowledge produced by these sciences has certainly a different status from that of exact and natural sciences, but has an equal legitimacy. Still, knowledge produced in this community is not termed as 'opinion', considering the negative image of this word.

The problem, precisely, lies there. The objectivist point of view has long been dominant – and it is probably still the case today – and so any emphasis on opinion, even locally, is negatively connoted and is faced with the depreciation carried by this notion. The massive attack led by the advocates of the second position, which turns scientific statement into just another kind of opinion, has not yet had any effect on this depreciation – except perhaps to cause an ironical depreciation of knowledge in general. The inferior status of opinion, whatever its field of application, is perhaps more strongly felt in countries like France and its severe Cartesian tradition of absolute distinction between science and opinion – 'what can be discussed is necessarily false' states Descartes, at the beginning of the *Discourse on Method* ([1637], 1996).

Two Hypotheses on the Relationships between Scientific Statement and Opinion

The above description and classification into three positions certainly do not exhaust the complexity of current debates on the status of knowledge. They are even, in a way, particularly reductive (as regards, for example, the debate between Feyerabend and Popper). But they help to organize some conceptions and better understand some oppositions.

It can be noted that the first two positions, as opposed to the third, often define themselves curiously as 'militant', polemist, or even aggressive. Gerald Holton does not hesitate, though he probably knows what words are worth in this domain, to speak about 'the watchdogs of adequate rationality in science' (1994: 150). The advocates of the objectivist point of view show only contempt for anything that relates to opinion or its defence, even in areas where science does not have much to say, like politics, which is thrown down to the hell of irrationality.

But, at the same time, it is clear that there is a close solidarity, within each conceptual framework, between scientific statement and opinion, *which seem to be able to exist only in their mutual relationship*, even in the third position presented here.

If the reader is ready to accept as a temporary premise the interpretative framework described above, and the partition into three distinct positions on the status of knowledge, two hypotheses can be made. The first regards the place given to audience and reception in the production of knowledge, the second regards the link between the status given to knowledge, and so to opinion, and the nature of the society in which the debate takes place.

The Role of Communication in the Production of Knowledge

The discussion of the role of communication in the production of ideas is another permanent feature of the debate on the epistemological status of knowledge. This role is itself extremely varied. The relation to the audience thus offers an interesting criterion to discriminate between opposed epistemological positions.

To come back to the interpretative framework (of this chapter), the 'objectivist' point of view implies a great solitude of the scientist in the concrete act of production of new scientific statements. This 'solitude' does not exclude team work and it is not opposed to it. Solitude rather means, in such a context, that one does not produce for somebody else or according to a given audience. The order of discovery is opposed to the order of display. And, if there is a search for a validation of worked-out results by the community of peers, this relation to an audience is only a second moment coming after the first movement of scientific discovery.

Invention thus becomes a matter of psychology and it is reduced to the dimension of the creative individual. The French mathematician Poincaré (1952) suggested, in a lecture in 1908, a scheme that has since been very popular among scientists. He distinguishes between, chronologically, a phase of preparation (investigation of the problem, empiricist approach, collection of data, testing of solutions and formulation of hypotheses), a phase of incubation when the problem disappears for some time in the 'inner-self' or 'subconscious' of the scientist, a phase of 'illumination' when the solution appears and a phase of validation of the relevance of the new, theoretical or experimental, idea.

Only this last phase is 'socialized'. In this conception, the 'degraded' status of opinion stems precisely from the fact that it is socialized from the start, that it must immediately take into account, *from its very conception*, its reception.

The metaphor of the 'ivory tower' which has long been used to describe the social position of the scientist, necessarily alone – even when he fulfils a social demand, as it is the specific moment of the production of new knowledge that is considered –, must be taken seriously. Even though her perspective is that of a radical criticism of science's ability to produce monsters, the poetess Mary Shelley has perfectly well understood the close relationship between the need for solitude and the inventive productivity of the scientist. This is one of the most penetrating themes of her book on Doctor Frankenstein's creature (Shelley, 1984).

On the contrary, the advocates of a more 'relativist' position see in the production of knowledge, including scientific statements, an eminently social activity, the 'truth' of a result being immediately and entirely subsumed under its social validation by the community of peers. The whole work of a scientist then consists in obtaining, thanks to appropriate rhetorical devices, the approval of his or her colleagues, even the most reluctant, who must be convinced with arguments, or even with power relationships established through institutional pressures.

The relation to the audience is a good indicator of the status given to knowledge. What is this status in Aristotle's initial conception? The divide is clear cut and there is no question of either imprisoning opinion into science, or the contrary. The search for truth through demonstrative means is clearly classified in the field 'of he whom searches for himself: whatever the premises of his reasoning, be they true and known, or disputed by the person who answers' (Aristotle, 1990: VIII, 1, 10).

The Aristotelian enterprise of objectivation clearly distinguishes between this 'isolated' approach of the people who seek the 'truth' and that of the dialectician or rhetor. The heuristic devices used by the latter directly include, as long as possible before the act of production, the audience which is addressed. Opinion is straightaway considered as *always* disputable, not only from the point of view of its validation and its acceptation by others, but disputable in its very own nature, which sets it apart from obviousness.

Thus, in the Seventh Book of *Topics*, devoted to the question of the 'rules of interrogation', Aristotle establishes a chronology of the invention of arguments which is also a protocol: 'it is necessary first, when one wants to formulate interrogations, to find the place from which the attack must be launched; second, to formulate interrogations and order them one by one; third, to pose them eventually to the adversary' (1990: VIII, 1, 1).

The movement of knowledge here unfolds itself in three moments: first, start from the audience ('the place of the attack'), then come back to one's self, finally argue. There is no better way to say that rhetorical knowledge is a *coproduction* of rhetor and audience.

Rhetoric thus renounces the idea of a 'universal audience' which lies at the foundation of analytics. In one case induction proceeds from 'universal' premises, in the other, example (rhetorical induction) proceeds from what is generally accepted by the audience addressed. The whole difference lies there.

As a matter of fact, this is why the text of Aristotle's *Rhetoric*, as Roland Barthes (1970) had smartly noted, is for a great part devoted to the analysis of audience and 'reception'. This is because reception is an essential mechanism of production itself.

All the authors who have, since then, perpetuated this Aristotelian perspective – like Chaïm Perelman (1982), Michel Meyer (1979) and the other members the 'Brussels School', who were the first to operate a revival of studies in this area, from the beginning of the 1950s onwards – attach a great importance to the role of the audience. Perelman, after a reminder that his conception of argumentation, taken up from

> Greek rhetoric and dialectics, is a breaking point with a conception of reason and reasoning taken up from Descartes [claims that] it is the idea of obviousness as a characteristic of reason that one must criticize if room is to be made for a theory of

argumentation, which accepts the use of reason to guide our action and influence the actions of others.

(Perelman and Olbrechts-Tyteca,1958/1970: 1 and 4)

In such a view, Perelman supports the radical point that

it is impossible to decide, beforehand, whether a determined structure [...] plays the role of argumentative figure or of figure of speech [...] it is the movement of speech, the adhesion of the audience to the form of argumentation it encourages, which determine the kind of speech at stake [...] a figure, whose argumentative effect is not achieved, falls down to the rank of figure of speech.

(Perelman and Olbrechts-Tyteca, 1958/1970: 229–30)

There is no better way of saying that it is the context of reception which decides the very nature of the rhetorical knowledge produced. It is also a way of being faithful to Aristotle's definition of rhetoric as 'the art of finding out what is persuasive in a specific cause' (1967). Rhetorical knowledge is here what is persuasive for a given audience.

The humanists in the Renaissance, like Erasmus, inaugurated the systematization of the confrontation of ideas within what Thomas More called *sodalitates* in his *Utopia*, informal 'networks' of intellectual friendship which enabled the discussion of all kinds of opinions over all Europe. More than ever, knowledge is conceived of as a coproduction within a debate whose rules and (specific) heuristics are under very close scrutiny. Yet, the Renaissance is also known for being the moment of a scission between the world of sciences – to which humanists were rather indifferent[3] – and the intellectual world, fed on the rediscovery of ancient rhetoric which provided for the rules of production of opinions. In their view, communication and production of opinion become inseparable: learning to think in order to convince is as important as learning to convince in order to think.

Knowledge becomes a matter of network, at least as far as opinion is concerned. It is from there, later, that some have tried to think all knowledge, including scientific knowledge, as produced within networks.

The Dependence of the Status of Knowledge on the Social Context

As it has just been mentioned, the status of opinion in relation to scientific statement is subject to great variations in its interpretation, just as the role given to communication and audience in the production of knowledge. How is this variability to be accounted for, which makes of epistemology and heuristics ever shifting domains, housing so contradictory to interpretative frameworks?

It is time to suggest a second hypothesis. Any interrogation on the status of knowledge takes into account, of course, the internal movement of the ideas produced, but does it not also depend on the social context in which these ideas take place? In other words, the epistemological status of opinion seems to depend, among other things, on the status of opinion – and, consequently, of scientific statement – within a given society.

To illustrate this question, let us comeback to the extreme but telling case of the reception of Aristotle's *Rhetoric* in the Arabic and Jewish worlds around the thirteenth and the fourteenth centuries. As Jean-Pierre Rothschild says it in a very synthetic and far-sighted way:

> rhetoric could not find, among the Arabic-speaking Jews, an application in the art of well-being, for more or less the same reasons as in Islam: there was no possible application either to the legal debate which (indeed) did not exist, the work of the dayyan, religious judge, and of the Muslim expert of fiqh, was to determine the law case through an exegesis of legal texts; or to political debate.
>
> (1998: 259)

The same conclusion could be drawn from the representation of rhetoric and opinion in the Middle Ages in Europe: the first was reduced, it has been mentioned, to its oratory dimension (the epistolary art or the art of preaching). The second simply did not exist because the mode of social organization allowed no room for such a type of knowledge. Evencio Beltran reminds us 'that the greatest ambition of Aristotle's Rhetoric was to confer this discipline a scientific status in such a way as to regulate the use of public speech' (1998: 162) and that the humanists that were closest to Aristotle followed this line and claimed, as Jean de Jandun, that it is with politics that rhetoric has the closest links. Heuristics corresponds to a political rectitude of speech, a question that is of course still relevant today (Breton, 2003a).

For opinion to have the status of legitimate knowledge, it is necessary that politics play a role in the society at stake (Breton, 2003b). That was not the case in the Arabic and Jewish worlds, just as in European Middle Ages. Because of that, their reading of Aristotle erased the whole dimension of rhetoric and opinion, which simply had no relevance to the people and elite of these societies. It is probable then that epistemological conceptions are partly socially determined (which is a different hypothesis than that of knowing whether knowledge itself is socially determined).

A heuristics of opinion becomes meaningful only in a democratic society, where a vast space is open for politics, that is to say for the three fields covered by opinion: the management of public affairs (political debate), the practice of justice (judicial debate) and the organization of public debate (the debate on the values of society). The current development of a generalized epistemology of opinion, as an analytical framework for the status of knowledge, can be, in that respect, associated to the spread of democracy in Western societies, at least as far as 'freedom of opinion' is concerned.

Similarly, there is a parallel to be drawn between the surge of individualism in the Renaissance and the development of a model for the production of scientific statement which puts into play the ideal of the isolated scientist facing the truth. The hypothesis that scientific knowledge can only take place in a social and political background which leaves a space open for the person and the individual's ability to create is quite bold, yet it is interesting to look at.

Since the nineteenth century, one can observe a tightening of networks of all natures (in fields like urbanism, energy, transport and later on information) and the very original kind of 'collectivization' – original because it goes with an extension of the place of the individual – of entire sectors of public life which correspond to these networks. This (evolution) can be linked to a vision of knowledge production as the result of a collective work involving a networking of qualifications. Understanding the new modalities of knowledge production and developing interpretative frameworks *ad hoc* has now become a major challenge, which does not only concern epistemology or the sociology of knowledge.

Endnotes

1 On this issue, see Dumont (1986).

2 See, for instance, Lawrence D. Green (1994).

3 It was here probably, and has been until today, one of the major failures of sciences and especially techniques to maintain a distance – with only a few exceptions – from humanism, which had begun a junction with them. This distance threw humanism into the arms of culture, and then higher culture, and has fed the current gap between technoscience and ethics.

References

Aristotle (1967) *Rhétorique*. Books 1, 2 and 3. Paris: Les Belles Lettres.

Aristotle (1990) *Organon*. Vol. V, *Les Topiques*. Paris: Vrin.

Aristotle (1997) *Ethique à Nicomaque*. Paris: Vrin.

Bachelard, G. (1977) *La formation de l'esprit scientifique*. Paris: Vrin.

Barthes, R. (1970) 'L'ancienne rhétorique', *Communications*, 16: 172–229.

Beltran, E. (1998) 'Les Questions sur la rhétorique de Jean de Jandun', in G. Dahan and I. Rosier-Catach (eds), *La rhétorique d'Aristote: Traditions et commentaires de l'Antiquité au XVIIe siècle*. Paris: Vrin, pp. 153–67.

Black, D. L. (1990) *Logic and Aristotle's Rhetoric and Poetics in Medieval Arabic Philosophy*. Leiden: Brill.

Black, M. (1962) *Models and Metaphors*. Ithaca, NY: Cornell University Press.

Bourdieu, P. (2004) *Science of Science and Reflexivity*. Chicago, IL: University of Chicago Press.

Breton, P. (2003a) 'Le "plaider en dehors de la cause" d'Aristote: un critère technique pour séparer argumentation et manipulation?', in S. Bonnafous, P. Chiron, D. Ducard and C. Levy (eds), *Argumentation et discours politique: Antiquité grecque et latine, Révolution française, Monde contemporain*. Rennes: Presses Universitaires de Rennes, pp. 153–63.

Breton, P. (2003b) *Eloge de la parole*. Paris: La Découverte.

de Coorebyter, V. (1994) 'Introduction. Science et rhétorique: dualisme ou dilemme', in V. de Coorebyter (ed.), *Rhétoriques de la science*. Paris: Presses Universitaires de France, pp. 1–4.

Descartes, R. ([1637], 1996) *Discourse on Method* and *Meditations on First Philosophy*. New Haven, CT: Yale University Press.

Dumont, L. (1986) *Essays on Individualism: Modern Ideology in Anthropological Perspective*. Chicago, IL: University of Chicago Press.

Green, L. D. (1994) 'Aristotle's Rhetoric and Renaissance Views of the Emotions', in P. Mack (ed.), *Renaissance Rhetoric*. London/New York: Macmillan/St Martin's Press, pp. 1–26.

Holton, G. J. (1986) *The Advancement of Science and its Burdens*. New York: Cambridge University Press.

Holton, G. J. (1994) 'La métaphore dans l'histoire de la physique', in V. de Coorebyter (ed.), *Rhétoriques de la science*. Paris: Presses Universitaires de France, pp. 149–69.

Knorr-Cetina, K. (1981) *The Manufacture of Knowledge: An Essay on the Constructivist and Contextual Nature of Science*. Oxford: Pergamon Press.

Lafontaine, C. (2003) *L'empire cybernétique*. Paris: Seuil.

Latour, B. and Woolgar, S. (1986) *Laboratory Life: The Construction of Scientific Facts*. Princeton, NJ: Princeton University Press.

Leavis, F. R. (1963) *Two Cultures? The Significance of C. P. Snow*. New York: Pantheon Books.

Mack, P. (1998) 'Aristotle's Rhetoric and Northern Humanist Textbooks (Agricola, Erasmus, Melanchthon and Ramus)', in G. Dahan and I. Rosier-Catach (eds), *La Rhétorique d'Aristote: Traditions et commentaires de l'Antiquité au XVIIe siècle*. Paris: Vrin, pp. 299–313.

Meerhoff, K. (1998) 'A la Renaissance, rhétorique, éthique et politique', in G. Dahan and I. Rosier-Catach (eds), *La Rhétorique d'Aristote: Traditions et commentaires de l'Antiquité au XVIIe siècle*. Paris: Vrin, pp. 315–30.

Meyer, M. (1979) *Découverte et justification en science*. Paris: Klincksieck.

Perelman, C. (1977) *L'empire rhétorique*. Paris: Vrin.

Perelman, C. (1982) *The Realm of Rhetoric*. Notre-Dame/London: University of Notre-Dame Press.

Perelman, C. and Olbrechts-Tyteca, L. ([1958], 1970) *Traité de l'argumentation: La nouvelle rhétorique*. Bruxelles: Editions de l'Institut de Sociologie de l'Université de Bruxelles.

Poincaré, H. (1952) *Science and Method*. New York: Dover Publications.

Ricoeur, P. (1981) *The Rule of Metaphor: Multi-Disciplinary Studies of the Creation of Meaning in Language*. Toronto: University of Toronto Press.

Rothschild, J.-P. (1998) 'La rhétorique dans la littérature hébraïque', in G. Dahan and I. Rosier-Catach (eds), *La Rhétorique d'Aristote: Traditions et commentaires de l'Antiquité au XVIIe siècle*. Paris: Vrin, pp. 257–82.

Shelley, M. (1984) *Frankenstein or The Modern Prometheus: The 1818 Text in Three Volumes*. Berkeley, CA: University of California Press.

Snow, C. P. ([1959], 1993) *The Two Cultures*. Cambridge: Cambridge University Press.

Thinès, G. (1994) 'Une rhétorique optimale du discours scientifique', in V. de Coorebyter (ed.), *Rhétoriques de la science*. Paris: Presses Universitaires de France, pp. 117–30.

8

High Cognitive Complexity and the Making of Major Scientific Discoveries

By J. Rogers Hollingsworth

Introduction[1]

This essay is derived from insights developed from a complex research project about major discoveries in the basic biomedical sciences of Britain, France, Germany and the United States during the entire twentieth century. Focusing on 291 major discoveries, that study was designed to understand the organizational and laboratory context in which major discoveries occurred.[2] In the process of conducting the study, I began to observe distinct social psychological characteristics of the scientists involved in making these discoveries. This essay reports some of these findings, with somewhat modest goals. And this essay is a preliminary report on some aspects of the social psychological profiles of many scientists who made major discoveries in basic biomedical science.

Focusing on individual scientists involved in making major discoveries, I do not attempt to develop a theory of discovery or of creativity. Because there is no consensus in the literature on the meaning of creativity, the essay deliberately avoids focusing on creativity. The term creativity has been used to address so many different problem areas that it has lost much of its utility as a research concept. People talk about the creative baker, the creative gardener, the creative taxi driver, the creative coach. One writer has listed over a thousand definitions of creativity. When a term is so overused and frequently misused, it is best to find an alternative concept for analytical purposes. For this reason, this essay employs the concept 'high cognitive complexity' to advance our understanding of the scientists who make major discoveries.

Those with high cognitive complexity have the capacity to understand the world in more complex ways than those with less cognitive complexity. For reasons described below, scientists having high levels of cognitive complexity tend to internalize multiple fields of science and have greater capacity to observe and understand the connectivity among phenomena in multiple fields of science. They tend to bring ideas from one field of knowledge into another field.[3] High cognitive complexity is the capacity to observe and understand in novel ways the relationships among complex phenomena, the capacity to see relationships among disparate fields of knowledge. And it is that capacity which greatly increases the potential for making a major discovery. Every one of the 291 discoveries in our larger research project reflected a great deal of scientific diversity. And in our larger body of work on scientists and major discoveries we argue that a major indicator of high cognitive complexity for scientists is the degree to which they internalize cognitively scientific diversity. Indeed, a necessary condition for making a major discovery was that the scientist had to internalize a high level of cognitive complexity. For this reason, an intriguing and important problem is to understand why scientists vary in having high levels of cognitive complexity. On the other hand, most scientists having high cognitive complexity do not make major discoveries.

This essay develops three separate but complementary agenda. First, it briefly reports on the social contexts of the laboratories in which the 291 major discoveries occurred. The structure of these laboratories enhanced their success in integrating novel perspectives on important problems from diverse fields of science. Second, the essay argues that most of the scientists who made the 291 major discoveries internalized a great deal of scientific diversity. It was that characteristic which facilitated their capacity to work in multiple fields simultaneously, and a major goal of the essay is to address the question of why they had high cognitive complexity. Third, the essay demonstrates the consistency of these findings about the process of discovery and high cognitive complexity with some of the literature which has been emerging for some years in certain areas of neuroscience. For example, some recent neurosciences literature provides insights to why a few individuals are able to make major breakthroughs which are highly relevant to scientists in many fields (though most scientists work on relatively narrow problems in highly specialized fields).

Laboratories where Major Discoveries Occur

Critical to our research has been the definition of a major discovery. A major breakthrough or discovery is a finding or a process, often preceded by numerous 'small advances', which leads to a new way of thinking about a problem. This new way of thinking is highly useful in addressing problems confronted by numerous scientists in *diverse* fields of science.

In this definition, the emphasis on 'diverse fields of science' is critical. Not only was each of the 291 discoveries in our research highly relevant to scientists in separate fields of science, but the discoveries were made by scientists who internalized considerable scientific diversity, who tended to be boundary-crossers, and could communicate with scientists in multiple fields. Since a trend in twentieth-century science has been towards increasing specialization, it is significant that major discoveries have tended to be highly relevant to scientists in multiple scientific specialities and were made by scientists who were not highly specialized but by those who internalized considerable scientific diversity.

This strategy for defining a major discovery is quite different from the rare paradigm shifts which Thomas Kuhn analysed in *The Structure of Scientific Revolutions* (1962). Major breakthroughs about problems in basic biomedical science occur within paradigms about which Kuhn wrote. Historically, a major breakthrough in biomedical science was a radical or new idea, the development

Table 8.1   *Indicators of major discoveries*

1 Discoveries resulting in the Copley Medal, awarded since 1901 by the Royal Society of London, insofar as the award was for basic biomedical research.
2 Discoveries resulting in a Nobel Prize in Physiology or Medicine since the first award in 1901.
3 Discoveries resulting in a Nobel Prize in Chemistry since the first award in 1901, insofar as the research had high relevance to biomedical science.
4 Discoveries resulting in ten nominations in any three years prior to 1940 for a Nobel Prize in Physiology or Medicine.*
5 Discoveries resulting in ten nominations in any three years prior to 1940 for a Nobel Prize in Chemistry if the research had high relevance to biomedical science.*
6 Discoveries identified as prize-worthy for the Nobel Prize in Physiology or Medicine by the Karolinska Institute committee to study major discoveries and to propose Nobel Prize winners.*
7 Discoveries identified as prize-worthy for the Nobel Prize in Chemistry by the Royal Swedish Academy of Sciences committee to study major discoveries and to propose Nobel Prize winners.* These prize-worthy discoveries were included if the research had high relevance to biomedical science.
8 Discoveries resulting in the Arthur and Mary Lasker Prize for basic biomedical science.
9 Discoveries resulting in the Louisa Gross Horwitz Prize in basic biomedical science.
10 Discoveries resulting in the Crafoord Prize, awarded by the Royal Swedish Academy of Sciences, if the discovery had high relevance to the biological sciences.

* I have had access to the Nobel Archives for the Physiology or Medicine Prize at the Karolinska Institute and to the Archives at the Royal Swedish Academy of Sciences in Stockholm for the period from 1901 to 1940. I am most grateful to Ragnar Björk, who did most of the research in the Karolinska Institute's archives to identify major discoveries according to the indicators in this table. Because the archives are closed for the past 50 years for reasons of confidentiality, I have used other prizes (Crafoord, Lasker, Horwitz,) to identify major discoveries in the last several decades.

of a new methodology, or a new instrument or invention. It usually did not occur all at once, but involved a process of investigation taking place over a substantial period of time and required a great deal of tacit and/or local knowledge. My colleagues and I have chosen to depend on the scientific community to operationalize this definition, counting as major discoveries bodies of research meeting at least one of the ten criteria listed in Table 8.1.

We have studied in considerable detail all the laboratories where each of the 291 major discoveries occurred as defined in Table 8.1. Among other things, we have attempted to learn for each of the 291 discoveries where, when and by whom was the research done? What were the characteristics of the culture and the structure of the laboratory where the research occurred?[4]

We have also studied in detail the characteristics of a large number of laboratories headed by highly visible scientists (members of the Royal Society, the National Academy of Sciences, College de France, etc.) who never made major discoveries, in order to discern whether there were significant differences in the two populations of laboratories. After conducting our research on laboratories, we observed two general types of labs: those with significant scientific diversity, headed by lab directors who had the capacity to integrate the diversity in order to address problems relevant to numerous fields of science – in Table 8.2 we label these as Type A Labs. The other type of laboratories was much more narrow in scope and was more oriented to the issues involving a single discipline. These we label Type B Labs (see discussion in Hollingsworth, 2006; Hollingsworth *et al.*, 2008).

Table 8.2   *Two general types of laboratories in the basic biomedical sciences*

Characteristics of Type A Laboratories
1 Cognitive: High scientific diversity
2 Social: Well connected to invisible colleges (for example, networks) in diverse fields
3 Material Resources: Access to new instrumentation and funding for high-risk research
4 Personality of lab head: High cognitive complexity, high confidence and motivation
5 Leadership: Excellent grasp of ways that different scientific fields might be integrated and ability to move research in that direction

Characteristics of Type B Laboratories
1 Cognitive: Moderately low scientific diversity
2 Social: Well connected to invisible colleges (for example, networks) in a single discipline
3 Material Resources: Limited funding for high-risk research
4 Personality of lab head: Lack of high cognitive complexity, limited inclination to conduct high-risk research
5 Leadership: Not greatly concerned with integrating different scientific fields

Almost all the 291 discoveries in our project were made in Type A laboratories. However, all Type A laboratories did not succeed in making a major discovery. Indeed, most did not. As many scientists and others have observed, there is a certain amount of chance and luck in the making of major discoveries (Edelman, 1994: 980–86; Friedman, 2001; Jacob, 1995; Merton and Barber, 2004; Simonton, 1988: chapter Two; Zuckerman, 1977). Most of the scientists who headed Type A labs internalized considerable scientific diversity and had high cognitive complexity, whether they succeeded in making a major discovery or not.

Type B laboratories are at the opposite end of the continuum on virtually all the lab characteristics. Significantly, none of the 291 discoveries in our research occurred in Type B labs. The heads of Type B labs tended to be scientists who internalized much less scientific diversity and had lower levels of cognitive complexity than those who were the leaders in Type A laboratories.

The more Type A laboratories there have been in a single organization and the more they have had high interaction with each other across diverse fields, the greater the likelihood that the research organization has had multiple discoveries having a major impact on diverse fields of science. Figure 8.1 characterizes the conditions under which an organization might have multiple breakthroughs. The number of research organizations having these characteristics in basic biomedical science during the twentieth century were very few, however. The one organization which had more major breakthroughs (defined by criteria listed in Table 8.1) than any other throughout the twentieth century was the relatively small research organization in New York City, Rockefeller University (for an analysis of why that organization had so many Type A labs see Hollingsworth, 2004; Hollingsworth *et al.*, 2008). Because Type B labs have tended to focus on relatively narrow problems, they have also tended to have fewer rich interactions across diverse fields, and for this reason, organizations dominated by Type B labs have had few or no major discoveries.

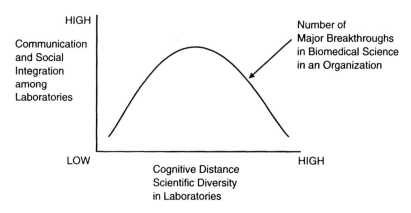

Figure 8.1   *The relationship among scientific diversity, communication/integration and making major discoveries.*

In our research, we have studied the institutional as well as the organizational context in which these labs were embedded. Variation in institutional environments leads to variation in the degree to which certain kinds of research organizations are dominant in a society. In sum, ours has been a multi-level analysis, concentrating on how institutional and organizational environments place constraints on how the types of labs and kinds of scientists are likely to be distributed across and within societies as well as across and within particular organizations within a society (Hollingsworth and Hollingsworth, 2000; Hollingsworth, 2004; 2006; Hollingsworth *et al.*, 2008). Others who have emphasized how the macro- and meso-environments of scientists have influenced innovativeness are Ben-David (1991), Cole and Cole (1973), Dogan and Pahre (1989), Merton (1973) and Zuckerman (1977). And while this essay also focuses on how these levels influence innovativeness, the distinctive argument of this essay is how those levels – combined with the social psychological features of scientists – influence the making of major discoveries.

High Cognitive Complexity and Major Discoveries

What is the relationship between high cognitive complexity and the making of major discoveries? The concept of cognitive complexity emerged some decades ago when research by psychologists failed to demonstrate that intelligence had much impact on individual performance. Because of their disappointment in being able to explain individual behaviour with various measures of intelligence, many psychologists began to focus their research on cognitive styles. Over time, cognitive complexity tended to be a better predictor of individual performance than measures of intelligence. The research on cognitive complexity suggests that cognitive traits of individuals tend to be stable over time, across subject areas and across tasks. There are numerous studies which suggest that individuals who have high cognitive complexity tend to be more tolerant of ambiguity, more comfortable not only with new findings but even with contradictory findings. Moreover, such individuals have a greater ability to observe the world in terms of grey rather than simply in terms of black and white. Psychologists have even defined a dimension of cognitive complexity with an emotional component: many with high cognitive complexity report that learning new things and moving into new areas is like play. They tend to be more intuitive and have a high degree of spontaneity in their thinking, to be individuals who enjoy exploring uncertainty and engaging in high-risk research rather than working in areas which are already well understood (Cacioppo *et al.*, 1996; Suedfeld, 2000). Moreover, cognitive complexity as a variable has been useful in helping to explain how individual scientists interact with their institutional and organizational environments (Grigorenko, 2000: 165; Grigorenko and Sternberg, 1995; Sternberg, 1997; Wardell and Royce, 1978).

Our data on scientists over the past century who have had high cognitive complexity and made major discoveries suggest that there are distinct social and psychological processes which influence the emergence of high cognitive complexity. We have derived our data from many different sources. We interviewed more than 450 scientists in the four countries and have worked in numerous archives containing correspondence and papers of scientists associated with making major discoveries. In addition, we have studied large numbers of biographies, autobiographies and obituaries of individuals, both those who made and did not make major discoveries. Because I wish to study the scientists who made major discoveries over a century, obviously I do not rely heavily on the kind of contemporary data which clinical psychologists normally use. Rather, much of the data are historical in nature.

Cognitive complexity tends to have its roots in various social psychological processes. Here I present two processes which were particularly notable in enhancing the cognitive complexity of high achieving scientists: the internaliza-tion of multiple cultures and having non-scientific avocations. The essay argues that distinguished scientific achievement results from the internalization of scientific diversity, but it is cognitive complexity which facilitates scientific diversity and high scientific achievement.

Internalizing Multiple Cultures

A very high proportion of those who have high cognitive complexity internalize multiple cultures in very meaningful ways. However, there are numerous path-ways by which one might internalize multiple cultures. Indeed, the defining of multiple cultures is not an easy task. At the most elementary level, an individual who internalizes multiple identities, each of which is defined by cultural traits, necessarily internalizes multiple cultures, and this facilitates the capacity of such an individual to observe the world in more complex terms than the individual who internalizes much less cultural diversity.

A common explanation as to why individuals have high cognitive complexity is because they have internalized multiple cultures based on ethnicity, nationality and/or religion (Hage and Powers, 1992). To acquire multiple cultural identities, it is not sufficient to live in a world where one is simply exposed to multiple cul-tures. Rather one must be sufficiently socialized by multiple cultures so that one actually internalizes the norms, habits and conventions of more than one culture. Such an individual then literally has the capacity to live intuitively in multiple worlds simultaneously. The argument here is that such an individual has the ability to observe the world in more complex terms and has the potential to be more innovative than those who internalize less cultural diversity.

There is an extensive literature pointing to the high achievements of German–Jewish scientists in the first-third of the twentieth century, achievements quite out of proportion to the Jewish fraction of the German population. A common explanation in the literature has been the emphasis which Jewish families placed on formal learning (Nachmansohn, 1979). This may be an important part of the explanation, but we need to broaden this perspective, for there were numerous non-Jewish scientists of high distinction who also internalized multiple cultures: some who were part Polish and part French, some had one parent who was Catholic and another who was Protestant, some had one parent who was French and another North African, some who internalized Latin American and British cultures and so forth. Because such individuals lived in intimate association with multiple worlds, they tended to have weak identities with each and for this reason they could more clearly perceive the world with a certain detachment, to have a higher level of cognitive complexity, and to have the potential to develop novel or creative views of the world.

The scientists in our population who internalized multiple cultures tended to be both insiders and outsiders, and it was this capacity to live in more than one world simultaneously that was the key to having high cognitive complexity. When they attended universities, it was almost second nature to cross from one field into another, to be both an insider and outsider. Just as in their personal lives they internalized multiple cultures, in their scientific lives they also internalized scientific diversity. And it is no accident that in this age of specialization, the discoveries by these scientists reflected a great deal of scientific diversity. Indeed, one of their key traits was the capacity to see and understand relations among multiple fields. From our population of scientists who made major discoveries in basic biomedical science as well as from the lives of many other scientists in the twentieth century, the capacity to internalize scientific diversity was virtually universal.

As suggested above, many observers have long been aware that some of the most renowned scientists of the twentieth century were Jewish. Within my population of scientists who internalized multiple cultures and who made major discoveries in the basic biomedical sciences were such well-known Jewish scientists as the following: Gerald Edelman, Fritz Haber, Roald Hoffmann, Francois Jacob, Aaron Klug, Hans Krebs, Karl Landsteiner, Rita Levi-Montalcini, Jacques Loeb, Andre Lwoff, Elie Metchnikoff, Otto Meyerhoff, Max Perutz and Otto Warburg. In my investigations of basic biomedical scientists who made major discoveries, I became increasingly interested in those who internalized multiple cultures so I could better understand some of the determinants of high cognitive complexity. I first focused on Jews who made major discoveries in basic biomedical science, as in our interviews and other investigations it became quite obvious that many of these were individuals who not only had high cognitive complexity but also internalized multiple cultures. Interestingly, the number of Jews in the population proved to be far greater than my colleagues and I originally suspected. Because of the very large number of Jews associated with major discoveries in basic biomedical science and closely related fields, I present their names in Table 8.3.

Table 8.3   *Jewish scientists who made major discoveries in basic biomedical and related sciences 1901–2005*[5]

Part One: Jewish Scientists Awarded Nobel Prizes in Physiology or Medicine		
Paul Ehrlich (1908)	Konrad Bloch (1964)	Michael Brown (1985)
Elie Metchnikoff (1908)	Francois Jacob (1965)	Joseph Goldstein (1985)
Robert Bárány (1914)	André Lwoff (1965)	Stanley Cohen (1986)
Otto Meyerhof (1922)	George Wald (1967)	Rita Levi-Montalcini (1986)
Karl Landsteiner (1930)	Marshall Nirenberg (1968)	Gertrude Elion (1988)
Otto Warburg (1931)	Salvador Luria (1969)	Harold Varmus (1989)
Otto Loewi (1936)	Julius Axelrod (1970)	Edmond Fischer (1992)
Joseph Erlanger (1944)	Sir Bernard Katz (1970)	Alfred Gilman (1994)
Herbert Gasser (1944)	Gerald Edelman (1972)	Martin Rodbell (1994)
Sir Ernst Chain (1945)	David Baltimore (1975)	Stanley Prusiner (1997)
Hermann Muller (1946)	Howard Temin (1975)	Robert Furchgott (1998)
Gerty Cori (1947)	Baruch Blumberg (1976)	Paul Greengard (2000)
Tadeus Reichstein (1950)	Andrew Schally (1977)	Eric Kandel (2000)
Selman Waksman (1952)	Rosalyn Yalow (1977)	Sydney Brenner (2002)
Sir Hans Krebs (1953)	Daniel Nathans (1978)	H. Robert Horvitz (2002)
Fritz Lipmann (1953)	Baruj Benacerraf (1980)	Richard Axel (2004)
Joshua Lederberg (1958)	Sir John Vane (1982)	
Arthur Kornberg (1959)	César Milstein (1984)	

Part Two: Jewish Scientist Awarded Nobel Prizes in Areas of Chemistry Relevant to Basic Biomedical Science		
Adolph von Baeyer (1905)	Ilya Prigogine (1977)	Rudolph Marcus (1992)
Henri Moissan (1906)	Herbert Brown (1979)	George Olah (1994)
Otto Wallach (1910)	Paul Berg (1980)	Harold Kroto (1996)
Richard Willstätter (1915)	Walter Gilbert (1980)	Walter Kohn (1998)
Fritz Haber (1918)	Roald Hoffmann (1981)	Alan Heeger (2000)
George de Hevesy (1943)	Aaron Klug (1982)	Aaron Ciechanover (2004)
Melvin Calvin (1961)	Herbert Hauptman (1985)	Avram Hershko (2004)
Max Perutz (1962)	Jerome Karle (1985)	Irwin Rose (2004)
Christian Anfinsen (1972)	John Polanyi (1986)	
William Stein (1972)	Sidney Altman (1989)	

Part Three: Jewish Scientists Awarded the Lasker Award in Basic Biomedical Science		
Selman Waksman (1948)	Sol Spiegelman (1974)	Joseph Goldstein (1985)
Sir Hans Krebs (1953)	Howard Temin (1974)	Rita Levi-Montalcini (1986)
Michael Heidelberger (1953)	Andrew Schally (1975)	Stanley Cohen (1986)
George Wald (1953)	Rosalyn Yalow (1976)	Philip Leder (1987)
Theodore Puck (1958)	Sir John Vane (1977)	Alfred Gilman (1989)
Heinz Fraenkel-Conrat (1958)	Hans Kosterlitz (1978)	Stanley Prusiner (1994)
Jules Freund (1959)	Solomon Snyder (1978)	Jack Strominger (1995)
Harry Rubin (1964)	Walter Gilbert (1979)	Robert Furchgott (1996)
Bernard Brodie (1967)	Paul Berg (1980)	Mark Ptashne (1997)
Marshall Nirenberg (1968)	Stanley N. Cohen (1980)	Aaron Ciechanover (2000)
Seymour Benzer (1971)	Harold Varmus (1982)	Avram Hershko (2000)
Sydney Brenner (1971)	Eric Kandel (1983)	Alexander Varshavsky (2000)
Charles Yanofsky (1971)	César Milstein (1984)	James Rothman (2002)
Ludwik Gross (1974)	Michael Brown (1985)	Randy Schekman (2002)

Table 8.3   *Continued*

Part Four: Jewish Scientist Awarded the Louisa Gross Horwitz Prize		
Marshall Nirenberg (1968)	César Milstein (1980)	Michael Rossmann (1990)
Salvador Luria (1969)	Aaron Klug (1981)	Stanley Prusiner (1997)
Harry Eagle (1973)	Stanley Cohen (1983)	Arnold Levine (1998)
Theodore Puck (1973)	Viktor Hamburger (1983)	Bert Vogelstein (1998)
Boris Ephrussi (1974)	Rita Levi-Montalcini (1983)	H. Robert Horvitz (2000)
Seymour Benzer (1976)	Michael Brown (1984)	Avram Hershko (2001)
Charles Yanofsky (1976)	Joseph Goldstein (1984)	Alexander Varshavsky (2001)
Michael Heidelberger (1977)	Mark Ptashne (1985)	James Rothman (2002)
Elvin Kabat (1977)	Alfred Gilman (1989)	Randy Schekman (2002)
Walter Gilbert (1979)	Stephen Harrison (1990)	Ada Yonath (2005)

Sources: JINFO, 2005a,b,c,d and e

The list in Table 8.3 identifies scientists as being Jewish in a number of different ways. In a very strict sense, there is no single definition of a Jew. All who are listed in Table 8.3 had some identity as being Jewish even if they were not Jewish in a religious sense, or did not associate with others who were Jewish. Indeed, some disguised their Jewish origins and married non-Jewish spouses. Some were extraordinarily secular or even atheist. In Table 8.3 we list high-achieving scientists in our population if their Jewish background – however defined – contributed to their (1) having some awareness of being Jewish and (2) contributed to their internalization of multiple cultures and having high cognitive complexity (Weisskopf, 1991: 27; also See Nachmansohn, 1979; Stoltzenberg, 1994).[6]

How a Jewish background worked out was very complex and varied from person to person and from society to society. Many were marginal to the society in which they grew up. Some like Nobel laureate Gertrude Elion were essentially 'multiple outsiders'. Her father had arrived in the United States from Lithuania and had descended from a line of rabbis who have been traced through synagogue records to the year 700. Her mother had emigrated from a part of Russia that is now part of Poland and her grandfather had been a high priest. Gertrude's maternal grandfather who had the greatest influence on her, was a learned biblical scholar who was fluent in several languages, and for years Gertrude and her grandfather spoke Yiddish together. But Gertrude as a young girl realized that she wanted to be a scientist – a man's profession. Hence, she not only internalized the culture of being Jewish and American, but also being a woman in an occupation dominated by men (Interview with Elion; McGrayne, 1993: 280–303).

Rosalyn Yalow was another Nobel laureate whose early life was being both insider and outsider. Her Jewish parents were immigrants to the United States who had little formal education, but they strongly encouraged her education. Hence during Yalow's early years, she tended to live in two separate worlds: one in which she received much encouragement from her uneducated immigrant parents and another in the public schools of the South Bronx. Later, she became very interested in physics, a male-dominated world. Again, she was an outsider. Fortunately for her, when she began graduate work during the Second World War there were not enough male graduate students to be research and teaching assistants. As a result, she was accepted in the Physics Department of the University of Illinois and given a stipend. Subsequently, she began to work with a group of physicians in the Bronx Veterans Administration hospital, but as a physicist she was again an outsider. It was as a result of this dual role of being both insider and outsider that she was able to establish bridges between the world of physics and medicine and to be one of the few scientists in the developing field of nuclear medicine (Csikszentmihalyi, 1996: 192–96; Howes, 1991: 1283–91; McGrayne, 1993: 333–55; Opfell, 1978).

As the sociologist Robert Park (1937: xvii–xxiii) observed many years ago, the marginal person is often a personality type who emerges where different cultures come into existence, and such an individual often assumes both the role of the cosmopolitan and the stranger. Because such an individual internalizes multiple cultures, he/she has the potential to develop a wider horizon, a keener intelligence, a more detached and rational viewpoint – the ingredients of a creative person (Park, 1937: xvii–xxiii). Somewhat earlier, the German sociologist Georg Simmel (1908) had developed similar ideas about the perceptiveness and potential innovativeness of the individual who is both insider and outsider (also see Dogan and Pahre, 1989; 1990). The psychologist Mihaly Csikszentmihalyi (1996: 177–78), a leading writer on creativity, has reminded us that there were also many routes by which high-achieving individuals have felt marginalized. Some experienced the life of the marginal individual because of their early success. Because they were so precocious, Nobel laureates John Bardeen, Manfred Eigen and Rosalyn Yalow were promoted to higher grades in school whereupon they were surrounded by older students with whom they were unable to establish any rapport.

Csikszentmihalyi (1996: 267) further suggests that many scientists have overcompensated for their marginalization with a relentless drive to achieve success, determination based on sacrifice, and discipline, but at the same time a fascination with constant learning about novel things. The American biologist E. O. Wilson, who experienced a painful childhood which generated a great deal of personal insecurity, has suggested that all great scientists must be marginal at times in their career. He too felt marginalized at moments in his highly successful and fascinating career (Wilson, 1994). According to Wilson, being a highly successful scientist requires 'enormous amounts of work and pain. And you have to accept a certain amount of rejection. [...] You have to be ignored for periods of time' (quoted by Csikszentmihalyi, 1996: 269; interviews with Wilson).

As the above paragraphs suggest, the emergence of multiple ethnic and national identities was not the only path for internalizing multiple cultures. Some scientists in our population internalized multiple identities or cultures by living simultaneously in two social worlds based on social class. For example, Sir James Black who was awarded the Nobel Prize in Physiology or Medicine in 1988 came from a relatively rural coal-mining community. He came from an upper-middle-class family in which his father was a mining engineer and colliery manager, but Black's peers were children of coal miners. In short, Black was living and negotiating in two different worlds – that of his professionally oriented home and that of the coal mining community where there was extremely high distrust of the mining management. Significantly, Black's tendency to live in two worlds concurrently has continued throughout his life: his scientific career was that of one living in multiple worlds, crossing boundaries and integrating in his own mind that which most of his scientific colleagues would never have been able to do (Black, 1988; interview with Black).

A similar case involved that of Gobind Khorana who was awarded the Nobel Prize in Physiology or Medicine in 1968. Khorana's cultural diversity was also derived from living in a small village in India, where his father was a civil servant and his family was the only one who could read English. In fact, most villagers had difficulty even in understanding English. Thus, Khorana grew up internalizing both the cultural world of the village and the more cosmopolitan world of his parents, and from this dual environment he was socialized to be both an insider and outsider, to be a boundary crosser – traits which facilitated his understanding relationships among multiple fields of science and making a major discovery.

Another case with a similar theme was that of Jacques Monod who was awarded the Nobel Prize for Physiology or Medicine in 1965. Monod also spent his childhood in multiple cultural worlds. His father was from a Protestant Huguenot family in Catholic France, while his mother was an American from Milwaukee and Iowa. His father was a painter who was an avid reader of science. This kind of socialization into a world of cultural diversity led to Monod's becoming a classical man of opposites, both an insider and outsider: growing up in a rigid Protestant culture but in a Catholic society, a man who was highly emotional but who insisted on great scientific precision, a man very musically oriented with democratic values but autocratic in his behaviour, a scientist who was able to integrate the best in both French and American styles of science.

There was the well-known case of Peter Medawar who was born in Brazil of a Lebanese father and an English mother. From there he was eventually sent to an English public school – Marlborough – and later became a student at Magdalen College, Oxford. Medawar indeed internalized an amazing amount of cultural diversity and this proved to be an enormous asset to him as he became a boundary-crosser in various scientific fields.

Another woman who excelled in the male-dominated world of science was Irène Joliot-Curie, awarded the Nobel Prize in Chemistry in 1935 with her husband Frédéric Joliot. A major factor in her ability to bring together disparate trends in chemistry and physics was her high cognitive complexity which was very much influenced by the cultural diversity she internalized. Irène was the daughter of Polish-born Nobel laureate Marie (Sklodowska) Curie and French-born Nobel laureate Pierre Curie. Irène grew up in Paris, but under the supervision of a Polish governess who spoke Polish to her on a daily basis. Irène also came under the strong influence of her French paternal grandfather who was very anticlerical in a culture under the dominance of the Catholic Church. While her peers attended the rather rigid schools operated by the French state, Irène attended a private cooperative school and was tutored in mathematics by her mother. In short, as a young girl she was intimately socialized to live in multiple worlds simultaneously (McGrayne, 1993: 11–36, 117–43).

Many individuals emerged from a multicultural world but never internalized in a deep sense the cultural diversity of their environment. All other things being equal, the greater the cultural diversity within a social space, the greater the likelihood that an individual will internalize multiple cultures and have potential to be highly innovative. However, there are many qualifications which must be made to such a generalization. The more structural and cultural barriers among those of different cultural backgrounds and the less the access to leading centres of learning, the lower the likelihood that individuals in a multicultural society will internalize cultural diversity. Hence, across multicultural environments there is variation in the degree to which individuals will internalize multiple cultures. Poland and Germany in the first third of the twentieth century were multicultural societies, but Polish Jews faced greater cultural and structural obstacles to scientific institutions than German Jews did. Even though anti-Semitism existed in both societies, it was more intense in Poland than in Germany, and partly for that reason, Polish Jews were less able to internalize cultural diversity and to be as innovative as German Jews at the same time.[7] This difference explains in part differences between the two populations in achievement of major breakthroughs in science in the first third of the twentieth century.

The United States is a multicultural society where many have internalized multiple cultures, and this has contributed to there being so many scientists in the United States who made major discoveries during the past century. A major exception involves African Americans. The extremely harsh experience of slavery and the intense racism throughout the twentieth century caused most African Americans to develop strong identities, but strong racial prejudice against them has made it very difficult historically to internalize in a very deep sense multiple ethnic or cultural identities. Because African Americans were long denied access to leading educational institutions, they were not as successful as Jewish Americans or other ethnic groups in making major discoveries. Indeed, the experience of African Americans suggests that if there is oppression and very strong discrimination against an ethnic group – even in a multicultural society – members of that group are unlikely to have the same levels of scientific achievement as those who internalize in a very deep way more than one culture. Because a number of indicators show racial oppression is diminishing in American society many more African Americans may come to internalize multiple cultures, and thus be more likely to be scientists of considerable distinction and achievement.

The Contributions of Avocations to High Cognitive Complexity

The basic argument of this essay is that the wider the range of experience and knowledge of the scientist, the more fields of science his/her work are likely to influence and the greater the importance with which it will be perceived (Csikszentmihalyi, 1996; Pelz and Andrews, 1966; Sternberg, 1988; Sternberg and Davidson, 1995). Thus far, the argument has been that cognitive complexity due to the internalization of multiple identities tends to enhance scientific diversity and scientific achievement. Cognitive complexity is further enhanced in those who already internalize considerable cultural diversity by engaging in mentally intensive avocations.

On the other hand, many scientists who did not internalize multiple cultures added to their cognitive complexity by mentally intensive engagement in avocations which on the surface did not appear to be related to their scientific work. On the basis of in-depth interviews (and from my study of biographical and rich archival materials), many scientists have made it abundantly clear that their avocations enriched the complexity of their minds and that many of their scientific insights were derived by engaging in what often appeared to be non-scientific activities. Impressive work in this area has been done by the Root-Bernsteins (1989; 1999) who argue that the skills associated with artistic and humanistic expression have positive effects in the conduct of scientific research. They contend that scientific accomplishments are enhanced by the capacity to be high-achieving in multiple fields – scientific as well as non-scientific – and by having the opportunity and ability to make use in science of skills, insights, ideas, analogies and metaphors derived from non-scientific fields. Many scientists have commented about the intuitive and non-logical factors in the act of discovery (Jacob, 1995; Medawar, 1991). Others have emphasized that the arts and humanities have the potential to stimulate the senses of hearing, seeing, smelling – enhancing the capacity to know and feel things 'in a multi-model, synthetic way' (Root-Bernstein, 2001: 65). Thus Einstein frequently observed that his theory of relativity occurred by intuition, but music was 'the driving force behind the intuition [. . .]. My new discovery is the result of musical perception' (Suzuki, 1969). Einstein's son observed of his father that '[w]henever he had come to the end of the road or into a difficult situation in his work, he would take refuge in music, and that would usually resolve all his difficulties' (Clark, 1971: 106). Root-Bernstein goes so far as to argue that 'no one with monomaniacal interests or limited to a single talent or skill can [. . .] be creative, since nothing novel or worthy can emerge without making surprising links between things [. . .]. To create is to combine, to connect, to analogize, to link, and to transform.' (2001: 66).

If fundamental discoveries are derived from experiencing unexpected connections from disparate fields and if discovery often has a strong emotional and intuitive quality to it, we should expect that many of the scientists in our population who were recognized for making major discoveries were also individuals who were quite accomplished performers in areas other than the scientific field for which they were renowned. There is indeed a very rich body of data revealing that highly recognized scientists in many fields were quite talented as writers, musicians, painters, sculptors, novelists, essayists, philosophers and historians. A number were also engaged in political activities – both closely and distantly related to their scientific activities. In Table 8.4, we list numerous scientists who made major accomplishments in the basic biomedical sciences who were also quite accomplished in various artistic and humanistic activities. While rather extensive, the list is probably an understatement. My colleagues and I still have incomplete data about the avocations of scientists who are in our population for being nominated for Nobel Prizes ten times in three different years but who never received a major prize for their achievement. Unfortunately, all of these 'ten-in-three' scientists are deceased, and the published materials about them is quite limited. We suspect that if we had had the same kind of extensive published materials on all of them as we do on those who received Nobel Prizes and other major prizes, we would have learned that most of the 'ten-in-three' scientists would also have been very talented in various avocational fields.

Table 8.4   *Twentieth-century scientists who made major discoveries and were also quite active in music, art, writing, crafts and politics*[8]

Musicians			
Luis Alvarez*	Physicist	Otto Meyerhof*	Biologist
Clay Armstrong*	Biologist	Albert A. Michelson*	Physicist
Oswald T. Avery*	Microbiologist	Jacques Monod*	Biologist
Georg von Békésy*	Physiologist	Rolf Nevanlinna	Mathematician
Walter B. Cannon#	Physiologist	Wilhelm Ostwald*	Physical Chemist
Ernst Chain*	Chemist	Max Planck*	Physicist
Louis De Broglie*	Physicist	Ilya Prigogine*	Physicist
Gerald Edelman*	Biologist	Mark Ptashne*	Biologist
Manfred Eigen*	Chemist	Ronald Ross*	Biologist
Albert Einstein*	Physicist	Solomon Snyder*	Biologist
Richard Feynman*	Physicist	Arnold Sommerfeld	Physicist
Otto Frisch	Physicist	Charles Stevens	Biologist
Michael Heidelberger#	Chemist	Joseph J. Sylvester	Mathematician
Werner Heisenberg*	Physicist	Axel Hugo Theorell*	Physiologist
Gerhard Herzberg*	Chemist	Georges Urbain	Physicist
William Lipscomb*	Chemist	Paul Urban	Physicist
Jacques Loeb#	Biologist	J.H. Van't Hoff*	Physical Chemist
Barbara McClintock*	Physicist	Emil Warburg*	Biologist/Chemist
Ernst Mach	Geneticist	Victor Weisskopf	Physicist
Lise Meitner	Physicist	Edmund B. Wilson	Biologist
Composers of Music			
Albert A. Michelson*	Physicist	Walter Thirring	Physicist
Ronald Ross*	Biologist	Georges Urbain	Chemist
Poets			
Marie Curie*	Physical Chemist	William Ramsay*	Physical Chemist
Fritz Haber*	Chemist	Charles Richet*	Physiologist
Otto Hahn*	Physical Chemist	Ronald Ross*	Biologist
A.V. Hill*	Biologist	Erwin Schrödinger*	Physicist
Roald Hoffmann*	Chemist	Charles Sherrington*	Physiologist
Otto Meyerhof*	Biologist	J. H. Van't Hoff*	Physical Chemist
S.H. Mueller	Mathematician	Selman A. Waksman*	Bacteriologist
H.J. Muller*	Geneticist	Richard Willstätter*	Chemist
Walther Nernst*	Physical Chemist		
Dramatists			
Fritz Haber*	Chemist	Charles Richet*	Physiologist
Novelists			
Carl Djerassi	Chemist	Charles Richet*	Physiologist
Fred Hoyle	Astrophysicist	Norbert Wiener	Cyberneticist

Table 8.4   *Continued*

Painters and Sketchers			
Edgar Adrian*	Physiologist	Howard Florey*	Chemist
Frederick Banting*	Physiologist	Roger Guillemin*	Physiologist
Joseph Barcroft[#]	Physiologist	Cyril Hinshelwood*	Physical Chemist
Theodor Boveri*	Biologist	Dorothy Hodgkin*	Chemist
Lawrence Bragg*	Physicist	Joseph Lister[#]	Physician
William Bragg*	Physicist	Otto Loewi*	Physiologist
Ernst Brücke	Physiologist	Konrad Lorenz*	Ethologist
S. Ramon y Cajal*	Neuroanatomist	Wilhelm Ostwald*	Physical Chemist
Harvey Cushing[#]	Surgeon	Louis Pasteur	Biologist
H. von Euler-Chelpin*	Biochemist	E.A. Scharpey-Schaefer*	Physiologist
Richard Feynman*	Physicist	Nico Tinbergen*	Biologist
Alexander Fleming*	Bacteriologist	E. O. Wilson*	Biologist

Sculptors			
Robert Holley*	Biochemist	Roger Sperry*	Biologist
Salvadore Luria*	Biologist	Georges Urbain	Physicist

Drafters			
Luis Alvarez*	Physicist	Linus Pauling*	Physical Chemist
George Beadle*	Biologist	William Ramsay*	Physical Chemist

Involved in Architecture			
Gunter Blöbel*	Biologist	Peter Mitchell*	Biologist
Otto Hahn*	Chemist	Robert G. Roeder*	Biologist

Photographers			
Patrick Blackett*	Physicist	Wilhelm Ostwald*	Physical Chemist
S. Ramon y Cajal*	Neuroanatomist	Wilhelm Roentgen*	Physicist
Gertrude Elion*	Biochemist	Ernest Rutherford*	Physicist
Howard Florey*	Chemist	E.A. Sharpey-Schaefer*	Physician
Tim Hunt*	Biochemist	Nico Tinbergen*	Biologist
Robert Koch*	Bacteriologist	Charles T.R. Wilson*	Physicist
Gabriel Lippman*	Physicist		

Woodworkers or Metalworkers			
Luis Alvarez*	Physicist	Walter Rudolf Hess*	Biologist
Joseph Barcroft*	Physiologist	Andrew Huxley*	Biologist
William Bayliss*	Physiologist	Barbara McClintock*	Geneticist
Georg von Békésy*	Physiologist	Wilhelm Ostwald*	Physical Chemist
Walter Cannon[#]	Physiologist	Louis Pasteur	Physician/Immunologist
Gerald Edelman*	Biologist	William Ramsay*	Physical Chemist
J. Willard Gibbs	Physicist	Theodor Svedberg*	Physical Chemist

Scientists Who Wrote Philosophy, History, Anthropology and/or Popular Science			
Paul Berg*	Biologist	John Eccles*	Biologist
Baruch Blumberg*	Biologist	Gerald Edelman*	Biologist
Niels Bohr*	Physicist	Manfred Eigen*	Chemist
Pierre Broca	Biologist	Albert Einstein*	Physicist
S. Ramon y Cajal*	Biologist	Richard Feyman*	Physicist
Alexis Carrel*	Biologist	Simon Flexner[#]	Physician/Psychiatrist
Erwin Chargaff	Biochemist	Sigmund Freud[#]	Biologist
Andre Cournand*	Biologist	Murray Gell-Mann*	Physicist
Frances Crick*	Biologist/Physicist	Stephen J. Gould	Biologist
Richard Dawkins	Biologist/Ethologist	Stephen Hawking	Physicist

(Continued)

Table 8.4   Continued

Werner Heisenberg*	Physicist	Max Perutz*	Chemist
J.H. Van't Hoff*	Chemist	Max Planck*	Physicist
Fred Hoyle	Astrophysicist	Henri Poincaré	Mathematician
Francois Jacob*	Biologist	Michael Polanyi	Chemist
Eric Kandel*	Biologist	Ilya Prigogine*	Physicist
Hans Krebs*	Biochemist	Martin Rees	Cosmologist
M.T.F. von Laue*	Physicist	Peyton Rous*	Biologist
Joshua Lederberg*	Biologist	Oliver Sacks	Neurologist
Richard Lewontin	Biologist	Carl Sagan	Astronomer
Ernst Mach	Physicist	Erwin Schrödinger*	Physicist
Ernst Mayr*	Biologist	Charles Sherrington*	Physiologist
Peter Medawar*	Biologist	Nikolaas Tinbergen*	Biologist/Ethologist
Otto Meyerhof*	Biologist	James D. Watson*	Biologist
Robert Millikan*	Physicist	Steven Weinberg*	Physicist
Jacques Monod*	Biologist	E. O. Wilson*	Biologist
Wilhelm Ostwald*	Physical Chemist		

Political Activists			
John Desmond Bernal	Physicist	Jacques Monod*	Biologist
Patrick Blackett*	Physicist	Salvador Luria*	Biologist
Niels Bohr*	Physicist	Matthew Meselson	Biologist
John Cockcroft*	Physicist	Nevill Mott*	Physicist
Paul Doty	Chemist	Robert Oppenheimer	Physicist
Albert Einstein*	Physicist	Linus Pauling*	Physical Chemist
James Franck*	Physicist	John Polanyi*	Chemist
Archibald Vivian Hill*	Biologist	Ronald Ross*	Biologist/Physician
Dorothy Crowfoot Hodgkin*	Chemist	Abdus Salam*	Physicist
Frédéric Joliot-Curie*	Chemist	Richard Synge*	Chemist
Irene Joliot-Curie*	Chemist	Leo Szilard	Physicist
Robert Koch*	Biologist	Edward Teller	Physicist
Joshua Lederberg*	Biologist	James D. Watson*	Biologist
Hendrik Antoon Lorentz*	Physicist	Victor Weisskopf	Physicist

Legend:
* Received Nobel, Lasker, Horwitz and/or Crafoord Prize and/or Copley Medal.
# Scientists whose discoveries resulted in ten nominations in three different years prior to 1940 for a Nobel Prize in Physiology or Medicine or in Chemistry if the research had high relevance to biomedical science.

The thesis of this essay is not that all scientists having high cognitive complexity made major discoveries. Rather, its main argument is that those with high cognitive complexity – for whatever reason – tended to have qualitatively different styles of doing science than those who did not have high cognitive complexity. The greater their cognitive complexity – whether as a result of internalizing multiple cultures and/or from participating in various artistic and humanistic fields – the greater the likelihood that they would be highly achieving scientists.

For many scientists, their activities as an artist, painter, musician, poet, etc., enhanced their skills in pattern formation and pattern recognition, skills that they could transfer back and forth between science and art. It was part of their ability to understand reality in more than one way. The great chemist Robert Woodward and many others marvelled at how their activities as artists reinforced their abilities to recognize complex patterns in nature. Roald Hoffmann, a Nobel laureate in chemistry who is also a poet, argues vigorously that scientists have no more 'insight into the workings of nature than poets'. Hoffmann's science describes nature with equations and chemical structures but he argues that his science is an incomplete description. By using ordinary language to describe nature, Hoffmann believes he has a richer understanding of the world. In short, the more different ways we can describe reality, the richer our description and understanding. For Hoffmann (1981; 1995) and many others, the roles of artist and scientist are mutually reinforcing. The physicist Victor Weisskopf in his autobiography (1991: chapter 14) makes a powerful argument that artistic and scientific activities complement one another in the mind of the scientist. Both are needed in order to have a more complete understanding of the world.[9]

Perspectives from Neuroscience and the Making of Major Discoveries

Thus far we have suggested that individuals who internalize multiple cultures and who have well-developed aesthetic interests will tend to have high cognitive complexity, enhancing their ability to understand the interconnectedness and relations among different phenomena. It is this ability to understand complex relations among things which is key to the ability to generate novel views about phenomena (Simonton, 1988). In short, internalizing multiple cultures and being highly engaged in mentally intense activities outside of science increase the likelihood that individuals will make major discoveries. In addition, our data suggest that being in organizational environments with other individuals who also internalize cultural and scientific diversity enhances the likelihood of making major discoveries (Hollingsworth, 2004). But organizational factors are not necessary or sufficient conditions for the making of a major discovery. Rather, these factors increase the probability of making a major discovery (Hollingsworth, 2004; Hollingsworth and Hollingsworth, 2000).

Neuroscientists and cognitive psychologists have long been concerned with the consequences of complex experiences for behaviour. The perspectives presented here are somewhat complementary with some of those which have emerged in the fields of neuroscience and cognitive psychology. To make the argument about high cognitive complexity and major discoveries more comprehensible, it may be helpful to relate cognitive complexity as discussed here to some of the views suggested by literature in neuroscience and cognitive psychology.

If internalizing multiple cultures leads to high cognitive complexity, perhaps we should ask why children in the same family or a similar social environment vary greatly in their cognitive complexity. This is not an easy problem to confront. Some sociologists and psychologists have long been intrigued with the fact that there is great variation in the performance of siblings and others raised in the same structural and cultural environment. Jencks *et al.* (1972) reported with a large sample of the American population that there is just as much variation in occupational attainment and income among siblings in the same family as in the population at large. Moreover, there is substantial literature which demonstrates that variation in the birth order of children within the same family leads to important differences in their behaviour, abilities and careers (Sulloway, 1996).[10]

Some neuroscience literature is suggestive for the problem of why children reared in the same family vary so much in their behaviour, and why different children growing up in the same multicultural environment may vary enormously in the degree to which they internalize cultural diversity and have high cognitive complexity. The starting point of this literature is that every brain is unique and distinctive. Nobel laureate Gerald Edelman and others inform us that even the brains, thoughts, emotions and levels of consciousness among identical twins raised in the same family are different (Edelman, 1987; 1989; 1992; 2004; Edelman and Gally, 2001; Edelman and Tononi, 2000; McGraw, 1935).

Each mind is made up of millions of neurons connected to neighbouring neurons across synapses, and the number and complexity of these connective patterns is almost unlimited. Within the cerebral cortex alone, there are approximately 10 billion neurons. If one were to count all the connections of neurons by synapses – one per second – one would finish counting them about 32 million years after one began (Edelman, 1992: 17). It is through extraordinarily complex sensory experiences that connections are generated among neurons. Throughout the life of the individual, each perception is modified by a person's genetic structure as well as by previous sensory experiences and connections. Each mind is constantly making complex classifications of phenomena related to previous sensory experiences. It is through the thickness of connections and in the almost limitless complexity and variety of experiences that the brain is able to detect patterns and to develop abstract relations among different phenomena. As a result of the billions and billions of different sensory experiences of individuals, each person – even when exposed to the same circumstances – codes or responds to the same observations or phenomena differently (Dempsey, 1996; Edelman, 1987; 1989; 1992; Hayek, 1952). As McGraw (1935) and others (Dalton, 2002: chapters 9 and 10) have demonstrated, this variation begins very early in the development of an individual. It is for this reason that even if several children in the same family are exposed to a similar multicultural environment, only one child may internalize a high level of cultural diversity and have high cognitive complexity.

Every new experience is influenced by all previous experiences. In short, the human mind is highly path-dependent (Rizzello, 1997; 2003). The synaptic reorganizations within the brain are continuously occurring with such enormous complexity that each individual perceives the world in a unique way. The mind with high cognitive complexity has a larger repertoire of patterns ready to be applied to the perception of each new situation.

One way that the uniqueness of each mind is revealed is in the connections among multiple parts of each brain. In each individual, every experience is related to all other experiences and each is mutually reinforcing (Dempsey, 1996; Hayek, 1952). There is no disjuncture between the end of one experience and the beginning of another. But each new experience has an effect on the entire mind.

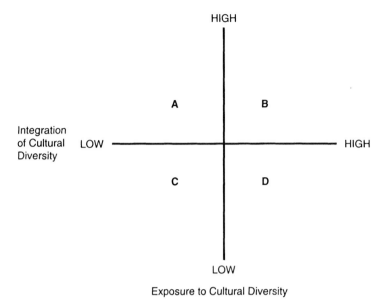

Figure 8.2   *Variations in the exposure to and integration of cultural diversity.*

Even when a single mind experiences the same set of external stimuli again, they are never experienced in the same way. Every experience is not only very personal but even for the same individual each experience is unique. As Michael Polanyi (1962) taught us many years ago, no two individuals see things in the same way.

The mind is biographical, but each step in the biography is highly unique and dependent on the previous step. Paraphrasing Stephen J. Gould (1989: 14), Dempsey writes: 'Wind the tape of the mind to its early days, [...] let it play again from an identical starting point, and the chance becomes vanishingly small that anything like the identical mind will grace the replay' (1996).

In Figure 8.2, two or more individuals may grow up in environments with exposure to high levels of cultural diversity (Cells A and B). However, even when children in the same family grow up in multicultural environments, perhaps only one child (Cell A) may internalize a high degree of cultural diversity and hence the potential to develop a high degree of cognitive complexity. As suggested above, children growing up in similar environments experience it differently. In short, growing up in a multicultural environment increases the likelihood of internalizing cultural diversity and of developing high cognitive complexity, but there is no certainty that this will occur. The cognitive development of individuals involves a high degree of chance and contingency (Edelman and Gally, 2001; Greenspan, 2001a; 2001b).

At one level, this poses a great difficulty for scientific work at the laboratory level. Replication is at the heart of the scientific enterprise. But at a very deep level, each scientist tends to see the same experiment in a very different way – even when repeated over and over – though very often the differences are extremely small. If two scientists, each with a mind having high levels of cognitive complexity and scientific diversity, can work together, there is much greater potential that because of their intense interaction, they may understand complex phenomena in novel ways. Because each mind experiences stimuli in very different ways, one of the great challenges to a scientist is to translate personal knowledge to codified knowledge, to communicate what is observed in one mind to a larger community (Judson, 2004: 39–40; Polanyi, 1962; 1966).

Individuals who have high cognitive complexity tend to have the capacity to understand the phenomena they study in multiple ways. They are rarely of 'one mind' about a problem. Because of their capacity to understand things in multiple ways, they often engage in paradoxical thinking (Dempsey, 1996; Minsky, 1995). And it is the result of this capacity to see things in very complex and novel ways that the scientific community occasionally labels as a major discovery (Hollingsworth *et al.*, 2008).

When I confront the question of whether my findings and hypotheses about high cognitive complexity and major discoveries are consistent with recent trends in neuroscience, it is necessary to place some constraints on the answer to such a problem. The scientific field broadly labelled neuroscience as extremely heterogeneous, consisting of dozens if not several hundred sub-specialities. However, my findings and hypotheses about the complexity of experiences, high cognitive complexity and major discoveries are consistent with the work of a number of theoretically oriented neuroscientists who are very macro-oriented and who attempt to understand the interconnections among multiple parts of the brain (Dalton, 2002: chapters 9 and 10; Dempsey, 1996; Edelman, 1987; 1989; 1992; Hayek, 1952; Rizzello, 1997; 2003).

Concluding Observations

The research reported herein is a small part of a large-scale, multi-level research project which attempts to understand why societies, organizations and within organizations, departments and laboratories vary in having major breakthroughs in basic biomedical science. This project is based on many years of research about these multiple levels throughout the twentieth century in the countries of Britain, France, Germany and the US. This essay has focused only at one of these levels – essentially the laboratory – and even there the focus has not been on the structure of the laboratory but on some of the personal characteristics of those associated most intimately with the making of major discoveries in basic biomedical science. Table 8.4 is somewhat broader in that it also includes a few scientists in physics and mathematics who also attained high distinction in science.

The reader should recognize that whenever one is writing historically about the psychology or social psychology of individuals or collections of individuals, the data are much less ideal than the data to which the psychologist has access in the laboratory or the clinic. In this essay, the data is retrospective in nature and is obtained from many sources. While the author has interviewed more than 450 individuals in connection with the larger multi-level, cross-temporal and cross-national research project, he has interviewed less than 25 per cent of the individuals on whom data is reported herein. As suggested previously, most of the data was obtained from the various types of sources discussed above.

This essay is heuristic in nature, written in the spirit of suggesting an agenda for further research about the kinds of individuals associated with the making of major discoveries. Hopefully, others will follow up with similar studies involving other fields of science and will subject the views presented herein to critical analysis. It is through the interactive process of proposing new ideas and subjecting them to rigorous testing that we may make fundamental advances in science. This essay is essentially at the stage of hypothesis and/or theory generation. As McDonagh (2000: 678) emphasizes, good dialogue in science requires that generalizations be replicated by researchers independent of the proponent of new ideas before the scientific community at large accepts the arguments as valid.

The essay has implications for those interested in the most effective way of organizing science in order to maximize the potential for major discoveries. Our research has identified the sociological properties associated with laboratories where major discoveries have occurred in basic biomedical science. But as this essay emphasizes, major discoveries are rare events. A scientist may design a laboratory with all the characteristics of a Type A lab and yet no major discovery may occur. The kind of mind of the scientist who makes a major discovery is a major factor in the explanation of the discovery process, and our knowledge of this subject has hitherto been underdeveloped. This essay attempts to contribute to the understanding of the kinds of minds associated with major discoveries.

At one level, the insights which this essay sheds on the process of discovery are somewhat discouraging. I have found that the minds of great discoverers tend to evolve in an unplanned, chaotic, somewhat random process involving a considerable amount of chance, luck and contingency. Cognitive complexity cannot be imparted in the classroom or curriculum by pedagogical technique. No matter how much we invest in training the young scientist to be excellent, this essay suggests that in the final analysis, it is idiosyncratic characteristics operating at the individual level which are decisive in determining who will make the major discovery. On the other hand, the individual who internalizes all the factors consistent with high degrees of innovativeness is unlikely to be very innovative without the opportunity to be in the structural and cultural environments where the scientist's potential can be realized (Hollingsworth and Hollingsworth, 2000). In the final analysis, those responsible for recruiting scientists would be well advised to give high consideration to individuals with high cognitive complexity.

Endnotes

1 Earlier versions of this essay were presented as lectures at the Neurosciences Institute in La Jolla, California; at the conference on Dewey, Hayek and Embodied Cognition: Experience, Beliefs and Rules, at the American Institute for Economic Research in Great Barrington Massachusetts; at the Society for Advancement of Socio-Economics Annual Meeting in Aix-en-Provence, France; and at the Atlanta Conference on Science and Technology Policy 2006: US-EU Policies for Research and Innovation. But it was Margie Mendell and her colleagues in Montreal in the Research Center on Social Innovations who provided the opportunity to write this essay while I was a visiting professor at the University of Québec in the fall of 2004.

2 My collaborators in the original study of discoveries and their organizational contexts were Jerald Hage and Ellen Jane Hollingsworth. Without their assistance this essay would not have been possible. David Gear's assistance in the larger project as well as in the research for and writing of this essay has been virtually indispensable. Ellen Jane Hollingsworth and David Gear kindly read multiple drafts of the essay and did much to improve it. Marcel Fournier and Arnaud Sales also made useful comments on an earlier draft. Katharine Rosenberry discussed the subject of creativity with me at length, and those discussions were very helpful in clarifying my thoughts on the subject. Much of the inspiration for this essay came from the work of Robert Root-Bernstein. His previous work about the achievements of scientists in various domains has been especially helpful. Over the years, my colleagues at the Neurosciences Institute in La Jolla, California, particularly Dr. Gerald Edelman, have taught me a great deal about neuroscience.

3 Some years ago, my colleague Jerald Hage first introduced me to the concept cognitive complexity, though subsequently he has used the concept somewhat differently from the way it is operationalized in this essay (see Hage and Powers, 1992; on cognitive complexity, also see Ceci and Liker, 1986; Conway *et al.*, 2001; Schaller, 1994).

4 In recent years we have had a number of excellent studies of single laboratories in basic biomedical science: Holmes, 1993; 2001; Kleinman, 2003; Latour, 1987; Rheinberger, 1997. But very few of these studies have been comparative in nature, and the authors have not developed theoretical generalizations about the types of individuals associated with particular types of laboratories. Thus, our research on laboratories departs from much of the existing literature.

5 More than 90 per cent of the individuals in this table had two Jewish parents. Also listed are a few individuals who had one parent who was Jewish and one who was not. Several (e.g. Karl Landsteiner and Gerty Cori) converted from Judaism to Catholicism. For purposes of this essay, this kind of issue is not highly relevant, for the concern is whether the individual internalized multiple cultures. Anyone who reads the biographies of Landsteiner (Rous, 1945; Speiser and Smekal, 1975) or Cori (McGrayne, 1993) will observe that they clearly internalized multiple cultures – partly because of their Jewish ancestry. For additional information on this subject, see Hargittai (2002).

6 For a thorough treatment of biological scientists under the Nazis, see Deichmann (1996).

7 Obviously, there were very innovative Polish Jews. An interesting case was the career of the Polish-born Nobel laureate Andrew Schally who was Jewish but whose father was a professional soldier who later became a major general in the Allied forces during the Second World War. The example of Schally is clear evidence that even in a culture where there is extreme discrimination, under certain circumstances it is possible for an individual to internalize the society's multiple cultures (Acker, 1991; Wade, 1981).

8 In the preparation of the material for Table 8.4, I am not only indebted to all of the individuals whom I interviewed for this essay (see references below) but especially to the scholarship of Robert Scott Root-Bernstein and to the following published references: Brandmüller and Claus, 1982; Curtin, 1982; Eiduson, 1962; Furguson, 1977; Hammond, 1985; Hindle, 1981; Kassler, 1982; Lepage, 1961; Levarie, 1980; Miller, 1984; Nachmansohn, 1979; Nickles, 1980; Nye, 2004; Ostwald, 1912; Rauscher and Shaw, 1998; Ritterbush, 1968; Roe, 1951; 1953; Root-Bernstein, 1989; Root-Bernstein and Root-Bernstein, 1999; Sime, 1996; Van't Hoff, 1967; Waddington, 1969; Wechsler, 1978.

9 Weisskopf uses the concept complementarity in the sense that Neils Bohr occasionally spoke about the subject. For further discussion on this issue, see Hollingsworth and Gear (2004).

10 There has been considerable controversy about the effect of birth order on the behaviour of children. Even so, there is considerable literature which demonstrates that birth order within families influences the behaviour of children. See *Politics and the Life Sciences* (2000) for an extensive discussion of the literature on the subject. Also, see Dalton (2004).

References

Published Sources

Acker, C. (1991) 'Andrew Victor Schally', in F. N. Magill (ed.), *The Nobel Prize Winners: Physiology or Medicine.* Vol. 3. Pasadena, CA: Salem Press, pp. 1271–79.

Ben-David, J. (1991) *Scientific Growth: Essays on the Social Organization and Ethos of Science.* Edited and with an introduction by G. Freudenthal. Berkeley, CA: University of California Press.

Black, Sir J. W. (1988) 'Sir James W. Black – Autobiography', http://nobelprize.org/medicine/ laureates/1988/black-autobio.html. Accessed 21 September 2004.

Brandmüller, J. and Claus, R. (1982) 'Symmetry: Its Significance in Science and Art', *Interdisciplinary Science Reviews*, 7: 296–308.

Cacioppo, J. T., Petty, R. E., Feinstein, J. and Jarvis, B. (1996) 'Dispositional Differences in Cognitive Motivation: The Life and Times of Individuals Varying in Need for Cognition', *Psychological Bulletin*, 119: 197–253.

Ceci, S. J. and Liker, J. K. (1986) 'A Day at the Races: A Study of IQ, Expertise, and Cognitive Complexity', *Journal of Experimental Psychology: General*, 115: 255–66.

Clark, R. (1971) *Einstein: The Life and Times.* New York: World Publishing.

Cole, J. R. and Cole, S. (1973) *Social Stratification in Science.* Chicago, IL: University of Chicago Press.

Conway, III, L. G., Schaller, M., Tweed, R. G. and Hallett, D. (2001) 'The Complexity of Thinking across Cultures: Interactions between Culture and Situational Context', *Social Cognition*, 19(3): 228–50.

Csikszentmihalyi, M. (1996) *Creativity: Flow and the Psychology of Discovery and Invention.* New York: Harper Collins.

Curtin, D. W. (1982) *The Aesthetic Dimension of Science: 1980 Nobel Conference.* New York: Philosophical Library.

Dalton, R. (2004) 'Quarrel over Book Leads to Call for Misconduct Inquiry', *Nature*, 431: 889.

Dalton, T. C. (2002) *Becoming John Dewey: Dilemmas of a Philosopher and Naturalist.* Bloomington, IN: Indiana University Press.

Deichmann, U. (1996) *Biologists under Hitler.* Translated by T. Dunlap. Cambridge, MA: Harvard University Press.

Dempsey, G. T. (1996) 'Hayek's Evolutionary Epistemology, Artificial Intelligence, and the Question of Free Will', *Evolution and Cognition*, 2(2): 139–50. Also available at www.cato.org/pubs/wtpapers/ hayekee.html. Accessed 15 November 2004.

Dogan, M. and Pahre, R. (1989) 'Hybrid Fields in the Social Sciences', *International Social Science Journal*, 121(1): 457–70.

Dogan, M. and Pahre, R. (1990) *Creative Marginality: Innovation at the Intersections of Social Sciences.* Boulder, CO: Westview Press.

Edelman, G. M. (1987) *Neural Darwinism: The Theory of Neuronal Group Selection.* New York: Basic Books.

Edelman, G. M. (1989) *The Remembered Present: A Biological Theory of Consciousness.* New York: Basic Books.

Edelman, G. M. (1992) *Bright Air, Brilliant Fire: On the Matter of the Mind.* New York: Basic Books.

Edelman, G. M. (1994) 'The Evolution of Somatic Selection: The Antibody Tale', *Genetics*, 128: 975–81.

Edelman, G. M. (2004) *Wider than the Sky: The Phenomenal Gift of Consciousness.* New Haven, CT/London: Yale University Press.

Edelman, G. M. and Gally, J. A. (2001) 'Degeneracy and Complexity in Biological Systems', *Proceedings of the National Academy of Sciences USA*, 98: 13763–68.

Edelman, G. M. and Tononi, G. (2000) *A Universe of Consciousness: How Matter Becomes Imagination.* New York: Basic Books.

Eiduson, B. T. (1962) *Scientists: Their Psychological World.* New York: Basic Books.

Friedman, R. M. (2001) *The Politics of Excellence: Behind the Nobel Prize in Science.* New York: Henry Holt and Company.

Furguson, E. (1977) 'The Mind's Eye: Nonverbal Thought in Technology', *Science*, 197: 827–36.

Goldstein, J. L. (1997) 'Comments and Acceptance Speeches, The 1997 Awards', www.laskerfoundation. org/awards/library/1997b_pp.shtml. Accessed 2 November 2002.

Goldstein, J. L. (2002) 'Comments and Acceptance Speeches, The 2002 Awards', www.lasker foundation.org/awards/library/2002_gold_intro.shtml. Accessed 21 March 2002.

Gould, S. J. (1989) *Wonderful Life: The Burgess Shale and the Nature of History.* New York: W. W. Norton.

Greenspan, R. (2001a) 'Biology, History, and Individuality', *Nimrod International Literary Journal*, 45: 141–51.

Greenspan, R. (2001b) 'The Flexible Genome', *Nature Review: Genetics*, 2: 383–87.

Grigorenko, E. L. (2000) 'Cognitive Styles: Intelligence', in A. E. Kazdin (ed.), *Encyclopedia of Psychology*. New York: Oxford University Press, pp. 163–65.

Grigorenko, E. L. and Sternberg, R. J. (1995) 'Thinking Styles', in D. H. Saklofske and M. Zeidner (eds), *International Handbook of Personality and Intelligence*. New York: Plenum Press, pp. 205–29.

Hage, J. and Powers, C. (1992) *Post-industrial Lives*. Newbury Park, CA: Sage.

Hammond, A. L. (ed.) (1985) *A Passion to Know: Twenty Profiles in Science*. New York: Scribner.

Hargittai, I. (2002) *Candid Science II*. London: Imperial College Press.

Hayek, F. (1952) *The Sensory Order: An Inquiry into the Foundations of Theoretical Psychology*. London: Routledge/Kegan Paul.

Hindle, B. (1981) *Emulation and Invention*. New York: New York University Press.

Hoffmann, R. (1981) 'Autobiography', in *Les Prix Nobel*. Stockholm: Nobel Foundation, pp. 168–72. Also available at www.nobel.se/chemistry/laureates/1981/hoffmann-autobio.html. Accessed 27 May 2004.

Hoffmann, R. (1995) *The Same and Not the Same*. New York: Columbia University Press.

Hollingsworth, J. R. (2004) 'Institutionalizing Excellence in Biomedical Research: The Case of Rockefeller University', in D. H. Stapleton (ed.), *Creating a Tradition of Biomedical Research: Contributions to the History of The Rockefeller University*. New York: The Rockefeller University Press, pp. 17–63.

Hollingsworth, J. R. (2006) 'A Path Dependent Perspective on Institutional and Organizational Factors Shaping Major Scientific Discoveries', in J. Hage and M. Meeus (eds), *Innovation, Science, and Institutional Change*. Oxford: Oxford University Press, pp. 423–42.

Hollingsworth, J. R. and Gear, D. (2004) 'The "Paradoxical Nature" of Complementarity in the Quest for a Research Agenda on Institutional Analysis', paper prepared for Workshop on Complementarity at Max Plank Institute for Study of Societies, Cologne, Germany, 26–27 March, 2004.

Hollingsworth, J. R. and Hollingsworth, E. J. (2000) 'Major Discoveries and Biomedical Research Organizations: Perspectives on Interdisciplinarity, Nurturing Leadership, and Integrated Structure and Cultures', in P. Weingart and N. Stehr (eds), *Practising Interdisciplinarity*. Toronto: University of Toronto Press, pp. 215–44.

Hollingsworth, J. R., Hollingsworth, E. J. and Hage, J. (eds) (2008, forthcoming) *The Search for Excellence: Organizations, Institutions, and Major Discoveries in Biomedical Science*. New York: Cambridge University Press.

Holmes, F. L. (1993) *Hans Krebs: Architect of Intermediary Metabolism, 1933–1937*. Vol. II. New York: Oxford University Press.

Holmes, F. L. (2001) *Meselson, Stahl, and the Replication of DNA: A History of 'The Most Beautiful Experiment in Biology'*. New Haven, CT: Yale University Press.

Howes, R. H. (1991) 'Rosalyn S. Yalow', in F. N. Magill (ed.), *The Nobel Prize Winners: Physiology or Medicine, 1969–1990*, Vol. 3. Pasadena, CA: Salem Press, pp. 1282–91.

Jacob, F. (1995) *The Statue Within: An Autobiography*. Translated by F. Philip. Cold Spring Harbor, NY: Cold Spring Harbor Laboratory Press. (This is a republication of the 1988 version by Basic Books.)

Jencks, C., Smith, M., Acland, H., Bane, M. J., Cohen, D., Gintis, H., Heyns, B. and Michelson, S. (1972) *Inequality: A Reassessment of the Effect of Family and Schooling in America*. New York: Basic Books.

JINFO.ORG (2005a) 'Jewish Nobel Prize Winners in Physiology or Medicine', www.jinfo.org/Nobels_Medicine.html (accessed 24 August 2005).

JINFO.ORG (2005b) 'Jewish Nobel Prize Winners in Chemistry', www.jinfo.org/Nobels_Chemistry.html (accessed 24 August 2005).

JINFO.ORG (2005c) 'Jewish Winners of the Lasker Award in Basic Medical Research', www.jinfo.org/Biology_Lasker_Basic.html (accessed 24 August 2005).

JINFO.ORG (2005d) 'Jewish Winners of the Louisa Gross Horwitz Prize', www.jinfo.org/Biology_Horwitz.html (accessed 24 August 2005).

Judson, H. F. (2004) *The Great Betrayal: Fraud in Science*. Orlando, FL: Harcourt, Inc.

Kassler, J. C. (1982) 'Music as a Model in Early Science', *History of Science*, 20: 103–39.

Kleinman, D. L. (2003) *Impure Cultures: University Biology and the World of Commerce*. Madison, WI: University of Wisconsin Press.

Kuhn, T. S. (1962) *The Structure of Scientific Revolutions*. Chicago, IL: University of Chicago Press.

Latour, B. (1987) *Science in Action: How to Follow Scientists and Engineers through Society*. Cambridge, MA: Harvard University Press.

Lepage, G. (1961) *Art and the Scientist*. Bristol: J. Wright.

Levarie, S. (1980) 'Music as a Structural Model', *Journal of Social and Biological Structures*, 3: 237–45.

McDonagh, J. (2000) 'Science without a Degree of Objectivity is Dead', *American Psychologist*, 55: 678.

McGraw, M. B. (1935) *Growth: A Study of Johnny and Jimmy*. New York: Appleton-Century; reprint, New York: Arno Press.

McGrayne, S. (1993) *Nobel Prize Women in Science: Their Lives, Struggles, and Momentous Discoveries*. New York: Birch Lane.

Medawar, P. (1991) *The Threat and the Glory*. Oxford: Oxford University Press.

Merton, R. K. (1973) *The Sociology of Science: Theoretical and Empirical Investigations*. Edited and with an introduction by N. W. Storer. Chicago, IL: University of Chicago Press.

Merton, R. K. and Barber, E. (2004) *The Travels and Adventures of Serendipity: A Study in Sociological Semantics and the Sociology of Science*. Princeton, NJ/Oxford: Princeton University Press.

Miller, A. I. (1984) *Imagery in Scientific Thought: Creating Twentieth Century Physics*. Boston, MA: Birkhäuser.

Minsky, M. (1995) 'Smart Machines', in J. Brockman (ed.), *The Third Culture*. New York: Simon and Schuster, pp. 152–66.

Nachmansohn, D. (1979) *German Jewish Pioneers in Science, 1900–1933: Highlights in Physics, Chemistry, and Biochemistry*. Berlin/New York: Springer-Verlag.

Nickles, T. (ed.) (1980) *Scientific Discovery: Case Studies*. Boston, MA: Kluwer.

Nye, M. J. (2004) *Blackett: Physics, War, and Politics in the Twentieth Century*. Cambridge, MA: Harvard University Press.

Opfell, O. S. (1978) *The Lady Laureates: Women Who Have Won the Nobel Prize*. Metuchen, NJ: Scarecrow Press.

Ostwald, W. (1912) *Les grands hommes*. Paris: E. Flammarion.

Park, R. E. (1937) 'Introduction', in E. V. Stonequist (ed.), *The Marginal Man*. New York: Charles Scribner's Sons, pp. xiii–xviii.

Pelz, D. C. and Andrews, F. M. (1966) *Scientists in Organizations: Productive Climates for Research and Development*. New York: John Wiley.

Polanyi, M. (1962) *Personal Knowledge: Towards a Post-critical Philosophy*. London: Routledge.

Polanyi, M. (1966) *The Tacit Dimension*. London, UK: Routledge/Kegan Paul.

Politics and the Life Sciences (2000), 19(2): 135–245.

Rauscher, F. H. and Shaw, G. L. (1998) 'Key Components of the Mozart Effect', *Perceptual and Motor Skills*, 86: 835–41.

Rheinberger, H.-J. (1997) *Toward a History of Epistemic Things: Synthesizing Proteins in the Test Tube*. Stanford, CA: Stanford University Press.

Ritterbush, P. C. (1968) *The Art of Organic Forms*. Washington, DC: Smithsonian Institution Press.

Rizzello, S. (1997) 'The Microfoundations of Path-dependency', in L. Magnusson and J. Ottosson (eds), *Evolutionary Economics and Path Dependence*. Cheltenham: Edward Elgar, pp. 98–118.

Rizzello, S. (2003) 'Knowledge as a Path-dependence Process', unpublished paper presented at the Third Annual Symposium on the Foundations of the Behavioral Sciences at the American Institute for Economic Research, Great Barrington, MA, 18–20 July, 2003.

Roe, A. (1951) 'A Study of Imagery in Research Scientists', *Journal of Personality*, 19: 459–70.

Roe, A. (1953) *The Making of a Scientist*. New York: Dodd, Mead and Company.

Root-Bernstein, R. S. (1989) *Discovering*. Cambridge, MA: Harvard University Press, pp. 312–42.

Root-Bernstein, R. S. (2001) 'Music, Creativity and Scientific Thinking', *Leonardo*, 34(1): 63–8.

Root-Bernstein, R. S. and Root-Bernstein, M. M. (1999) *Sparks of Genius*. Boston, MA: Houghton Mifflin.

Rous, P. (1945) 'Karl Landsteiner', *Obituary Notices of Fellows of the Royal Society*, 5: 295–324.

Schaller, M. (1994) 'The Role of Statistical Reasoning in the Formation, Preservation, and Prevention of Group Stereotypes', *British Journal of Social Psychology*, 33: 47–61.

Sime, R. L. (1996) *Lise Meitner: A Life in Physics*. Berkeley/Los Angeles, CA: University of California Press.

Simmel, G. (1908) 'The Stranger', in K. H. Wolff (ed. and tr.) (1964), *The Sociology of Georg Simmel*. Glencoe, Il/London: Free Press/Collier-Macmillan Limited, pp. 402–8.

Simonton, D. K. (1988) *Scientific Genius: A Psychology of Science*. New York: Cambridge University Press.

Speiser, P. and Smekal, F. S. (1975) *Karl Landsteiner*. Translated by R. Rickett. Vienna: Verlag Brüder Hollinek.

Sternberg, R. J. (1997) *Thinking Styles*. New York: Cambridge University Press.

Sternberg, R. J. (ed.) (1988) *The Nature of Creativity*. New York: Cambridge University Press.

Sternberg, R. J. and Davidson, J. E. (eds) (1995) *The Nature of Insight*. Cambridge, MA: MIT Press.

Stoltzenberg, D. (1994) *Fritz Haber: Chemiker, Nobelpreisträger, Deutscher, Jude*. Weinheim, Germany: VCH Verlagsgesellschaft.

Suedfeld, P. (2000) 'Cognitive Styles: Personality', in A. E. Kazdin (ed.), *Encyclopedia of Psychology*. New York: Oxford University Press, pp. 166–69.

Sulloway, F. J. (1996) *Born to Rebel: Birth Order, Family Dynamics, and Creative Lives*. New York: Pantheon Books.

Suzuki, S. (1969) *Nurtured by Love: A New Approach to Education*. New York: Exposition Press.

Van't Hoff, J. H. (1967) 'Imagination in Science', *Molecular Biology, Biochemistry, and Biophysics*, I: 1–18. Translated by G. F. Springer.

Waddington, C. H. (1969) *Behind Appearance: A Study of the Relations between Painting and the Natural Sciences in This Century*. Edinburgh: Edinburgh University Press.

Wade, N. (1981) *The Nobel Duel*. Garden City, NY: Anchor Press.

Wardell, D. M. and Royce, J. R. (1978) 'Toward a Multi-factor Theory of Styles and their Relationships to Cognition and Affect', *Journal of Personality*, 46: 474–505.

Wechsler, J. (ed.) (1978) *On Aesthetics in Science*. Cambridge, MA: MIT Press.

Weisskopf, V. (1991) *The Joy of Insight: Passions of a Physicist*. New York: Basic Books.

Wilson, E. O. (1994) *Naturalist*. Washington, DC: Island Press.

Zuckerman, H. (1977) *Scientific Elite: Nobel Laureates in the United States*. New York/London: Free Press.

Interviews

David Baltimore, Professor of Biology, Massachusetts Institute of Technology and former President of Rockefeller University. Interview in his MIT office, 28 April 1995.

Paul Berg, Professor of Biochemistry, Stanford University School of Medicine. Interview in his office, 6 May 2003.

Sir James Black, Emeritus Professor of Chemistry, University College, London. Interview at McGill University, Montreal, 23 September 2004.

Günter Blobel, Professor at Rockefeller University and HHMI investigator. Interview in his office, 12 April 1995; Subsequent interviews in his office, 16 March 2001, 18 March 2001, 21 December 2004, 12, 14 March 2007.

Konrad Bloch, Higgins Professor Emeritus of Biochemistry, Harvard University. Interview in his office, 25 April 1995.

Sydney Brenner, Professor, Salk Institute, and Former Director of Laboratory of Molecular Biology, Cambridge, UK. Interview in La Jolla, CA, 7 April 2003.

Francis Crick, President Emeritus and Distinguished Professor, Salk Institute; former scientist at Cambridge University and at the Laboratory of Molecular Biology. Interview in his office in San Diego, 6 March 1996 and 11 March 1998. Interview at UCSD, 6 June 2002.

Thomas C. Dalton, Professor, California Polytechnic State University, San Luis Obispo, California. Interview by phone, 18 November 2004.

Renato Dulbecco, Emeritus President and Distinguished Professor, Salk Institute; Former Professor California Institute of Technology. Interview in his office in San Diego, 23 February 1996. Second interview in his office, 22 May 2000.

Gerald Edelman, Research Director, The Neurosciences Institute, San Diego, California and former Professor and Dean, Rockefeller University. Interviews in Klosters, Switzerland, 17 January 1995, and at Neurosciences Institute, 13 January, 16 January, 19 January, 30 January, 14 February, 20 February, 22 February, 5 March, 16 March, 17 March 1996; 12 February 1998; 4 April, 11 April, 18 November 2000. Interview by phone, 3 April 2001.

Gertrude Elion, Scientist Emeritus, The Wellcome Research Laboratories, Research Triangle Park. Interview in her office, 17 March 1995.

Walter Gilbert, Carl M. Loeb University Professor at Harvard University. Interview in Chicago, 14 October 1993. Interview in his office at Harvard University, 26 April 1995.

Joseph Goldstein, Professor, Department of Molecular Genetics, University of Texas Southwestern Medical Center. Interview at Rockefeller University, 13 March 2007.

Paul Greengard, Professor at Rockefeller University. Interview in his office, 16 May 2001.

Eric R. Kandel, Director of Center for Neurophysiology and HHMI Investigator, Columbia University School of Physicians and Surgeons, member of Board of Trustees, Rockefeller University. Interview at Columbia University, 19 April 2001.

Aaron Klug, former Director, Laboratory of Molecular Biology (LMB), Cambridge England, President of the Royal Society, Honorary Fellow of Trinity College. Interview by telephone, 24 May 1999. Interview in his office at LMB, 11 July 2000. Interview at Trinity College, Cambridge, 3 April 2002.

Arthur Kornberg, Emeritus Professor of Biochemistry, Stanford University School of Medicine (Nobel laureate in Physiology or Medicine, 1959). Interview in his office, 5 May 2003.

Joshua Lederberg, President Emeritus, Rockefeller University. Former Chair, Medical Genetics, Stanford University School of Medicine and former Professor of Genetics, University of Wisconsin, Madison. Interviews at Rockefeller University, 16 September 1993, 13 April 1995; interview by telephone, 27 August 1999, interviews in his office, 25 January 2001, 4 April 2001.

Rita Levi-Montalcini, Professor Emeritus of Biology, Washington University, St. Louis. Interview at her home in Rome, Italy, 15 June 1995.

Dan Nathans, Professor, Department of Molecular Biology and Genetics, Johns Hopkins University, Baltimore. Interview in his office, 21 July 1997.

Paul Nurse, President, Rockefeller University. Interviews in his office, 23 December 2004, 13 March 2007.

Max Perutz, former Director, Laboratory of Molecular Biology, Cambridge, England. Interview at Peterhouse College, 15 March 1997; interview at Laboratory of Molecular Biology, 11 June 1999.

John Polanyi, Professor, University of Toronto. Interview at the Center for Advanced Cultural Studies, Essen Germany, 5 September 2001.

Howard Temin, Professor in McArdle Cancer Laboratory, University of Wisconsin, Madison. Interview at McArdle Cancer Laboratory, 26 November 1993.

Harold Varmus, Director of the National Institutes of Health and former Professor at University of California, San Francisco. Interview in his office, Bethesda, Maryland, 6 March 1995.

Torsten N. Wiesel, President, Rockefeller University. Interviews in his office, 14 April 1995, 14 July 1997, 7 February 2001, 4 May 2001, 25 May 2001.

Edward O. Wilson, Pellegrino University Professor and Curator of Entomology, Museum of Comparative Zoology, Harvard University. Interviews in his office, 4 May 1995, 17 December 2002.

9

The Creativity of Intellectual Networks and the Struggle over Attention Space

By Randall Collins

Creativity takes place in networks. There is of course a large research literature on networks. But we immediately encounter a problem in relating this literature to intellectual networks. There are two main substantive theories. The first concerns dense networks – that is to say, networks in which almost everyone is connected to everyone else. This makes for a tightly linked community. Dense networks are sometimes called 'support groups', since they are correlated with higher levels of mental health, greater longevity and other social benefits (Wasserman and Galaskiewicz, 1994). From a cultural viewpoint, they are the type of networks which have the greatest degree of conformity and the least individuality, what Emile Durkheim called mechanical solidarity.

The other main pattern in social network theory is what is called 'holes in networks', or sometimes 'the strength of weak ties' (Burt, 1992). Here the emphasis is on places where there are few network ties. The individual who uniquely has access to a distant network – occupying the bridge between different networks – has a competitive advantage, because he or she is the only one to get the information or resources that flow across that bridge. Bridge ties or holes in networks are important especially for economic success, such as making a career in business management, or for organizations entering a new market before their competitors.

The problem is that neither of these two patterns – dense support networks, or bridges across holes in networks – fit very well for the kind of networks I am concerned with, which are intellectual networks. Networks appear to operate differently in different institutional arenas; I will speak mainly about intellectual networks but we should be aware that economic and political networks seem to operate on yet different principles still.

The patterns that I will describe come from a study of philosophers in China, Japan, India, ancient Greece, the medieval Islamic world and medieval and modern Europe. This may seem like an impossibly large task; what made it manageable was that I have concentrated first of all on the networks that connected the important philosophers with each other. For more detail I refer you to my book *The Sociology of Philosophies* (Collins, 1998).

The Clustering of Creativity in Networks

Eminent intellectuals cluster together more closely than lower-ranking intellectuals do. Here I am measuring eminence by the amount of influence they exert on future generations, indexed by how much attention they receive in the writings of their successors, and the space they get in histories of the field. Thus I distinguish between major thinkers, secondary and minor. This clustering together by eminence occurs in two different dimensions: vertically across time, and horizontally within their own generation.

Vertically, the higher ranking, more influential intellectuals are more likely to have eminent teachers and pupils; and since intellectual parentage, unlike for people in their ordinary capacities, does not require exactly two parents, one may have just one intellectual parent, or many. Students who are going to become eminent tend to have several important teachers. And these ties concatenate across generations, giving rise to lineages of star grandteachers, great-grandteachers and so on. In all these ways, the more eminent intellectuals have more ties to other eminent intellectuals than less eminent ones do.

Horizontally, intellectuals who are going to become eminent tend to have close ties to others who are also going to become eminent. They often make up groups of youthful friends, such as the circle that formed around Jean-Paul Sartre in the 1920s and 1930s when they were studying for their various exams, a group which included Simone de Beauvoir, Merleau-Ponty, Raymond Aron (who was Sartre's roommate at the Ecole Normale Superieure) and Jacque Lacan. Another such group existed in London in the 1850s through the 1870s, and included Herbert Spencer, T. H. Huxley and Mary Ann Evans (who took the pen name George Eliot). Sometimes these groups had formal names and meetings, like the so-called Apostles at Cambridge, which at the turn of the twentieth century included Whitehead, Russell, More, Keynes and McTaggart; or *Die Freien* – the Free ones – who met in a Berlin coffee house in the late 1830s and early 1840s and included Marx, Engels and the anarchist Max Stirner. Horizontal ties could include both friends and enemies; indeed, as we shall see in a moment, there is a structural reason why these ties should create enmities.

To repeat: the more eminent the intellectual, the more ties he or she has with other eminent intellectuals, both vertically across the generations, both backwards to their teachers and grandteachers, and forward to their own protégés; and horizontally, in direct personal acquaintanceship, as well as conflict, with other intellectuals who are also in the process of becoming historically famous. And the two kinds of network ties further concatenate, since horizontal ties lead to further indirect ties to the previous generation as well as further outwards among contemporaries. Those who become most eminent come from the places in the networks where both past eminence and prospective eminence is most densely clustered.

Now this leads us to some critical issues. Perhaps all this is a banality. After all, isn't everybody linked to everybody anyway, if we allow indirect links? American researchers have studied what is called the 'small world problem': they claim to show that any person can connect to any other person in the United States within six links, as documented in studies using postcards sent from one link to the next (Milgram 1967; see Watts 2003). I have some doubts about the methodology of these 'small-world' studies; and further, they do not bear on the point of how intellectual networks operate. For one thing, studies of rumour, in which a chain of people repeat a message from one person to the next, show that the message becomes quite garbled within a few links. High-quality intellectual influences would hardly survive a six-link network structure. Moreover, intellectual networks do not just connect anyone to anyone else – it is not a matter of Wittgenstein's landlady shopping at the same butcher as Russell's landlord – but that Wittgenstein and Russell know each other personally and engage in intense intellectual exchanges. If we restrict the network to those who are actually engaged in intellectual discourse, the differences are quite clear: the more eminent intellectuals are more closely tied to each other than less eminent intellectuals are to the more eminent – accumulate more eminence both directly and indirectly than less eminent intellectuals do. When Martin Heidegger, himself a pupil of Husserl, has an affair with a student named Hannah Arendt, something is flowing through these networks that is distinctive to intellectual creativity; intellectual success breeds success, in more ways than one.

Hark back now to the main substantive theories of network research: Intellectuals do not operate like economic networks; their success does not come from loose networks full of holes where they can be the unique bridge from one isolated network to another. Intellectual networks more resemble dense networks, where most people know each other. The trouble is that such networks produce not innovation, but conformity – at least among non-intellectuals – the like-minded-thinking characteristic of the closed fraternity, the club, the small town and the tribal clan. What is it that intellectual networks do that is different?

Let us add one more problem. If intellectual networks operate by the principle, 'eminence attracts eminence', doesn't this beg the question of what causes what? I have already noted that many intellectual ties start early in life, before anyone has done the work that will make them famous: Hegel, Schelling and Hölderlin were roommates together before they met Fichte and were introduced to Idealist philosophy; Whitehead was Russell's mathematics teacher before either of them started the kind of work that would make them famous philosophers. Young Karl Marx used to walk around the streets of Paris with poet Heinrich Heine. How does future fame attract future fame? Another version of the same problem is visible when we note that the bigger the intellectual star, the more eminence he/she has both upstream – in previous generations of predecessors – and downstream – among his/her followers. How can the future create the present?

The answer, I suggest, is to reconceptualize the nature of intellectual creativity. Perform a gestalt switch: instead of conceiving of a series of individual thinkers, conceive of the network itself as the actor on the intellectual stage. That is to say, individuals do not have qualities – as intellectuals – before they encounter the network; it is the network which allocates positions for them and makes them what they are. I am well aware of the criticism, raised by analytical philosophers that a network is nothing but a set of connections among individuals; hence it cannot be an actor, and it is the individuals that make the network do whatever it does. But this is confusing individual human bodies with their minds and actions; although I cannot here go into the full sociological evidence, intellectuals are charged up by interactions in their network, in their thoughts, concepts, techniques of thinking and arguing, as well as in their ambitions, energies and emotions. Individuals are not fixed essences – least of all intellectual individuals – but are, so to speak, programmed from the outside. Nor is this a once-for-all, fixed program, an initial socialization, so that the intellectual after a period of schooling is programmed like a wind-up doll that will go on thereafter producing certain kinds of ideas. Ideas and currents of emotional energy flow in networks, from one generation to another, and horizontally among contemporaries who put certain of these ideas in the centre of attention. And this is an emergent process: confrontations in the network rearrange these ideas, foster new points of attention and rearrange all the positions at the same time. The so-called great thinkers, the famous names of subsequent history, are those who are in those places in the networks where these transformations take place. In this sense, the great thinkers are those who get credit for what happens in the network, who come to symbolize what the network has done.

The Law of Small Numbers

We see this collective character of creativity in what I call the 'law of small numbers'. If there is any creativity, any important intellectual innovation within a generation, there are typically three to six rival positions appearing simultaneously. There is never one single towering figure who dominates a generation, but always rival innovators who appear at the same time.

The Vienna Circle of logical positivists is contemporary with the phenomenology and existentialism of Husserl and Heidegger; and this kind of pattern is found throughout world history. We see the same thing in terms of networks: there are typically between three to six rival lineages which carry on across the generations during a time of creative intellectual activity. The law of small numbers is demonstrated by what happens when it is violated: if the upper limit of six positions is exceeded, some of the innovators fail to find continuers in the following generation; their lineages break off. An intellectual field is an attention space with only a limited amount of room in it. If there are too many positions – more than six, and indeed often, more than three or four – some of them fail to attract attention. It does not matter how much substantive value there is in their innovations, how creative their new positions; the field acting as audience or attention space cannot clearly focus on all of them, and some of them drop out, and fail to make it into historical memory as important creations.

An intellectual field, then, is a limited attention space, in which creativity occurs by conflict among rival positions. This is why there never occurs a single, major position, without contemporary rivals. If a single position holds sway, reproducing itself as a single lineage – such as has happened at various times, for example, in the history of Chinese philosophy, there is no creativity but only intellectual tradition. Each new position is created in a field of argument; each time the field of argument is transformed, several new positions appear on rival sides. If two positions are created, a third is always possible, by a stance of plague on both houses; and since lines of argument are generally multidimensional, it is possible to combine elements in various ways to create a fourth and fifth position, and indeed several more. But too much recombination of intellectual elements makes for a crowded and murky attention space; it appears to contemporaries as a cacophony of positions, and a mood of scepticism tends to prevail until the attention space is simplified in the following generations.

Intellectual creativity occurs, not simply by solving problems and making discoveries, but by creating problems. The major historical changes across intellectual generations happen when new topics are formulated, new tools of argument are established; these generate a space on which the new generation of intellectuals, coming from the existing lineages, can take rival positions. Thus when Kant formulated the transcendental method, of arguing in terms of what presuppositions must be necessary for an idea to be formulated in the first place, he opened up a problem space into which rushed an array of idealist, and eventually anti-idealist, philosophers. Again in the early twentieth century, the movement to develop the foundations of mathematics from logic gave rise not only to a range of logicist philosophies of the type promoted by Russell, but a dispute over whether the nature of language itself could be encompassed by the tools of formal logic, thus generating an ordinary language movement as well. I am simplifying both of these intellectual situations, of course, since there were several other strands which played into the philosophical fields in those generations; but these complications would reinforce the point that the intellectual field moves onward by dividing up into rival camps around the same complex of problems.

Intellectuals depend on their rivals, whether explicitly or only tacitly and unconsciously, for the lines of dispute which attract the most attention and force them to marshal the tools of discourse most acutely.

Cultural Capital and Emotional Energy

We are now in a position to understand what it is that star pupils get from their star teachers. As we have noted, the vertical pattern of intellectual networks is for eminence to be passed along from teacher to pupil across the generations. But pupils cannot merely be acquiring substantive knowledge from their teachers; one does not become a major intellectual simply by acquiring what Bourdieu calls 'cultural capital'. To learn and repeat what one's eminent teacher has taught does not make one an eminent intellectual, but only a follower; without departing from one's teacher's position, one is swallowed up in his/her reputation. What then is the advantage that comes from being in the heart of the network, close to the teachers who have made the previous round of innovations? Two advantages: first, star pupils acquire a sense of what it is like to be on the forefront of a fight; they learn the orientation of their teachers in dealing with rivals, and in pushing the level of argument to its most acute. Being initiated at the core of the old scenes of battle gives a first-hand sense that is not visible from a distance, and that cannot be transmitted merely by reading books; it is a sense of the level of abstraction at which arguments are pitched, and the degree of reflexive consciousness of what is at stake. What one acquires at the core of the older networks is a sense of intellectual sophistication.

The second advantage of learning from the eminent players of the previous generation, by sound of voice and face to face, is not so much strictly cognitive as emotional. The great teachers make an impression, above all by the tone in which they deliver their teachings: sometimes it is quite literally their tone of voice, their idiosyncrasies and habits in lecture hall or seminar room. Wittgenstein was a living legend among Cambridge students, for the bizarreness of his behaviour in seminars, his obliviousness to ordinary amenities, his fits of silence, his sudden torrents. Whatever the specific features, the great teachers impress by their seriousness – treating intellectual life as a realm far above ordinary concerns. And they impress by their concentration, by the energy they put into the world of abstractions in which they live. I have said above that the intellectual field is an attention space of concentrated argument; by viewing the persons who live at the highpoints inside that space, we find that it is also a space of emotional energy. It is a kind of Durkheimian collective effervescence, prolonged and perpetuated as arguments are carried on at the core of a network; a portion of that effervescence is embodied in the so-called great thinkers who are at the centre of the action. Thus part of what can make a pupil into a future star is a process of contagion, taking on the emotional energy of their teachers, taking on their seriousness, their concentration, their elevation of their intellectual work into a quasi-religious realm.

The result of this transmission of emotional energy is the peculiar alternation between social contact and solitary work which is characteristic of intellectuals. Major thinkers generally begin in the heart of the networks; which is to say they are connected by those intense gatherings with other major intellectuals that precede and accompany them; in due course they become teachers in their own right who are intensely followed by others. But in between these intellectual gatherings, there are long periods of inwardness. The dominant intellectuals throughout history have generally been fanatically attentive to their work; from Socrates to Newton to Wittgenstein and Heidegger there is the pattern of devoting long hours to one's mediations, ignoring the amenities of ordinary life. And leading intellectuals typically produce large amounts of work, far more than they become famous for, sometimes huge numbers of published papers, sometimes huge volumes of notes, or of conversations left to others to transcribe. The star intellectuals are those who take the ideas and techniques passed along in the networks, and concentrate on them most intensely, working through their combinations and oppositions most energetically and ferociously. Thus they rise to the top of the attention space, over the mass of other intellectuals who also populate those networks. It is their heightened emotional energy that puts them out in front of the others; and as they get out in front, the distance steadily widens until a point at which they seem to be different in kind, elevated to the status of 'genius'. In reality, there are immense stretches of hours during which they pore over the stock of ideas available to them; when the great insights come, the gestalt is rearranged, new patterns fall into place, this may happen rapidly, in moments which are mythologized like Newton observing the fall of an apple, but in fact occurring in the midst of a long chain of concentration.

Networks, I have argued, are the actors on the intellectual stage. But networks, for the most part, are not easily visible at a distance; they personify themselves in the names and reputations of a few figures in whose writing and speaking the cultural ingredients passed around in the network find their most convenient form.

The great thinkers, canonized by history and adulated by students, are a concentration, a distillation of what the network has done. Furthermore, I would hold that this is almost literally a description of what goes on in the process of creative thinking when these thinkers retire into their solitude – whether it is Socrates standing guard for an entire night engrossed in his thought, Newton in his chambers amidst his papers, or Wittgenstein in his hut on a Norwegian fjord. The intensely focused thinker, primed by the key arguments of the core networks, is oblivious to the immediately surrounding world because he or she is entrained in the internalized conversations of the network; creativity is a process of making coalitions in one's mind, fitting together arguments that feel successful. To repeat again, from a sociological viewpoint, it is the networks which are carrying out the action, even though at any particular instant the ideas are in someone's brain or being formulated on their tongue or their writing implement. The ideas are passed around, distributed, partitioned, fought over and in the process are transformed into new concepts and new techniques of argument building on older ones. This passing around, this transformation, can be located in the conventional way as the thinking of particular individuals; in the most conventional hero-worshipping way, we truncate the process and notice only the completed ideas expressed by the most famous individuals at the centre of the attention space. As we add more historical detail, as we widen the screen, we see the flow of ideas throughout the network; with our reversed gestalt, we can see the famous individuals, the great thinkers, as the places where the network crystallizes the most important of these processes of changing earlier ideas into newer ones.

This is both a cognitive and an emotional process. Ideas and techniques flow in the network, crystallize in certain hot circles of argument and in the internal conversations of individual minds. Emotions flow in the network as well, indeed, are built up primarily in those times when people are assembled – when the famous teacher is expounding and impressing his or her students as a bundle of energies concentrated on the horizon; when debates erupt; when the circles gather to drink and discuss. The star thinkers are not necessarily smarter or better educated than everyone else; at the cores of intellectual networks, there are no doubt many persons who are both intelligent and well informed, well endowed with elite cultural capital. What separates out those in the process of becoming great are their higher levels of concentration, their emotional energy and their fanatical focus.

I have been advancing a sociological interpretation of why networks of the intellectually eminent breed success at their cores. One dimension of these networks, the vertical lineages from teacher to pupil, passes along a sense of intellectual sophistication, an attunement to arguments at the forefront of an attention space; equally importantly, it passes along the emotional intensity of being at the core, and of treating ideas as quasi-religious objects to which all else is committed. There remains to consider the horizontal dimension of the network, especially the groups of young contemporaries who know each other before they become eminent, who work their way up together into the forefront. What happens in these discussion groups, besides drinking beer and coffee or smoking pipes late into the night? The group situation itself generates a focus of attention on the problem forefront; it heightens the oppositions which are the driving force of transforming the attention space. Being intensely involved in such a group is a way that the young intellectual becomes charged up with an additional fund of emotional energy that goes into solitary work manipulating networks in the interior of one's mind. The two dimensions of networks, vertical and horizontal, are often combined; the members of the youthful group are frequently the pupils of one or more of the major teachers. As for instance in the case of the *Die Freien*, several are pupils of Hegel, Schelling, or Schleiermacher; Marx, who is not a direct student of any of these, is closely connected with their substance and the ethos of their arguments through his association with Bauer, Engels, Stirner and Ruge, who had heard their lectures.

The horizontal group transforms the cognitive problem space, and the focus of emotional energy, in at least two ways. First: these are typically youthful followers of previous network stars; the Berlin coffee-house group was the most organized node of the Young Hegelians, which is really a shorthand for the intermingled networks of the various Idealist philosophers and their early critics such as Feuerbach and D. F. Strauss. Thus the group focuses intense attention upon their teachers, raising them into even greater figures in their minds; the circle operates as a kind of cult engaged in intellectual hero-worship. But, and this is the second process, the hero-figures are also intensely scrutinized; they become transformed into devil-figures, into evil tyrants to be overthrown; or ambivalent father figures, from whom to borrow techniques with which to mount a rebellion. The horizontal group generates the energy, the confidence and enthusiasm, to break with the vertical lineage, which is to say to turn its techniques in a new direction. Here again, we see innovativeness as a collective phenomenon. The spell of famous teachers over their pupils is not easily broken; the group collectively builds up the energy to make the break in the safety of numbers. *Die Freien* mobilized the break from German Idealism into militant materialism. Two generations later, in the sedate chambers of Cambridge, the Apostles discussion group first touted English Idealism, and then was the site of the break from it led by Moore and Russell.

The Structure of Intellectual Conflict

Finally, I want to underline one more aspect of the conflictual nature of intellectual networks. The law of small numbers indicates that several new positions can break with the older generation at the same time; thus there is a structural incentive, or opportunity, for the young rebels to break in different directions, and thus to break with each other. And there is an upper limit, somewhere around three to six positions; beyond this, innovators will not get recognized. But famous teachers have far more than six pupils; and no doubt there are many more youthful discussion groups, drinking their beer and smoking their pipes and arguing late into the night, than the few groups that become famous later on because their youthful members go on to become the central figures of the new attention space. There is what I call a 'structural crunch': there are more candidates than niches for them to be successful in. Many, perhaps most of those individuals who start out in a favourable position, in the core of the old network, will not be able to remain at the core of the new one. The process in which individuals sort themselves out, in the early to mid-phase of their intellectual career, is largely a process of dispersion of emotional energies.

I have argued that ideas and techniques of argument are circulated around in a network; and also that the personal contacts that make up the network, the tones of voice and the facial and bodily demeanour that give a distinctive flavour to encountering dedicated intellectuals in the flesh, generate an intense emotional energy. Although it is natural for us to think of emotions as properties of individuals, it is more fruitful to think of them as energies ebbing and flowing in social encounters. This energy of intellectual life is built up by the network, and is distributed unequally to particular locations in the network. One becomes initiated into the emotional flow of intellectual life, contaminated with it as by a kind of emotional magnetism, by contact with teachers who have it, or sometimes by one's rivals or youthful compatriots. Then, retiring into the interior of one's own mind where intellectual work is done, comes another fateful transformation: creativity hinges on whether the energy grows or dims; whether in the internal conversations of one's mind, one hits upon coalitions in the imaginary representation of the intellectual network, which lead onward to ideas that feel successful; or encounter blocks in the flow of thought, or peter out in the routine of banal everyday thought.

The structural crunch is experienced on the individual level: by some, as a feeling of increased confidence that one's ideas are meeting a favourable reception in the attention space; by others, as a diminishing sense that what one is doing is possible, important, or worthwhile. Those who become the great thinkers are those who get onto the upward path; their ideas become even more important to them, taking on the quasi-religious devotion of sacred objects in collective attention space; they become increasingly energized by their work, more capable of long hours of concentration, more familiar with the experience of shifting the gestalts and feeling them encompass the world in a new pattern. On the other side of the divide, the great majority of young aspirants start to feel themselves upstaged and outdistanced; they lose energy, enthusiasm, they concentrate less, experience fewer breakthroughs. Many soon recognize that their best career path is not to struggle for the centre of the attention, but to attach oneself to some one else's movement, to become a follower, a disciple, a retailer of ideas to the provinces, an applier of established techniques to specialities. Some individuals, of course, occupy the middle ground between incipient stars and confirmed followers; some get minor recognition as secondary figures, interesting sidelights in the more detailed historical accounts; others become isolated, idiosyncratic, getting a local reputation as strange dreamers, stubborn egotists, or embittered cranks.

These are not enduring personality traits; they are positions in the social structure of the intellectual field. The attention space, structured by the law of small numbers, allows a few individuals to become built-up into stars, full of energy, inspired processors of the most sophisticated ideas and techniques passing through the network; others must settle for whatever minor niches are available to them, or to fight it out unsuccessfully in the interstices. Viewed as a whole, in every generation a large population of intelligent young people are initiated by contact with the last generation of intellectual networks; this population becomes winnowed and differentiated as it passes through the structural crunch. Though the cognitive ingredients are a collective pool shared by a large network, the emotional energy of being nearer or farther from the limited points of attention makes individuals quite different in the way they handle their intellectual heritage. Such become elevated to the rank of leading thinker, even genius; others, starting perhaps from very similar locations, are relegated to modest positions in the transforming attention space; their thinking becomes competent, scholarly, uninspiring and conventional. The role of genius, like the role of follower, or of intellectual crank, are masks donned for one's place in the show. Though intellectual history is written in a discourse of individuals, they are only the facade, the glamorous images on the advertisements that surround the theatre; inside, it is truly the networks who are the actors on the stage.

References

Burt, R. S. (1992) *Structural Holes*. Cambridge, MA: Harvard University Press.
Collins, R. (1998) *The Sociology of Philosophies: A Global Theory of Intellectual Change*. Cambridge, MA: Harvard University Press.
Milgram, S. (1967) 'The Small World Problem', *Psychology Today*, 2: 60–67.
Wasserman, S. and Galaskiewicz, J. (1994) *Advances in Social Network Analysis*. London: Sage.
Watts, D. J. (2003) *Six Degrees: The Science of a Connected Age*. New York: Norton.

10

Evaluating Creative Minds: The Assessment of Originality in Peer Review

By Michèle Lamont, Marcel Fournier, Joshua Guetzkow,
Grégoire Mallard and Roxane Bernier

What a good thing Adam had – when he said a good thing, he knew nobody had said it before.

Mark Twain

Introduction

Originality plays a key role in academic research: the main objective of scholarship is to discover something new, to say something that nobody has said before. In psychology, one finds many studies concerning the creative, imaginative, or inventive personality and its early identification (Brockman, 1993; Czikszentmihalyi, 1996; Dervin, 1990; Simonton, 1988). Historians of science often use the term 'genius', or more modestly, the notion of 'divergent thinking' (Kuhn, 1970), to point to innovators and their contributions. Sociologists, for their part, have tended to focus their attention on the social factors that lead to innovation (Collins, 1998). Researchers have largely ignored the question of how scholars assess originality (but see Dirk, 1999). However, as clearly revealed by the most elementary involvement in the scholarly reviewing process, how to recognize originality is a question that looms large in academic evaluation.

The peer review system – a central institution of the scientific world – plays an important role in institutionalizing definitions of 'originality'.[1] Borrowing implicitly or explicitly on the Mertonian (1942/1973) dichotomy between universalism and particularism, previous studies of the peer-review system have been concerned with issues of fairness. They focus their attention on whether judgements about 'irrelevant', particularistic characteristics, such as the author's age and reputation, affect the evaluation of his or her work (Bell, 1992; Cole, 1992; Cole and Cole, 1973; Cole *et al.*, 1978; Dirk, 1999; General Accounting Office, 1994; Liebert, 1976; Merton, 1996; Roy, 1985). The questions posed by these researchers often imply that a pure evaluation would be possible, once particularistic considerations are eliminated. Moreover, these questions imply that judgements about the qualities of the researcher, as opposed to the research itself, are inappropriate and corrupt the peer-review process. In our research, we break with these assumptions and show that qualities imputed to researchers are often central to judgements made about the creativity of their work. To do so, we draw on systematic interviews with individuals serving on American and Canadian funding panels in the social sciences and the humanities to explore how they think and talk about originality.

In taking a cultural approach to the study of peer review, we join a growing line of work in the sociology of knowledge that focuses on the cultural dimensions of knowledge creation (Abbott, 2001; Becher, 1987; Bender and Schorske, 1997; Bourdieu, 1984; Clark, 1983; Wagner *et al.*, 1990). This literature often posits important differences across disciplines. For example, Bourdieu (1984), Knorr-Cetina (1981; 1999) and Somers (1996) examine how the production of knowledge is guided and bounded by the beliefs and practices (in a word, the culture) of disciplines and disciplinary organizations. These authors would lead us to hypothesize that specific beliefs about originality also differ between disciplines. In fact, our interviews suggest weak disciplinary differences in the significance attached to originality.[2]

Bourdieu (1975; 1984) and colleagues (Bourdieu and de Saint-Martin, 1975) are among the few scholars who have examined qualitatively academic evaluation systems. Drawing on the structuralist tradition, they 'read' or identified matrices of hierarchically ordered oppositional categories at work in evaluation processes. Rather than presuming that originality is defined through such binary matrices, we focus on the meaning actually given to originality by panelists, paying particular attention to the types of arguments they deploy when judging originality. Our findings suggest that binary matrices cannot adequately capture the types of arguments scholars make when talking about originality.

Our study also reveals that panelists often conflate the originality of the proposal with qualities of character attributed to researchers themselves – qualities such as integrity, courage, independence and audacity. At the same time, originality is also often identified through the substance of the project itself: the questions it asks, the topic it focuses on, the theory it offers, its research design and the data itself are all elements around which arguments about originality get to be articulated.

Because we find character is key to how originality is conceptualized by panelists, our research resonates with the work of Steven Shapin (1994: xxvii), who, in his study of the evaluation of scientific credibility in seventeenth-century England, shows that judgements about scientific value are often social judgements: a scientist's character (defined in terms of honor, modesty, civility and courtesy)[3] largely determined the extent to which his results were trusted and credibility established. However, our study goes beyond Shapin's. While in his conclusion, he suggests that in the contemporary world, credentials, training and expertise have eclipsed character in establishing trust and credibility – 'Modernity guarantees knowledge not by reference to virtue but to expertise' (1994: 413) –,[4] we show the continuing salience of character in evaluations. We find that when panelists interrogate the qualifications of the researcher, which is akin to evaluating trustworthiness (is he/she likely to deliver what he/she promises?), they do look to credentials, training and track record. But when they interrogate the originality of the potential contribution, they often turn to arguments about the applicant's character and particularly their personal moral and mental qualities. Finally, we find that panelists often express their reaction to proposals they perceive as original in emotional terms, in terms of what is exciting to them and that some panelists offer their emotional reaction as proof of the project's originality and of its potential contribution: if the project 'excites' the panelists, it will surely excite others.

Despite this centrality of 'character' in the evaluation of originality, panelists tend to view personal characteristics as irrelevant to scholarly evaluation when questioned on their self-understanding of their own standards. As if they were abiding by a Mertonian description of the ideal-universalist norm in science, many of them insist on keeping the sphere of knowledge and the sphere of the social separate. And they do describe what they do as attempting to be neutral, objective and 'fair'.

We briefly position our argument in relation to the available literature on originality in science. We then move on to discuss our results, showing how respondents judge originality on the basis of substantive aspects of the proposal, the character traits that they ascribe to authors, and their emotional reaction to proposals. But first we will discuss the data used in this study.

Data

The study is based primarily on interviews with individuals serving on five different funding panels that distribute research fellowships in the social sciences and the humanities in the United States. A total of ten funding panels were studied over a period of two years, with interviews being conducted with panelists at the following institutions: the Social Science Research Council, the American Council for Learned Societies, the Woodrow Wilson National Fellowship Foundation, an anonymous Society of Fellows at a top research university, and an anonymous foundation in the social sciences.[5] All of these panels are interdisciplinary, meaning that each panel was composed of people from different disciplines, though some panels were more oriented towards the humanities while others were more oriented towards the social sciences. In two cases, we were able to observe the panel deliberation process. Otherwise, the Principal Investigator, Michèle Lamont, conducted an hour-long in-depth interview with panel members about what happened during the panel deliberation, about the criteria of evaluation they used to assess proposals, and in some cases, about how they understood the criteria used by other panelists. Other questions concerned how panelists interpret the process of selection and its outcome, and how they recognize excellence in their graduate students, among their colleagues and in their own work. We also interviewed programme officers about the selection of panelists. Panel members originated from a wide range of disciplines: anthropology, art history, economics, English, geography, history, musicology, philosophy, political science, sociology and women's studies. A total of 78 interviews were conducted, but this essay is based on an analysis of the first wave of interviews only, which included 42 individuals.

A Canadian study, conducted by Marcel Fournier, is adding a comparative dimension. This study analyses over the course of three years (2000–2003) seven disciplinary and interdisciplinary funding panels of the Standard Research Grants Program of the Social Sciences and Humanities Research Council of Canada (SSHRC), the federal agency responsible for promoting and supporting advanced scholarly research and research training in the social sciences and humanities in Canada. In the Standard Research Programme distributes research grants in the various social sciences and humanities disciplines. There are 24 adjudication committees, including one interdisciplinary/multidisciplinary committee. The committees that have been selected for this study are Panel 2 'History' (e.g. history of science, technology and medicine), panel 7 'Economics' (e.g. macro/micro-economics), panel 15 'Interdisciplinary/multidisciplinary' (e.g. sociology, linguistics and literature), panel 16 'Anthropology and archeology' (e.g. Latin America and China), panel 19 'Literature' (e.g. Canadian and contemporary literature), panel 20 'Health, women and social work' (e.g. nursing and feminist studies) and panel 24 'Political science' (e.g. public administration and law). This essay is based on an analysis of 18 interviews conducted in the first year of the project. Although we have not begun to systematically compare the cases, these interviews will provide a number of points of cross-national comparison.[6]

Prior Research on Originality

Originality as an Institutional Norm of Science

In the canonical literature in the sociology of science, originality is described as a primary goal of research and an institutional norm of science: 'It is through originality, in greater or smaller increments, that knowledge advances' writes Merton (1957/1973: 293). This institutional emphasis on originality can be counteracted by other institutional norms, mainly modesty and humility. But the first virtue is given priority: 'Great modesty may elicit respect, but great originality promises everlasting fame' (Merton, 1957/1973: 308). In his text on 'The Normative Structure of Science', Merton does not identify originality as an institutional imperative, as a part of the ethos of science (Merton, 1942/1973). But in his article, 'Priorities in Scientific Discovery', he states that:

> Recognition for originality becomes socially validated testimony that one has successfully lived up to the most exacting requirements of one's role as scientist. The self-image of the individual scientist will also depend greatly on the appraisals by his scientific peers of the extent he has lived up to this exacting and critically important aspect of his role.
>
> (Merton, 1957/1973: 273)

The cultural emphasis on originality is so great that it can produce 'deviant' behaviour when scientists try to obtain credit for an original discovery by all means available. Merton suggests that fraud and plagiarism are two types of response to this emphasis, but there are also alternative responses, such as retreatism.

Scientists are rewarded for making original contributions; they therefore wish to be the first to announce 'original' discoveries and for this reason, they frequently engage in 'priority disputes' over who was the first to make a discovery. Presumably, scientists can always agree that a particular discovery is original, but often it is not clear who should get credit for it. Other researchers have also defined originality in similar terms (e.g. Gaston, 1973; Hagstrom, 1974). Gaston compares art and science: 'In art, the chances that two creative artists will produce exactly the same sculpture or painting are extremely low, but in a competitive field of science the chances are very high that two or more scientists will make simultaneous discoveries.' In other words, 'we would not have the Fifth Symphony without Beethoven, but we would have had relativity without Einstein.' In science, 'original research consists', according to Gaston, 'of not just doing something on a topic that no one has ever worked on before, but rather in doing something that no one ever worked on before and that will add to knowledge appreciated and acknowledged by the scientific community'(Gaston, 1973: 3–4).

This understanding of originality is doubly restricted: first, it equates originality with making a new discovery or developing a novel method, ignoring other forms of innovation, such as proposing a middle-range conceptual shift; second, 'making new discoveries' in the name of scientific progress is a conception of originality that more aptly applies to the natural sciences than to the humanities or even the social sciences. Indeed, even in the natural sciences there is reason to believe that innovation is not the overarching imperative Merton believed it to be – at least in the specific context of peer-review panels. Indeed, Chubin and Hackett (1990: 13) argue that reviewers' propensity to recognize innovativeness is limited. For instance, established scientists who reach beyond the 'conventional wisdom' or pursue topics outside their areas of acknowledged competence are frequently rebuffed. Far from being an objective matter, defining and establishing originality is itself the object of conflicts and negotiations.[7]

Studies of Peer Review

Defining originality is an arduous enterprise. Indeed, 'the difficulty in being original is made more difficult by the problem of evaluating originality' (Dirk, 1999: 765–66). It seems that it is difficult for some panelists to define what originality means in the abstract. When we ask the panelists what is the difference between an innovative and an original project, they don't find an easy answer:

> An innovative project? Hum, that's a good question (coughs). There's a bit of tension, I think, by definition, an innovative project is one that addresses a topic in some sense no one else has addressed. But that of course conflicts with the idea that the topic has to be grounded in the existing literature. So I guess, the innovation comes from the answers that a person wants to, the potential answers to the question the person wants to explore. I look for people to be suggesting innovative answers to those questions and innovative methods for exploring or testing those hypothetical types of answers (Political Scientist).

By definition, 'originators have no peers' (Horrobin, 1990). Therefore, who can judge them? And how? Peer review is a critical gate-keeping mechanism in academia, and it has been the object of numerous studies. Social scientists working on the topic have been particularly concerned with the fairness of the outcome and the biases of panelists, and they often equate fairness with consensus.[8] The question then is whether consensus about quality is typical of funding panels. The answer is not clear. On the one hand, studies of evaluation processes point to a relatively high level of consensus (Cole, 1992). One study finds a common 'language' used in the evaluation of the quality of research, with a focus on scientific excellence (Aguilar *et al.*, 1998). Referees use the same descriptors to discuss proposals such as 'exceptional quality' and use a few common categories of classification, such as the distinction between original and unsurprising research (Fournier *et al.*, 1988). On the other hand, other studies point to low consensus. For instance, based on a review of the literature, Langfeldt (2001) concludes that there is a low degree of agreement between referees who tend to have various kinds of contradictory biases. Along similar lines, in an attempt to improve reviewer consensus, Dirk (1999) conducted an experiment where she developed a typology of eight different types of originality (in relation to hypotheses, methods and results) and asked respondents to rank their publications according to each type. In response to her questions, 40 per cent of respondents declared themselves uncertain of whether the typology she proposed would help make journal peer review fairer, and an additional 16 per cent believed it would not.[9] This outcome also suggests low consensus among evaluators. Paying attention to the meaning that panelists give to various criteria, such as originality, may shed light on this ambiguous question of consensus by stressing the construction of quality as defined by the panelists, as opposed to objective qualities embodied in scientific projects that panelists come to recognize.

The Meaning of Criteria: From Cognitive Categories to Types of Arguments

The assumption that objectivity in the evaluation of knowledge often goes hand in hand with the assumption that judgements about scholarship and judgements about scholars are clearly independent from one another. In this context, assessments based on personal characteristics (such as reputation) are often viewed as contaminating the peer-review process. Hence Merton argued that there are two meanings of excellence: one which refers to the personal qualities of scholars and one which refers to the work itself.[10]

In recent years, sociologists of science have repeatedly questioned the Mertonian firewall dividing the sphere of the social and the sphere of knowledge. Pierre Bourdieu (1984; 1989) and colleagues (Bourdieu and de Saint-Martin, 1975) are among the few who have examined criteria of evaluation of scholarly knowledge. Drawing on the structuralist tradition, they uncovered hierarchically ordered, bipolar oppositions, such as those contrasting work and scholars qualified as original/banal, brilliant/dull, gifted/motivated, distinguished/vulgar, cultivated/academic, eloquent/awkward and refined/crude. This system of oppositions is what Bourdieu and de Saint-Martin (1975) called the 'catégories de l'entendement professoral' ('the categories of professorial understanding').

In Bourdieu's sociology, these oppositions correspond to two underlying ideal types of academic success: the most highly valued type evokes an image of charismatic qualities based on *individual talent*, while the other suggests that success comes through *hard work* and determination. Bourdieu and de Saint-Martin (1975) argued that the most highly valued criterion, 'talent', tends to be used to describe the work of students from higher social backgrounds. Hence, they demonstrate that the categories of perception through which work is assessed are inherently social.

Their research on scholarly evaluation stands in stark contrast to most research on the peer-review process that sharply and normatively divides the spheres of the social and of knowledge. While this research inspires our study, we also go beyond it. Contra Bourdieu, we do not presume that originality is defined primarily through a pre-existing hierarchically ordered matrix of oppositional categories. Rather, we pay attention to the various meanings given to originality by panelists, and we focus in particular on the types of arguments they deploy to establish the originality of specific researchers and proposals. Classifications are always flexible, and categories and boundaries between categories are often uncertain (Knorr-Cetina, 1999: 137). Hence, they are the result of ongoing argumentations, interpretations and negotiations: they need to be justified, that is to be accompanied by sets of arguments.

Moreover, we take issue with Bourdieu's focus on disciplinary differences. He argued (1984; 1989) that constructions of worth vary between disciplines. Focusing on struggles surrounding the legitimization of various dimensions of academic activities (e.g. the opposition between research and teaching), he showed that some disciplines value and promote the pole of the opposition that they are most closely associated with. For instance, literary scholars put more emphasis on teaching than scientists in evaluating their peers.[11] Other studies have also focused on the cultural dimensions of disciplinary boundaries (Abbott, 2001; Becher, 1987; Bender and Schorske, 1997; Clark, 1983; Heilbron, 1995; Wagner et al., 1990). Rather than positing that disciplines are strongly differentiated, we show that the types of arguments used by panelists – how they talk about originality – span disciplinary boundaries. For example, people from any of the disciplines we studied might have referred to a proposal as 'daring' or said that it 'brings new evidence to bear on an old question'. However, the specific content academics give to 'daring' or 'an old question' appears to be determined by their disciplinary (or sub-disciplinary) background and their expertise. Finally, we contribute to the literature by showing, contra Shapin (1994), that judgements about character remain intrinsic to academic recognition, and to judgements about originality in particular.

Findings

Our analysis of interviews suggests that panelists point to three types of evidence when describing how they go about identifying and evaluating scholarly originality: evidence having to do with the substance of the proposals themselves; with the applicant's character, defined as personal virtues (such as courage) and other qualities (such as brilliance); and with the panelists' own emotional response to the proposals and the researchers. While the distinction between these types is generally clear, panelists may use them in combination with each other when discussing any particular proposal.

Substantive Qualities of the Proposal

Unsurprisingly, in assessing the originality of a proposal, panelists often point to evidence having to do with the substance of the proposal itself. They make reference to the topic, question, theory, method, or data of the proposed research – and often the relationship between two or more of these components. In discussing these various dimensions, they typically point to small-scale innovations that are identified as innovative based on the panelists' own expert knowledge of the field – knowledge that allows them to *recognize* what constitutes new data or a new perspective. This is expressed by a historian who describes in general terms the extent to which the proposals reviewed by the panel on which he served exhibited originality. He explains that the panelists recognized as original 'those things that drew on especially new sources of information, that added new perspectives to relatively complacent fields of research – that was what we found interesting.' Echoing these remarks, but adding more specificity, an English literature specialist states that originality is about bringing new perspectives to established research fields. He praises a proposal that approaches the study of Aramaic through a socio-historical perspective, which he contrasts with the more traditional philological and 'new criticism' perspectives. Another interviewee, an anthropologist, praises a proposal because it deftly recycles old theories to apply them to new problems 'in a generative way'. Finally, an economist illustrates innovative research in the following terms:

> An innovative project would be something that, for example, would use lots of techniques that have not been used before [...]. A project that brings methodologies that have not been applied to economics, in econometrics, yet, and has a lot of potential for the analysis of time-series in the future.

Clearly, the cornerstone of originality lies in a delicate balance between the old and the new, and assessment of originality concerns as much the predicted substantive impact of research as its generativity for understanding other questions. But this substantial definition brings us only so far. A fuller understanding has to take into consideration the heroism associated with originality, and this requires crossing the sacred firewall that separates knowledge from those who produce it.

Talking about Character

The *Concise Oxford Dictionary* mentions the moral and mental qualities of a person as key dimensions of character. A systematic analysis of the interview transcripts reveals many mentions of such qualities – and particularly moral qualities – by our panelists. Wining applicants were deemed 'courageous', 'ambitious', 'risk-taking', 'independent', 'curious' and 'intellectually honest'. They were also characterized as 'challenging the status quo' and as 'exhibiting a passion for ideas'. Likewise, the vocabulary used by panelists for describing lack of originality had a clear moral tone. Those at the losing end of the competition were deemed to lack ambition, energy, or creativity. The terms used by panelists to describe them include: 'complacent', 'tired', 'hackneyed', 'rehashing', 'spinning their wheels', 'traditional', 'gap-filing', or alternatively, 'trendy' and 'facile'.

While panelists were ostensibly evaluating proposals, they very frequently and easily slipped from discussing the substance of the proposals – the imputed qualities and traits of their authors (as if the latter suffered from guilt by association and as if proposals could be read as templates of character). And this, despite the fact that several panelists professed their desire to maintain a clear distinction between proposals and proposers – following the Mertonian dictat. In doing so, they employ what we call the metonymic mode, using 'the name of one thing for that of another of which it is an attribute or with which it is associated' (*Merriam-Webster's Dictionary*, 2002). Just as 'the oval office' is often used to refer to the president, the panelists will describe a proposal as 'risk-taking', while they are in fact describing the author as risk-taking (since the proposal does not act by itself). They will also describe a proposal as conformist or trendy, suggesting that the author is a crowd-pleaser, perhaps someone who lacks backbone, independence and individuality. In some cases, the judgements that bear on character are not made in a metonymic mode, but refer explicitly to the author's character (this is what we call the 'personalistic mode'). The metonymic mode, which is most often used, helps panelists legitimize their assessments by framing them as concerned with substance as opposed to people.

One panelist, an art historian, slipped in the metonymic mode to discuss the courage and passion of the researcher as embodied in his/her work, which she takes to be an equivalent of originality. Among the criteria of evaluation she privileges,

> [c]ourage is important [...] to go against the received so-called consensus, to be suspicious of that, to ask interesting questions [...] none of us can be original, but certainly I think amongst all of us, and for myself as well, [what we are looking for is] a nose for, a real passion for ideas, regardless of whether they get the grant or not, a real love of working with their minds [...]. And somehow, it's an aroma.

The 'aroma' let off by the proposal helps the panelist develop an impression of the level of emotional commitment of the researcher ('a real passion for ideas') which she equates with intellectual quality. Similarly, a historian extrapolates a lack of independence and a certain laziness in a proposer from his proposal when he mentions:

> I don't flop over with joy when somebody in history comes in and says 'I use race, class and gender as my categories'. That could be OK, that could be fine for a different project, but it's what everybody does. It's the line of least resistance now. When people do the line of least resistance and flow that in the rhetoric of subversion, I tend to get very turned off.

Also criticizing the character of the proposer via the proposal, in a perfect metonymic mode, a philosopher states about a particular project: 'I thought it was very trendy, politically correct, [a topic] that we've all tired of'. The author could be nothing but politically correct if his/her work is described as such.

Another way in which judgements of originality are made about people rather than proposals is when the proposed research is seen in light of the author's prior work or that of his advisor. As a musicologist puts it, '[y]ou know, if they're just rehashing what they did as a doctoral dissertation, that's probably where they're going to be stuck for the rest of their academic career'. For doctoral students, this mimetism can be directed towards their advisor's work. A historian explains that 'I react very strongly when I see work that's extremely derivative. When I see dissertation projects which are spin-offs of the advisor, I always say: 'Oh well, I'm not sure about this person'. And why is being derivative a problem? As one sociologist stresses it:

> I believe that there is a tremendous inertia in academic life, a tremendous inertia to reproduce what's going on, to reproduce advisors, projects, frameworks, theories or whatever. There is a tremendous self-imposed constraint about emulating what's considered hot, which obviously generates its own form of conformity.

This quotation implicitly constructs personal dynamism as tantamount to originality and excellence. Note however, that working within one's area of expertise and extending one's past work can be seen by panelists as strengths, since it is read as indicative that the researcher will be able to carry out the proposed study. Thus, what might under some circumstances be considered a weakness can be construed as a strength under different circumstances. This observation is incompatible with Bourdieu's (1989) method which consists in analysing the categories through which scholarly work is assessed as ordered in a relatively rigid and stable hierarchy of oppositional categories. His approach ignores context in true structuralist fashion.

While these examples show how panelists cast judgement on character conceived as moral virtue (independence, personal strength), we also find that they often highlight more cognitive or mental aspects of the proposer's personal characteristics, such as creativity and intellectual ability, when making substantive judgements about a proposal. These judgements often bear simultaneously on the substance of the proposal and the personal qualities of the proposer, and suggest once again the impossibility of establishing a clear distinction between the social and scientific criterion salient in the evaluation process. For example, in describing what originality is, one historian said, it is 'the ability to take two ideas that have nothing to do with one another', thus pointing directly to the researcher's personal ability to make unexpected analytical connections. Or, describing the craft of research, a political scientist points to the importance of creative capacities, saying: 'to be a craftsman without insight or creativity, you know, that wouldn't work to create good objects, you have to be creative as well'.

Similarly, panelists will define originality in terms of the way that the researcher's distinctive skills in approaching the empirical material. In describing one of his best graduate students, one political scientist explained: 'he was able to kind of dig up interesting sources of data and was able to bring those data to bear on some thorny issues that people had been debating, but they were just kind of arguing with each other'. Along similar lines, this is what a historian says of a proposal in English literature:

> I liked that she was doing textual analysis in a very elegant and creative way, and using these chronicle texts, as I recall. She shed a real light, not just on history, but

historiography and the intellectual history as through writing about [Indian] society and culture. And she seemed to me to be doing a very deft, elegant and non-obvious, non-trivial reading of these texts.

These panelists point to the merits of the research by discussing the qualities of the researcher – the two being deeply intertwined.

Emotional Reaction as Proof of Originality: 'Surprising',
'Disturbing' and 'Exciting'

Earlier we mentioned the role of emotions in assessments of originality, arguing that although reviewers recognize originality at the cognitive level, they often experience that recognition as an emotional reaction, which is read by panelists as evidence that they are encountering originality. The language of 'excitement' and surprise thoroughly permeate discussions of originality, and the two are often conflated. For instance, an anthropologist describes a proposal he views as original by saying 'that's a good example of what I would call an exciting proposal'. A historian explains why another proposal is original by saying 'I just found that one really exciting'. Another panelist in interdisciplinary/multidisciplinary (e.g. sociology, linguistics and literature) talks about originality in terms of what captures imagination. Speaking of winning proposals, she says:

> They were innovative in some way, they captured the imagination of the committee, they captured the imagination of the assessors, they kind of sparked, they had something original, they were doing things that were, you know? Many times, we would have said: 'Oh! I'd like to read this when it's published'. 'Oh, I'd like to follow, you know, to know more'. So it captures the imagination of the committee as a whole.

A historian even more clearly equates excitement and originality when she underlines:

> And then there is that 'something', there's that edge, there's that spark, there's that freshness. And it can happen in any discipline [...]. You get the sense and several people will **agree**: 'Oh, this is exciting'. And often people will say: 'Oh, I wish I had time to pursue that **myself!**'

'Edge', 'spark', 'freshness': these words associated with emotions make research exciting and heroic, as opposed to words – dusty, musty and humdrum. It is these emotions that keep researchers going. It is the hope of producing such emotions in others that keep them hunched at their desk (Collins, 2004). It is not surprising that these emotions are central to how panelists talk about originality – using emotional as opposed to cognitive terms.

Emotional evidence of originality is often offered together with more substantive and personalistic evidence in the panelists' descriptions of what makes a winning proposal. One anthropologist, for instance, describes a winning proposal and, in a metonymic mode, its author, in the following terms: '[it's] unusual and unique. It's breaking a paradigm [...]. Something that really steps outside of those boxes in a way that [...] in a sense takes a risk. [...] And it's pretty hard: innovative, exciting, new, different work'.

A Note on Disciplinary Differences

In general, the same vocabulary of originality was used by panelists from all disciplinary backgrounds. For instance, panelists from all disciplines appreciate what is courageous and daring, and reject what is hackneyed and trendy. Of course, what a philosopher finds challenging or trendy may be very different from what someone in English considers challenging or trendy. These judgements are grounded in the distinctive disciplinary history and substantive foci. For example, in literary studies, work that focuses exclusively on analysing texts (which is typically called 'close reading') without taking into consideration the social context in which that text was produced is now seen as old-fashioned. In this case, the criteria in use are specific to a particular discipline at a particular historical period. While the specificity of such criteria varies enormously across disciplines, and presumably, overtime, we find that they are likely to be couched within a broader rhetoric of excellence that stresses substantive, character and emotional evidence. These were overall very salient across all fields, and more so than distinctively disciplinary classification systems. But this remains to be examined further in light of a complete analysis of our interview data. The results indicate that disciplinary differences are much less salient than the literature would suggest, at least as far as the discourse of excellence is concerned.

Conclusion

In this essay, we have discussed some preliminary findings of our research on the evaluation of originality in peer review. In contrast to the predominant Merton-inspired scholarship on the peer-review system, we adopted an inductive approach by examining how panelists assess grant proposals.[12] We found that when they discuss originality, panelists employ different types of arguments, sometimes focusing on the substantive aspects of the proposal itself, the character of the proposal's author, or their emotional reaction to the proposal. The finding that panelists often make judgements about the author's character resonates with a rich line of culturally oriented research on knowledge-making that breaks down the divide between the sphere of knowledge and the sphere of the social. We go beyond the disciplinary focus of much of this research (at least for the time being) by showing that the types of arguments made about originality span disciplines.[13] We also show that Merton's contention about the norm of universalism in science holds to the extent that it is important for researchers to legitimize their evaluations as based solely on 'objective' scholarly criteria.

Following Shapin (1994), we showed that assessments of character (having to do with trustworthiness for Shapin and with courage and ambition for us) are central in academic evaluations. Although Shapin contends that character judgements in modern science have been largely surpassed by the importance of credentials and expertise, we showed that the discourse of character is alive and well, albeit used in a different context. Interestingly, the general evaluation of quality concerns not only originality, but also trust. These two terms correspond to a tension in grant proposal-funding decisions between admiration and bureaucratization. On the one hand, judgements about originality are based on an ideology of the talented genius, which is central in literature, science and art (Dirk, 1999; Fuchs, 2001). But the process of evaluation of the quality of research is also a part of a bureaucratic enterprise of grant-giving, and panelists also give weight to more practical considerations based on establishing trust (in the qualities of researchers, their competence, accountability, scientific dispositions and so on). Different panelists, panels, organizations and disciplines may tend to weigh originality more heavily than trust. We have yet to generate grounded hypotheses to predict these variations.

There are a number of open questions and further aspects of this topic that we plan to explore in future essays. Our discussion here, for example, has completely ignored the fact that the decisionmaking takes place in the context of a dynamic panel process. First, the proposals are reviewed by one or more external reviewers whose area of expertise is much closer to the proposed research than that of the panel members. What influence, if any, do these reviews have on the opinions of panel members? How are arguments shaped by the disciplinary composition of the panel? Are arguments framed differently if they are meant to convince a philosopher, a political scientist, or an English literature expert? How about the order in which proposals are considered? Does it have a stronger impact at the beginning of a meeting than it does at the end? And what impact do the exigencies of the panel decision-making process, such as limited time, have? Another line of questions would concern whether there is any correspondence between statements in a proposal attesting to its originality and the assessments of external reviewers or panel members.

At a time of important discipline-spanning debates about the construction of the canon and the meaning of academic excellence, studying such issues in a concrete context can be an important complement to more abstract debates. Scholars do tend to debate epistemological issues as if theoretical discussion existed in a vacuum. In the context of peer-review panels, methodological and theoretical issues are discussed and hashed out in a practical context, with all kinds of factors affecting judgement, including the number of proposals needing to be reviewed and the pace of the discussion. Indeed, one would be hard pressed to find a single exchange in the context of our panels in which epistemology is employed without reference to such factors. The constitution of a disciplinary canon and the definition of academic excellence are activities that happen in real time, with real people and real organizational constraints. Our contribution is to examine these au 'ras-du-sol', with the hope of shedding new light over important debates in the sociology of knowledge and science.

Endnotes

1 Peer-review panels are a part of the general system of academic recognition. Members of these committees act as 'gatekeepers' who are also part of a bureaucratic process of evaluation, involving formal rules, explicit criteria and bureaucratic organization. The purpose of these panels or committees is to assess the quality of a proposal and the excellence of applicants in order to give them resources they need to conduct research and thereby gain more recognition. In a more constructivist line of reasoning, we would argue that rather than 'recognizing' intrinsic qualities, peer-review panels designate and elevate proposals and their authors, marking them with a stamp of excellence. See also Fuchs (2001) in this regard.

2 Some of the findings presented in this essay are presented in Guetzkow *et al.* (2004), in a somewhat altered form. That paper goes beyond this one by developing a typology of definitions of

originality, examining disciplinary differences in the definition of originality, and elaborating the argument about the conflation between original work and individual moral worth.

3 At the time, the English gentry believed they were the only ones who possessed this combination of virtues.

4 In the epilogue, he speculates that the personal knowledge gained in face-to-face interaction still plays an important role in establishing trust, but this only applies to the close-knit communities of scientific core-sets, which is a far cry from the impersonal nature of the peer-review panels we studied.

5 The specific competitions studied were the following: the International Dissertation Field Research Fellowship program at the Social Science Research Council at the American Council for Learned Societies, the Women's Studies Dissertation Fellowship program at the Woodrow Wilson National Fellowship Foundation, and the fellowship program in the humanities at the American Council for Learned Societies.

6 Differences between the Canadian and American panels we studied include the following: The Canadian panels are uni-disciplinary, while the American panels are multi-disciplinary; the Canadian system of grant-making is centralized, while the American system is decentralized; the Canadian panels tend to be more conservatives than the American ones and to be more sceptical about claims concerning originality.

7 This is illustrated by the peer-review system in Canada, which has repeatedly been criticized for its unmistakable bias towards conservatism in the name of quality control (National Commission on Research, 1980). In the 1990s, a report commissioned by the Canadian government found that many academics view their funding agencies as supporting the 'tried and true rather than the risky and innovative' (Social Science Research Council of Canada, 1998: 7). This report concludes that members of the scientific community often believe that in view of small budgets and its resistant history of conservative committees', research councils do not tend to receive 'the best or most innovative applications'. While these perceptions are not widely shared, they are of serious concern about the Council. The Council must ensure that its programmes and committees are willing to push the boundaries of existing paradigms and should not be perceived as the funding body for most pedestrian researchers (Social Science Research Council of Canada, 1998: 8). Hence, originality is now listed in the official guidelines of the Council as one of the most important criteria for evaluation to be considered by reviewers. Furthermore, colleagues who provide evaluation letters are directly asked to assess the originality and influence of the researchers previous work on others, as well as the expected contribution to the advancement of knowledge for social sciences and humanities in the research proposal. The other 'Official' criteria are: intellectual, cultural and social importance, pertinence of the theoretical approach, relevance of research strategies, methodological significance, dissemination of results within the population, and publication output in the academic milieu.

8 See the special issue of *Science, Technology and Human Values* (1985) on 'Peer Review and Public Policy'.

9 If you identify hypotheses, methods and results as the three main elements of a scientific paper, and if you define originality as 'a permutation of old and new information' (previously reported in the scientific literature/newly reported), the eight originality types are rated by the majority (84 per cent) of the respondents (indicating that they could recognize her typology), and the most frequent type (42 per cent) of originality seems to be new hypothesis/previous-reported methods/new results. But many (40 per cent) are uncertain whether this typology might help to make the journal of peer review fairer, and some of them are not able to grasp all the types (Dirk, 1999).

10 Merton called these two meanings 'excellence in the sense of quality' and 'excellence in the sense of performance' (Merton, 1960/1973). According to Merton, these two definitions of excellence embody two 'doctrines of justification': one by *faith in the individual*, who has yet to prove himself and the other, by *works*; the first is reminiscent of Luther, and the second reminds us of Calvin (Merton, 1960/1973: 424). Examining methodically the connections between excellence and recognition for excellence (and how they often diverge), Merton recognizes at one point that the question of the criteria of excellence is complex and he asks: 'What qualities of a seeming achievement are to be judged?' His response is that 'there is a difficult problem, in many spheres of human activities, of discriminating the authentic innovation that merits recognition from the mere novelty that doesn't' (Merton, 1960/1973: 433–44).

11 Literary studies, social sciences and sciences correspond to different ways of defining legitimate professional orientations: whereas the sciences value research at the expense of professorship, the professional orientation in literature studies is highly correlated with professorship and the acquisition of 'academic power' rather than with research activities. Social sciences stand between the two. Bourdieu explains conflicts of evaluations within disciplines by the fact that disciplinary boundaries can blur. For instance, authors in literature can import categorizations from the social sciences into their disciplines: the figure of Roland Barthes is exemplar in the sense that he emphasized research over professorship by orienting his career towards the social sciences.

12 By inductive, we mean both that we abandoned the normative assumptions typical of research on peer review, and also that we did not predefine the categories of evaluation, nor do we assume that they are ordered into a hierarchy of oppositions.

13 We did not study the natural sciences. It may be that the rhetoric of originality is more oriented towards discussions of discovery, but it may also be similar to what we found.

References

Abbott, A. D. (2001) *Chaos of Disciplines*. Chicago, IL: University of Chicago Press.

Aguilar, A., Ingemanson, T., Hogan, S. and Magnien, E. (1998) 'Peer Review Evaluation of Proposals in the Biotechnology Program of the European Union', *Research Evaluation*, 7(3): 141–46.

Becher, T. (1987) 'The Disciplinary Shaping of the Profession', in B. R. Clark (ed.), *The Academic Profession*. Berkeley/Los Angeles, CA: University of California Press, pp. 271–303.

Bell, R. (1992) *Impure Science: Fraud, Compromise and Political Influence in Scientific Research*. New York: John Wiley and Sons, Inc.

Bender, T. and Schorske, C. (eds) (1997) *American Academic Culture in Transformation*. Princeton, NJ: Princeton University Press.

Bourdieu, P. (1975) 'The Specificity of the Scientific Field and the Social Conditions of the Progress of Reason', *Social Science Information*, 14: 19–47.

Bourdieu, P. (1984) *Homo Academicus*. Paris: Minuit.

Bourdieu, P. (1989) *La noblesse d'État: Grands corps et grandes écoles*. Paris: Minuit.

Bourdieu, P. and de Saint-Martin, M. (1975) 'Les catégories de l'entendement professoral', *Actes de la recherche en sciences sociales*, 3: 68–93.

Brockman, J. (ed.) (1993) *Creativity*. New York: Simon and Schuster.

Chubin, D. E. and Hackett, E. J. (1990) *Peerless Science: Peer Review and US Science Policy*. Albany, NY: State University of New York Press.

Clark, B. (1983) *The Higher Education System: Academic Organization in Cross-National Perspective*. Berkeley, CA: University of California Press.

Cole, J. and Cole, S. (1973) *Social Stratification in Science*. Chicago, IL: University of Chicago Press.

Cole, S. (1992) *Making Science: Between Nature and Society*. Cambridge, MA: Harvard University Press.

Cole, S., Rubin, L. and Cole, J. (1978) *Peer Review in the National Science Foundation: Phase One of a Study*. Washington, DC: National Academy of Sciences.

Collins, R. (1998) *The Sociology of Philosophies: A Global Theory of Intellectual Change*. Cambridge, MA: Harvard University Press.

Collins, R. (2004) *Interaction Chain Rituals*. Princeton, NJ: Princeton University Press.

Czikszentmihalyi, M. (1996) *Creativity: Flow and the Psychology of Discovery and Invention*. New York: Harper Collins.

Dervin, D. (1990) *Creativity and Culture: A Psychoanalytic Study of the Creative Process in the Arts, Sciences, and Culture*. London: Associated University Press.

Dirk, L. (1999) 'A Measure of Originality: The Elements of Science', *Social Studies of Science*, 29(5): 765–76.

Fournier, M., Gingras, Y. and Mathurin, C. (1988) 'L'évaluation par les pairs et la définition légitime de la recherche', *Actes de la recherche en sciences sociales*, 74: 47–54.

Fuchs, S. (2001) *Against Essentialism: A Theory of Culture and Society*. Cambridge, MA: Harvard University Press.

Gaston, J. C. (1973) *Originality and Competition in Science*. Chicago, IL: University of Chicago Press.

General Accounting Office (1994) *Peer Review: Reforms Needed to Ensure Fairness in Federal Agency Grant Selection: Report to the Chairman, Committee on Governmental Activities, US Senate*. Washington, DC: General Accounting Office.

Guetzkow, J., Lamont, M. and Mallard, G. (2004) 'What is Originality in the Humanities and Social Sciences?', *American Sociological Review*, 69(2): 190–212.

Hagstrom, W. (1974) 'Competition in Science', *American Sociological Review*, 39(1): 1–18.

Heilbron, J. (1995) *The Rise of Social Theory*. Minneapolis, MN: University of Minnesota Press.

Horrobin, D. F. (1990) 'The Philosophical Basis of Peer Review and the Suppression of Innovation', *Journal of American Medical Association*, 263(10): 1438–41.

Knorr-Cetina, K. (1981) *The Manufacture of Knowledge: An Essay on the Constructivist and Contextual Nature of Science*. Oxford: Pergamon Press.

Knorr-Cetina, K. (1999) *Epistemic Cultures: How the Sciences Make Knowledge?* Cambridge, MA: Harvard University Press.

Kuhn, T. (1970) *The Structure of Scientific Revolutions*. 2nd edn. Chicago, IL: University of Chicago Press.

Langfeldt, L. (2001) 'The Decision-Making Constraints and Processes of Grant Peer Review, and their Effects on the Review Outcome', *Social Studies of Sciences*, 31(6): 820–41.

Liebert, R. (1976) 'Productivity, Favor, and Grants among Scholars', *American Journal of Sociology*, 82(3): 664–73.

Merton, R. K. (1942/1973) 'The Normative Structure of Science', in R. K. Merton (ed.), *The Sociology of Science*. Chicago, IL: University of Chicago Press, pp. 267–78.

Merton, R. K. (1957/1973) 'Priorities in Scientific Discovery', in R. K. Merton (ed.), *The Sociology of Science*. Chicago, IL: University of Chicago Press, pp. 286–324.

Merton, R. K. (1960/1973) 'Recognition and Excellence: Instructive Ambiguities', in R. K. Merton (ed.), *The Sociology of Science*. Chicago, IL: University of Chicago Press, pp. 420–38.

Merton, R. K. (1996) *On Social Structure and Science*. Edited by Piotr Sztompka. Chicago, IL: University of Chicago Press.

National Commission on Research (1980) *Review Processes: Assessing the Quality of Research Proposals*. Washington, DC: National Commission on Research.

Roy, R. (1985) 'Funding Science: The Real Defects of Peer Review and an Alternative to It', *Science, Technology and Human Values*, 10(3): 73–81.

Science, Technology, and Human Values (1985), 10(3); s. i.: 'Peer Review and Public Policy'.

Shapin, S. (1994) *Social History of Truth: Civility and Science in Seventeenth-Century England*. Chicago, IL: Chicago University Press.

Simonton, D. K. (1988) *Scientific Genius: A Psychology of Science*. Cambridge, MA: Harvard University Press.

Social Science Research Council of Canada (1998) *Report of the Research and Dissemination Committee on Revitalization of Peer Review*. Ottawa: Social Science Research Council of Canada.

Somers, M. (1996) 'Where is Sociology after the Linguistic Turn? Knowledge Cultures, Narrativity and Historical Epistemologies', in T. McDonald (ed.), *The Historic Turn in the Human Sciences*. Ann Harbor, MI: University of Michigan Press, pp. 53–90.

Wagner, P., Wittrock, B. and Whitley, R. (eds) (1990), *Discourses on Society: The Shaping of the Social Science Disciplines*. Dordrecht: Kluwer, pp. 331–57.

Name Index

Subject Index

Note: The letter n indicates a note